THE ENLIGHTENED MAN'S EVOLUTION

into

THE FAMILY OF MAN

THE ENLIGHTENED MAN'S EVOLUTION

into

THE FAMILY OF MAN

Shido of Sukhavati

THE ENLIGHTENED MAN'S EVOLUTION
INTO THE FAMILY OF MAN

iUniverse books may be ordered through booksellers or by contacting:

iUniverse
1663 Liberty Drive
Bloomington, IN 47403
www.iuniverse.com
1-800-Authors (1-800-288-4677)

ISBN: 978-1-4917-4945-6 (sc)
ISBN: 978-1-4917-4946-3 (e)

Library of Congress Control Number: 2014918201

Printed in the United States of America.

iUniverse rev. date: 10/25/2014

Forward

At Last! All the Knowledge and Wisdom You Need about Dating and Sex Play to Be the Perfect Husband

First realize you need to be married with children to be complete.

Ten better ways to have better dates.

Seventeen ways to pursue her.

Twenty nine ways to attract her.

Eight steps to plan for better performance.

Twelve ways to improve your persuasion by speaking, listening, and acting.

Plenty of Warnings.

The Seven Heights of Love

Give and Receive Hundreds of Caresses

How to Be in Demand at Parties

Five ways to be invited to lots of parties.

Sexual Thrills beyond the Earthly Existence

Mental Preparation: the Main Sexual Organ is Your Mind-Brain

Four Physical Preparations for Extreme Connection with Your Most Appropriate Woman

Emotional Preparation Is the Source of Vitality for Sexual Games and for a Long Term Marriage

Eleven Weeks of Spiritual Preparation for Extreme Sexual Fulfillment and for Married Bliss

Mastery of Communication on All Levels

Continuous Improvement to Make Your Marriage the One that Is Happy Ever After

Are you the next man to accelerate your pace into the family of mankind?

How can this small book contain so much vital help? How can you avoid the troubles of dating and married life?

This book explains the results of a lifetime of experience with dating and marriage by an intelligent man.

Shido succeeded as a physicist, an engineer and an administrator. His life has been flooded with women who were attracted to him and by those women he pursued. He applied the methods of scientific research to solve the problems of how to find appropriate women, to attract them, to pursue them, to improve himself so the women would perceive him as a valuable mate, to marry the best possible women, to behave as a husband who improves the marriage and to achieve a lasting and satisfying marriage.

This took about 40 years.

Since Shido did all the work. You can learn the details of his extensive research and avoid the pain and the failures.

You do not have to fail over and over in order to learn how to get satisfaction. You do not have to endure a lifetime of trial and error. You do not have to leap into marriage with an inappropriate woman for life.

You can choose to use the methods in this book to have a life of dating, or enjoying short terms of being close to many different women, or marrying a woman whose excellence is fitted to you. If a near-perfect woman shows up, then you can marry her and use the methods in this book to improve your marriage for a lifetime.

Shido observed that almost all men lacked the fundamental knowledge about relating to women. He learned that most women lacked the most basic knowledge of how men think and what drives men to take action. Society is composed mostly of men and women who do not know how to relate. Therefore he set out to teach men the many skills necessary to relate to women.

He also wrote an equivalent book for women to relate to men. *The Art and Science of Dating: Use these Suggestions, Methods, and Tools to Get the Relationship with the Man You Want by* Shido of Sukhavati available at iUniverse.com, Bloomington, IN: iUniverse (2012). If you have a superior woman you are pursuing, give her this book. Then you will find it easy to persuade her to choose you.

If the reader uses the suggestions, methods and skills proposed in this book and if he makes a major effort to apply the information in this book, he will produce the best possible marriage with the best possible woman who have made the best possible effort. This book cannot pretend to apply to all men in all situations due to the many limits on each man, on his available women, and on the political, social, and economic conditions.

This book guides men into fulfillment of their need for one woman with which to connect and to merge. It guides men into five channels of communication with their wives. Continuous and never ending improvement in the skills in this book may lead to a lifelong satisfaction with the marriage.

Disclaimer

The ideas and methods presented worked for the author. The author arrived at the conclusions presented here after he made many mistakes and achieved many excellent successes using the ideas and methods presented.

Some of the information will not work for you. Also you may discover better methods than those presented. Each person is different. Thus there are no approaches that will work for all men who want to identify the kind of woman they will want. There are special cases among men and women that are not covered here for finding perfect women, for interviewing her, and for qualifying her as a wife.

However, any man who applies these ideas and methods as they are stated, will definitely locate the best possible woman for himself considering the limitations of his abilities and the town or city in which he hunts.

As a condition for reading this book, or experimenting with the ideas provided herein, you agree that you are solely responsible for the good or bad results that occur. If you do not agree then you are forbidden to read this book and you will give it to someone else. This book, the author and the publisher do not claim this is valuable advice for medical nor physical body nor legal nor psychological nor religious nor financial nor any other kind of use.

Each reader will use this book in a different way which cannot be anticipated. Meeting people, dating, partnering, accompanying, and marrying are serious events and can result in good benefits or in bad troubles in consequence to your speech, or actions. All results are your glory and your fault. You are liable for the consequences, for the resulting excellent experiences, for the bad feelings, the good feelings and damages. You are responsible for enjoying the excellent results and the distasteful results. You are responsible for making whole anyone you damage and for taking the credit for all the good you spread. You are responsible for reaping the benefits and for curing yourself for all emotional, mental or any other kind of consequential damage. You are solely the winner of all the wealth you create. You are solely the loser of any wealth you lose due the risk you take. You are responsible for any threat or compliment you receive.

Your life is separate from, and not connected in any way to the lives of the author and the publisher. The author and the publisher are not liable for any good or bad consequences whether they are mental, emotional, financial, psychological, bodily, or medical. Each reader will create a different and un-knowable achievement or failure based on reading this book. Each reader will have different expectations and different understanding of the language used in this book.

Table of Contents

The dominating thoughts of your mind have a tendency to change into the physical reality of your life.

GUARANTEE

If you act and speak as recommended in every chapter and you keep a journal of progress, speech, and actions, make a strong effort, the maximum you can gain is a sense of completion even if you are not physically near your lover or your wife. This will only work if you have an appropriate woman who keeps journal and makes a strong effort.

Use the following true claim to find, pursue, attract, interview, check out your cooperation with the best possible woman:

The dominating thoughts of your mind have a tendency to change into the physical reality of your life.

Give and take in getting a date.

If a man is a powerful support, he is attractive.

Almost all women think they are Cinderella.

You have high body vitality even lust.

You can raise her lust up to your level.

How attractive are you today in terms of senses, appearance, smell, voice sound, and touch?

Why do you need to answer these questions?

How to be more desirable, communicative, magnetic, and attractive.

Consider how to make yourself more attractive.

Another fundamental problem is a woman who does not understand men or who is ignorant of how to speak or act around men. This book will help her relate to you:

The Art and Science of Dating: Use These Suggestions, Methods, and Tools to Get the Relationship with the Man You Want

A list of attractions you can learn that will help women (and other people) love you.

First Attraction: Make yourself joyful and contented.

Second attraction: Express yourself with words, vocal expressions and body movements.

Third attraction: express your feelings to let your woman understand you.

Fourth attraction: let pleasure lead your relationship into joy and contentment.

Fifth attraction: Joyful and contented people laugh more than angry and dissatisfied people.

Sixth attraction: Your best possible woman will be good company if she feels you love her. Then you will feel joyful inside yourself.

Seventh attraction: Confidence and erect posture make you attractive as a date.

Eighth attraction: The feelings of determination, ambition, and seeking to achieve a goal impress women.

Ninth attraction: You are as happy as you want to be

Tenth attraction: The most attractive men have a healthy mind and healthy feelings in a healthy body.

Eleventh attraction: A woman's need for support can mean she needs a powerful man, not just one who can support her.

Announcing eighteen more ways to attract that outstanding woman who interests you and who you crave.

Twelfth attraction: the basic requirement is that you feel terrific and your body is in good shape.

Thirteenth attraction: to meet a woman you do not know yet, say a neutral observation with a smile or a joke.

Fourteenth attraction: Engrossing conversation.

Fifteenth attraction: Listening.

Sixteenth attraction: Communicate what you want from her.

Seventeenth attraction: recognize that most women, not all, want to have a sexual event with you.

Eighteenth attraction: your speech, your senses, and your body movements are in harmony with a particular woman.

Nineteenth attraction: never have sexual contact with a woman on the first date.

Twentieth attraction: Wait for sexual gratification and other more meaningful goals.

Twenty-first attraction: indirect seduction.

Twenty-second attraction: when you are on a first date, complain about small defects in the woman. In particular, complain about her not giving you anything in exchange for all the money you spent, all your time, and all your entertaining company. When she is defensive, let her promise to give you something in return.

Twenty-third attraction: withhold information about your past, your assets, your experiences, especially about other women.

Twenty-fourth attraction: This is the opposite of the last attraction. This is her being attracted to you because you want to know everything about her.

Twenty-fifth attraction: show impeccable respect, appreciation, and admiration.

Twenty-sixth attraction: Always be aware of your feelings and always control them.

Twenty-seventh attraction: Listen.

Twenty-eighth attraction: use the full range of your speaking voice to sooth her or to excite her.

Twenty-ninth attraction: Look behind her mask to have a heart to heart communication.

You are making progress.

To pursue her means to take active measures to make friends with a desirable woman.

Ten skills you must have to enjoy the dates you want.

Dating skill one: how to ask for a date.

Dating skill two: Planning a date to get results.

The thirteenth winning tool: it is easy to make new acquaintances.

The fourteenth winning tool: list all the possessions you want. Many women also want similar things with variations.

The fifteenth winning tool: The seven basic needs of a sane person.

The sixteenth winning tool: expend the time and effort to ask questions and answer them.

The seventeenth winning tool: hunting for the best woman and connecting with her.

Focus on what results you want on a date.

This book gives you most of the methods you need.

Always consider her needs and feelings.

The details of the rules do not matter as much as the three principles.

Be a woman's friend before you are her lover or husband.

Eight step plan for peak performance.

Twelve ways to improve your speaking, listening, and acting.

Improvement one: Communicate in every possible way.

Improvement two: Speak clearly.

Improvement three: Control your voice.

Improvement four: Communicate by touching.

Improvement five: Listen completely.

Improvement six: Read body language, clothes language, and face expressions.

Improvement seven: Learn to speak the same language that she speaks.

Improvement eight: Show integrity.

Improvement nine: Use skilled methods of thinking and feeling.

Improvement ten: Use the skills of communicating through the channel of clothes and appearance.

Improvement eleven: Control your feelings.

Improvement twelve: Learn to give and to take information.

Can you imagine sex without friendship or love?

You can create the foundation to have a best possible friend.

Arguing and differences of opinion are part of almost all relationships.

Remember giving in exchange for getting.

How well do you know her? How would you describe your best possible woman now that you have met her? What is she really like?

There are at least seven levels of love.

First level of love: Attraction.

Second level of love: Infatuation.

Third level of love: Communion.

Fourth level of love: Intimacy.

Fifth level of love: Surrender and non-attachment.

Sixth level of love: Passion.

Seventh level of love: Ecstasy.

You want to be free of pain and suffering; therefore your emotions are a major influence in your life. You have control over most of your feelings.

You use your feelings to guess the immediate future.

An exercise when you can feel anything you want.

Your feelings send you information on the threats and opportunities near you.

Another exercise when you can feel anything you want.

Five ways to be invited to lots of parties.

Three basic rules of etiquette.

Use the rules of etiquette to earn friends at work.

In America, there are about two hundred different immigrant groups and about 50 different economic and social classes.

How a man and woman connect in every possible way.

Tantric Sexual Practice from ancient India

Remember that the purpose of sexual congress is to reproduce human beings.

These complications of making babies evolved in such a short time for three main reasons.

A contemporary and embarrassing problem arose.

Some changes in the American Society that have caused a few men to have sexual dysfunctions.

Many men have sexual trouble, so do many women.

Are you willing to stick with this learning process until you have made all the connections?

The main aphrodisiac is your thinking. You think yourself into lust and the reflexive sexual drive.

Somehow you learned that you are one separate individual person.

You may be able to learn a new way of being a part of a group.

To prove your interdependence on other people, try this mind experiment.

What do you want from a sexual adventure?

Physical approach one: Your body needs the basic preparations.

Physical approach two: Sexual experience is so demanding that you must provide all your physical body and other basics if it is to rise to its possible payoff.

Physical approach three: Your body must be built so it can withstand 1 to 5 hours of aerobic exertion.

Physical approach four: Plan how to express your love through massage or other physical touching.

Prepare for your encounter with your best possible woman.
The seven levels of love.

This chapter could be called Eleven Weeks to Sexual Thrills beyond the Earthly plane.

Caution: the high energy you may feel may be pleasure but it can also be pain.

Do you have the aptitude to allow yourself to be a part of a large group or even a part of all human kind?

Requirements of the environment of this as a group course.

The following is a guide to a course in love leading to a higher state of Being leading to the ultimate in connection with your best possible woman.

Week one: Preparing to rise in love.

Week two: learning overall concepts of love.

Week three: experiencing the state of being in love.

Week four: removing barriers that exist between you and your best possible woman.

The Root as used in this book means:

1.) The thought of Me, Myself, and I.

2.) The thought, "It belongs to me." Example, my arm belongs to me.

3.) "I belong to it." Example, I belong to my country.

4.) "I am real and important." Example, I am better than anyone.

5.) "It is part of me." Example, I am a person who is polite.

Week five: allowing yourself to concentrate on your best possible woman.

Week six: learning to meditate in a specific way.

The first jhana.

Possible results from the first jhana.

Week seven: Learning to meditate the second way.

Prepare for second level jhana.

Exercise in consciousness.

Week eight: Adding the third jhana.

Remove barriers to love.

Week nine: the fourth jhana.

A benefit from the four jhanas.

Tenth week: absorption.

Increasing the power of concentration, meditation, and absorption.

Constructive use of your emotions, your feelings.

Autosuggestion for changing feelings.

Eleventh week: You and your woman loving on five channels.

Description of water crystallization.

Continuous, never-ending improvement.

Limitation one: Your pursuit of women and your enjoyment of sexual thrills cannot be the focus of your whole life.

Consider the levels of desire.

Limitation two: Attract and pursue a woman who is a possible wife, not a woman who will be forever impossible to relate to.

Limitation three: Your sexual life is best if it is a part of balanced life that you and your best possible woman are building together.

Limitation four: This book is most useful and efficient for a man who will invest the effort, who will focus on long term possible outcomes, and who will continue making the effort until he achieves the entire process being taught.

An example of the Tantric Way to Paradise.

After receiving from your woman, give an equal or better experience back to her.

The Tantric ceremony can be a healing experience through release of blocked chi, vitality, thoughts, or feelings.

Tantric methods increase vitality and health.

What is a happy marriage?

An ancient discovery about marriage.

Eleven efforts you must make to create a good marriage and family.

First effort. Find a wife, the best possible wife.

Second Effort. Learn the skills necessary for getting along in a marriage condition.

Some of the skills necessary for a positive marriage.

Third Effort: General guidance. Create a basis of friendliness with your prospective wife.

Fourth Effort: Learn skilled methods of relating.

Fifth Effort: The fourth effort is very difficult but if you can do it and she can do it, about half the major problems will not exist.

Sixth effort: The objective is to agree on a satisfying marriage relationship before the marriage is announced. Put it in a legal prenuptial.

Seventh effort: Plan the wedding in detail; way ahead of time.

Eighth effort: Lessons you must learn and use every day with your intended wife.

Ninth effort: An extended family as part of your marriage plan.

Tenth effort: Understand male impotence and female loss of interest in sexual action.

Eleventh effort: Assess both of your levels of desire.

After

What are some clues to guide you into being perpetual best friends and lovers?

Any skill improves with repetition

Continuous and never ending improvement is a process to forge a satisfactory marriage

All married couples meet situations that appear to be impossible

More skilled methods and masterful means of relating to your wife

Unskilled thinking of ordinary people would degrade and hinder your married life were you to think and act ordinarily

Legal problems and real problems of family formation

Decide what you want with a woman.

This is a learning process.

Your change in thinking will show you the best possible woman.

Your improvement takes time and practice.

Yes, this improvement is difficult but it will lead you to what you want.

Why I am giving you this information.

You can believe this book is full of advice that will guide you to the best women and to the best possible marriage for you depending on your individual abilities and limitations.

Knowing a woman has a beautiful body, youth and low body weight is not enough information to decide whether a woman is worth being friends with.

Focus on observing couples.

Main lessons of the book.

Three concepts you must know to use this book effectively.

Introduction

You are an enlightened man. This is obvious because you are reading this book. In a few weeks, after you have applied the lessons in this book, you will be substantially more enlightened about being a real man and connecting with the most appropriate woman and entering the family; the complete state of a human being.

The intent of this book is to coach you into several kinds of behavior that will result in your finding, pursuing, attracting, interviewing, checking out our cooperation, and marrying the best possible woman for you. The objective of this book is to guide you to a sacred relationship—a connection that will enrich your life.

You can have a sense of connection with your lover and other people. You can feel whole and completed even if you are not physically near your lover.

This book recommends several other books in addition to several experiences you need to sharpen up you skills. Another book you may like to read is:

Be Your Own Dating Coach: Treat yourself to the ultimate relationship makeover. By Hemmings. The full reference is in the Appendix of this book.

Use the following true claim to find, pursue, attract, interview, and check out your cooperation with the best possible woman:

The dominating thoughts of your mind have a tendency to change into the physical reality of your life.

Yes! That is the key to success. These few words have been used by thousands of men and women to succeed up to their goals.

1

Begin immediately to invent your dominating thoughts.

Man's oldest occupation was finding a mate and keeping her.

Marriage to the best possible woman will usually but not always improve a man's life. Unfortunately, many men do not realize this. Today, American men are not as directed in their efforts to find the best possible woman.

Master the art and science of finding the best possible woman, confirming that she is the best possible, convincing her that you are the best possible man, and marrying her.

Then the hard work begins. How to improve your marriage so it lasts forever.

This book leads you through the stages of achieving this process. This is a learning process. It is part science but much of what you learn depends on your ability to learn and to apply what you learn. You will need to imagine the lessons that you must teach yourself: that is the art of this serious endeavor.

This book is not funny. This is a serious book with over a hundred lessons. If you study this book and experiment with the solutions to your problems, you will learn how to have relationships with women that are satisfying and that last for as long as you want.

A man has a tendency to crave a certain woman or to cling to a woman who rejects him.

The lessons in this book will only work of you are willing to give up craving, to release clinging, and to experiment with the lessons in situations with as many women as it takes to become adept I using the lesson.

GUARANTEE

You can always have all your suffering and loneliness back when you decide to stop reading this book, when you stop getting the recommended books, when you stop experimenting with the valuable information, and when you give up.

As you continue to read this book, watch for the following advice.

The need to go out and be with people: why love and dating are so important.

How to make yourself a powerful support, a major attraction for women.

How to attract a woman.

How to actively pursue a woman.

How to plan ahead for a perfect date.

Skilled communicating, speaking, listening and acting.

How to be a good friend before being a lover.

How you can give and receive hundreds of caresses.

How to be in demand at parties.

How to survive a serious event like a wedding.

How to experience sexual pleasure beyond the earthly plane.

Where you are going with all this knowledge and wisdom (you are becoming the perfect husband).

How to be married happily ever after.

Does that seem like too much to learn? You can to learn these ways of thinking. You can learn to practice it. In the Appendix of this book you will find another book full of amazing lessons.

Luciani, J. J. (2004). *The Power of Self-Coaching: The Five Essential Steps to Creating the Life You Want.*

The way to learn enough to find your best woman and to find out if she is the best possible woman for you is

Continuous and Never-ending Improvement.

This is self coaching. Are you ready to grow into a greater life? Would you like to discover your limits and rise above them?

Chapter 1
The Need to Go Out and Be with People and Why Dating Is So Important

All people everywhere want to be with other people. They want to leave home and go to interesting places with a group of other people.

Most people are fond of the company of other people. It is natural to live in a herd. This could be called a need or an instinct. The need to be loved, to feel love within oneself, to be part of a group, to connect, to have someone belong to you, and to be part of a group of friends. All these needs are strong in almost all people.

The impulse to find companionship fills the emptiness of being disconnected from all people. The emptiness is a terrifying abyss of nothingness. The loneliness causes anxiety. The vacuum hints of madness. There is a threat of a lack of self or a loss of self esteem due to deviation from the norm. There is a sense of inferiority due to being "out of line" or abnormal. The sense of worth is based on approval as a reward for conformity.

You can be approved for being a part of the herd. Everyone has different concepts of reality or what is best to spend time on; you are going to have personal desires and habits that are different from the norm. It is normal to be a little different. It is alright to present a face of conformity even when this requires some mental contortions. So the fear of disapproval causes a little deviation from your own personality. This deviation is the worth the feeling of being in close touch with the "herd."

Being in close touch with the herd may be the instinct of surviving. It is one of the spiritual laws that govern our mental and emotional functions. The spiritual law is not made by government. It is not a law made by people, but it hard to violate.

Jackall describes the extension of this instinct to the practice of corporate management. (Jackall, 1980)

Even when all your bodily needs are satisfied, your experience of aloneness drives you to establish union with other people. Without this union, you would feel insane. Your sanity depends on the necessity to unite with other living beings. This necessity is behind all human intimate relations and all passions that are called love.

The reproduction of humans depends on this necessity. A definition of love is union with other people or things outside oneself under the condition that one retains one's separateness and integrity.

It may be a sharing or a communion. Sharing and loving permits you to transcend your individual existence. The value of the experience is that you feel love within yourself. Love is the experience of solidarity with other living beings. There is also the love for non-living things. Love may exist between parent and child, between man and woman, within the brotherhood or sisterhood, and between animals and humans.

The requirement for love is that you love yourself. You can only love other people as much as you love yourself. One cause of suicide is the lack of connection with another person. Another cause is the lack of influence on other people. The connection with their lovers is more important than anything for some people. That's how important connecting is. Maybe it is that strong for you. So recognize consciously that you want a lover who will connect with you long enough to accomplish a higher level of love. Then you hope that the bonds of love will keep you going when there is conflict. There will indeed be conflict.

Most people feel the drive to connect, not to connect for five minutes, but for days or years. Make the effort to find and connect with a mate who also will recognize this drive consciously.

This is sophisticated behavior. At this high level of love, it may be much more than sexual expression. This could lead to a sacred relationship with your lover; not a temporary sexual release but a valuable investment that grows in value.

Once a woman discovers you are a powerful support, then she only has to smell you, to hear you, to taste you, to touch you, and maybe see you, then she will want you.

After you master the dating game, you can find such a relationship. After you try out the methods in this book on many women, you will be a dating expert. The way you will become an expert is to be a powerful support, a treasure that women will discover. This could lead to the sacred bond of marriage.

Chapter 2
You Are the Powerful Support:
Now Make Yourself a Major Attraction

Give and take in getting a date

Negotiating a date means you are selling something. She is using her time or her beauty or her company so you will pay for her fun time. She is selling something. You are buying the time to evaluate her; to know her better or to have an intimate connection with her. You have to offer something to a woman so she will date you. She has to offer you something because she wants to know you better and she wants you to entertain her at your expense. She has to convince you to give her your precious hours. Are buying and selling enough?

Or do you try the same tricks to get something for nothing? Do you think you can stay the way you are and get awesome dates that you want? If you continuously improve yourself, your will find better women. You have to put out the effort, the time, and the practice to get the dates you want.

Since you bought this book, I am going to make a rich promise.

Here is a full, precise, and guaranteed promise

After you follow the lessons in this book. After you practice the lessons over and over with different women, even when you do not get what you want for a while, you will find yourself with more satisfying women. If you make the effort to become close to an available woman who is within the range of what is possible, your reasonable requirements from a specific woman will be available for you.

Yes, it is humiliating and frustrating to experiment with the lessons and get nothing. If you get what you want without effort, you learn nothing. But you learn valuable behavior when you do not achieve your goal. If you recall the date when you got nowhere and you point out your mistakes you learn more than from successes.

How many times did you date between age 10 and now? How many times did you change something and try again? Many times, right? You achieved more after while. But you still did not get all your goals.

I am guessing you want a better quality of woman and you want more satisfaction from a woman. That is why you bought this book.

Now you are going to get some results. Keep experimenting with the suggestions in the lessons. Make the effort to meet more women to experiment on. Imagine other events to set up with women. Get the other books listed at the end of this book and study them. Practice what you learn. If you keep it up, you will get results. It becomes hard work because you do not always think right nor do you act right. Persist. You will get better. That is a promise.

If you are not willing to put out the effort, the time and the practice to get the dates you want, then stop reading now. Give this book to someone else who will make the effort. Wait a month and ask him how the lessons worked.

Let's be honest. Most men, just like women, are overweight, plain looking, or too old for the women they desire. There are only a few terrific looking men. And there are few really pretty women, and almost no stunning women. So you have to start with what you have, improve it, and locate the best possible woman. Not the perfect woman. But it does not matter how old you are, nor that you are overweight, nor what you look like. You can prove this to yourself by watching couples wherever you go. Most couples are ordinary people; overweight, and not particularly good looking. But they still found each other. Some percentage of these couples are happy. Some are contented. A percentage of any million couples are miserable. There are women who will not speak to you. But there are many who will adore you as you improve.

An important feature to note; most couples found an end to loneliness. This is obvious from the fact that a majority of people are in a couple or a group. They found a contented home life with each other. Each couple decided what contentment meant to them and found it. You can, too.

If you use this book, learning, experimenting with the way you think and act and speak you will be in a happy couple.

Be realistic, love is not based on looks, age, or weight. Many people were convinced to get into a relationship based on appearance, age or body weight. These features become worth little in comparison to the behavior, energetic attitude, morality and other characteristics.

You will know what love is by the time you follow up all the suggestions in this book. You want to be loved. You want to love at least one person, maybe lots of people. However, you are not likely to know the heights of love yet. There is a chapter on this later in this book.

You can have a rich and varied array of dates, regardless of your looks, age, or weight. Remember that younger people do not have a depth of experience, wisdom, or education. Older people do have these. That's why older people are so intriguing, fascinating, and attractive when you get past their looks and their common bodies. Remember that fashion models, movie stars, and sports heroes are not ordinary. Nor are they available. Do not try to be like them. Remember that many of the skinny young beauties (that you are craving) are living scripted lives dictated by their managers. The football stars are on a rigorous time table under the thumb of a coach. They are not free like you. They often are miserable and die young. They have to please everyone. Remember that you only have to please a few people. You will learn how to please a few people well if you follow the directions in this book.

This book does not discuss, body fitness, nor looks, nor age. These are the common measures that men use to evaluate a woman. This is a waste of time. A woman can act out the part you want to see her play. Then you are part of her fake act.

Fitness, looks and age do not measure the valuable qualities you will need from her in a serious engagement. These aspects are superficial and only mean a lot when you first meet. True, the first meeting can make or break the connection and unfortunately, some men care too much about these aspects of a first meeting.

Even though, as you know, these appearances do not support a long-term fulfilling relationship, you still have to cope with the first meeting. If you are not a rich, brilliant conversationalist, you have to be a powerful support. If you are a magnificent hunk, you must be a powerful support anyway. Or you will lose the interest of that fascinating, slightly overweight, wealthy prospective honey. Being a powerful support is the main solution to the problem of marrying the best possible woman that you will gain from this book.

Think about the usual case. A man meets a perfect date. He is awestruck. She is conniving how to get him into bed as much as he is conniving. You are overlooking her annoying habit of smoking and playing with her hair. You are overlooking her sour faced silence and lack of education, her absence of interesting conversation. You are ignoring her drunken voice and heavy German accent. After she notices you and likes your voice, she wants to show how interested she is in you by talking all night. You would have more power to attract if you had the full use of your speaking voice. Or she may listen to you by the hour to boost your ego so you will like her and ask her out again.

She is also purposefully ignoring your mistakes and habits. She even pays the whole bill for your extravagant taste in beer. She will see you often until you refuse to show commitment. You will see her every day if she will do sexual games with you. After a while, you both wake up to the impossible fact of living together. Then you separate, glad that fake, insane sex game is over. You joke about her with your circle of friends. She complains to everyone. What went wrong?

Visualize another case. The woman is ten years older than you are. She is 30 pounds overweight and has a birthmark on her face. But her voice is controlled and powerful. She artfully uses her voice to sooth you and seduce you. You have a hard-on in ten minutes because of her voice. She is witty enough to keep you laughing. She tells entertaining stories. She is sexier than any woman you have ever imagined.

You are amazed that you can be so sexually aroused by an older woman. You are concentrating on doing everything possible to support her. You show her how powerful you are. You support anything she does. You are part of her act, a powerful part. You listen well and are sympathetic when she talks, mirroring her feelings. You notice that she speaks with an exact and educated vocabulary. You search inside yourself for ways show respect and admiration. Taking her to bed is low on your priorities. You insist on paying the whole bill. You find it difficult to persuade her to meet you again. The difficulty gains your respect. You want her more. You are a powerful support who needs her and cares deeply about her.

She feels honored to be with you, to speak with you because you are so powerful and so supportive. She decides she would like to feel the thrill of your obvious appreciation. Going to bed with you is an easy decision to make. When she sees her buddies, she praises you. Even though she may not want them to see you because of your ordinary looks. But she dwells on you until she can meet you again. She is particularly astonished that such a plain man can be so alluring. This makes you even more magnetic.

This is just two of a thousand different combinations and behaviors of women. So here is the problem. You, and most women, are visually judgmental on the first date. This means that how you look, how your voice sounds, how you smell, are the basis for their decision to meet you again. And for your decision to meet them again. Face it. This is true when getting to know most women. Even plain women who are overweight and much too old for you think this way. You will solve this problem as you read this book and follow the directions here. You will change the way you think and you will look for the treasure in women, not looks.

To interest a woman, you have to get through the first date by exhibiting your deep caring for her precious company and by showing that you are a powerful support for her. If you are a normal, plain looking man, you may note her sneer or her cold shoulder at first. You will change her attitude with glow and dazzle or whatever you are good at. In spite of the first trouble, charm her and seduce her according to the type of woman she is and the type of man you are. Your voice, your eyes, your confidence, your grooming, your engrossing conversation, your mysterious distance, your appropriate level of rapport, whatever you bring to the date—these soon blur your appearance.

By the time you finish this book, find many women to experiment on, try out some of the recommended books, you will know how to be a caring and powerful support. If you take action so you are indeed a treasure, you will be in control of your destiny with women.

If a man is a powerful support, he is attractive

Most women want to be supported in some ways, not just money. What else is attractive?

What does it mean "to attract?" Attracting a woman means you motivate her toward you. You act, speak, flirt, and emote, intending to get a result. One woman observes you and, as a result, she acts, thinks, behaves, or emotes. She has her own internal rules in her mind. She may like trying to do what every one else is doing. Or she may be trying to hit on a date as soon as possible. At a party, there are several women. But you want to attract a certain woman. So you have to motivate your desired woman specifically. Other women may respond to your flirting; perhaps your "flirtee" does not pick up the ball. So you motivate her based on her rules and desires (not yours), and you have to get the results you want. How do you motivate her to do what you want? Keep reading and you will know.

Almost all women think they are Cinderella

Especially younger or immature women want a man to be everything to them, to take care of them, to whisk them out of their ordinary life into a fast and glamorous life, to be rich enough to give them all the material things that flash and sparkle. They want to do little while the prince does everything. He gives them a big thrill just because they are themselves. They want a young prince who does not notice all their shortcomings and treats them like a princess. He begins this star treatment at the magical moment that he first sees them.

Go see Walt Disney's film.

One way to attract is to be that prince.

Instead of attracting her, you may try persuading her.

Sometimes attracting does not work. Persuading her to come to you may take several attempts. You change your flirt, speech, action, or emotion each time until you motivate her. You keep it up until she responds. This approach is called, "change something and try again." Persuading may not work either. See Chapter 3 which explains how to pursue her later in this book.

You have high body energy even lust

You can relate to your own motivation toward sexual adventures. If you sense your own sexual drive, then you can understand and motivate thru her drive better. Women are motivated by romance more than sex; the thoughts and feelings of sex more than the physical sex.

You can raise her lust up to your level

Give her the book,

The Art and Science of Dating: Use These Suggestions, Methods, and Tools to Get the Relationship with the Man You Want by Shido of Sukhavati from iUniverse

It was written for women.

Directions to get it online are given at the end of this chapter. You could print out the directions and give them to your best woman so she can get the book.

The direct way to get her started at your level is to give her the book. Go online and buy it for her.

How attractive are you today in terms of senses, appearance, smell, voice sound, and touch.

At first, you attract by appealing to a woman's five senses and her imagination. Ask yourself the following questions. Write the answers in your journal.

> ➢ Why would a woman want to go out on a date with you?
> ➢ Do you appear to be desirable, friendly, trustworthy, powerful, rich, or fun?

> Does your speech sooth a woman or irritate her?
> Do you have a delicious, manly scent, or do you smell like garlic, or is your cologne too strong?
> How about your breath? What do you eat or drink that affects your aroma?
> Are you a drunken slob or are you cozy and huggable?
> Do you listen to your lady friend or do you talk all the time?
> Do you encourage her to talk or is there an embarrassing silence?
> Are your clothes trendy or sloppy, raggedy or clean?
> Do you have the boring habit of talking about trivial things, or are you witty?
> What kind of feelings do you have: negative, curious, lighthearted, sad?

In any case, you'd better figure out how to feel joyful and positive because women can usually guess your feelings.

Why do you need to answer these questions?

Questions spark your inventive mind to come up with answers. When you imagine the answers, you believe them. If you read the answers, you think they are my ideas. Your ideas are more exactly suited to you than mine.

When you answer the questions, you will discover what you have that is so wonderful that you need to offer it to the right woman. You have to offer something to a woman so she will date you.

Do you think you can stay the way you are and get awesome dates?
Do you know what you need to improve?
Are you writing the answers?

The answers will make you a treasure.

A later chapter is about how to be a treasure. You will make yourself into a treasure that women can detect.

Women love supportive men, men who show how much they love women, men who show the power and ability to support them. Women love to talk endlessly, so listen as much as you can. To be a powerful support, you have to put out the effort, the time, and the practice experimenting to get the dates you want.

How to be more desirable, communicative, magnetic, and attractive

In what ways do you want to be more desirable, communicative, magnetic and attractive? Give it some thought. Did you answer? Is becoming desirable worthwhile? Is it worthwhile to use your time and money to be more communicative? You are motivated are you not? You will be grateful that you took the time and invested the money.

Consider how to make yourself more attractive.

One type of attraction is to be a happy person. When you are happy, you influence your woman to be happy. When she is happy near you, she thinks you are a powerful support. Think about the opposite. Does you lover like it when you are grouchy or depressed? Or does she like you better when you are joyful, and contented? You do not have to answer this question. The answer is obvious.

When does she treat you the way you like; when you are complaining, grouchy, or depressed? Or when you are joyful, playful, or contented? When you are happy, you have a high probability of accepting her and appreciating her. Then she treats you right.

What you do and how you feel depends on what you are pondering. It depends on your opinions and your preconceived evaluation of the world. So you could dwell on being happy. You could decide to feel joyful and contented. You could tell yourself you have the best possible life. You could tell yourself that you are getting better each day in terms of your feelings. Every time you feel like complaining, you could insist on saying something positive. You could decide to say how much you appreciate the blessings in your life, or think of all the advantages you have. You could even think of all the people who do not enjoy all your advantages. You can invent your joyful life.

So what is happiness? We could define it by its opposite. The opposite of happiness is depression, the inability to feel. Depression is being dead while your body is alive. It is the inability to express joy, and also the inability to express sadness or anything. It is not fun and pleasure. It may be boredom.

Happiness is not being glad to kill another hour. It is not being aware of the lurking demon of boredom.

Then happiness is a state of intensified vitality. It fuses our effort to understand people and to be a part of humanity. Happiness results from touching the rock bottom of reality. We touch ourselves and our oneness with others. We are connected to all life. We feel a productive relatedness to all living things and to ourselves. Happiness is to experience fullness, joy, vitality. It results in an inner peace and contentment—but not in the sense of buying and consuming. Consuming is an attempt to fill an emptiness. Happiness is using love to realize our oneness with something greater.

The aim of your life is to live it intensely. Meaning arises out of being fully born and being fully awake.

The subject of this book is dating, sort of acting out a fantasy. When two people act out a fantasy together, happiness spreads out to connecting with people, or at least the whole community living nearby. Many people realize that happiness results from connecting with pets, or gardens, or the forest or all life. So awareness of your being part of all life is happiness.

Another fundamental problem is a woman who does not understand men or who is ignorant of how to speak or act around men

You must have met these immature, self-centered, and impossible women. The solution is to inform her of a book that will teach her about men and dating. You could even give her the book. Email her these directions.

The Art and Science of Dating: Use These Suggestions, Methods, and Tools to Get the Relationship with the Man You Want
To buy online an eBook which she can read on your smart phone or on other reader: go online
Go to iuniverse.com
Click bookstore
At top is a search window: type Shido of Sukhavati in the window
A screen appears: Advanced search
Scroll down to The Art and Science of Dating by Shido of Sukhavati. She can buy a hard copy or an eBook for your electronic book reader.
Click add to cart.
Click checkout.
Enter address and credit card number and so on

OTHER PLACES YOU CAN BUY IT ON THE INTERNET

Barnes & Noble, Inc. [ONLINE IT IS

HTTP://WWW.BARNESANDNOBLE.COM

Look for "books" on the left side and click it

A menu of book types appears

Look for "Self improvement" and click it

"Self-Help & Self-Improvement"

AT the top is a window, type in Shido of Sukhavati and click "search"

"The Art and Science" shows

Buy it

Retail -- Online Sales include outlets like:

Amazon Marketplace [ONLINE IT IS AMAZON.COM]

Click "BOOKS"

TYPE into window "Shido of Sukhavati"

Push "return" button

"The Art and Science" will show BUY IT

www.ebay.com

look for "all categories" click it

look for "books" and click it

The book screen will appear

type into the window "Shido of sukhavati"

"The Art and Science" will appear, Buy it

Other web sites:

Abebooks

eBay

Froogle

Alibris

Overstock.com

GOOGLE.COM

Here are some more questions for you. They will help you to think of ways to be a powerful support. When you are s powerful support, women will be drawn to you.

> ➤ Who can you expect to attract today with your physical appearance?
> ➤ Who is interested in your mind today?
> ➤ Are you ready to learn to speak well at all times, to listen well?
> ➤ Can you enter into spiritual harmony with people you adore?

Write your answers so you can realize your progress later. Then you can have all the qualities women look for.

How you can attract women is the subject in the next chapter.

Chapter 3
How to Attract Her

You have learned how to be a powerful support by experimenting with the ideas in the last chapter. So, you are ready to attract a new woman.

How are you going to attract? Have you noticed the attention women give you when you feel terrific and your body is in good shape? That is a way to attract. The basic requirement is that you feel happy and your body is neither fat nor skinny. That is how you start attracting. You do not have to be skinny or tan to be in good shape. You are more attractive when you show glowing skin and firm muscles (not sagging or atrophied muscles). You are more attractive when you are energized and positive, even joyful. This is how you signal health at any age.

The objective of attracting women is to be loved. Chances are that you would welcome an environment of love. If everyone loved you, that would be a better surrounding. That would be a good position to start.

A list of attractions you can learn that will help women (and other people) love you.

Then try them out so they become habitual and come to you when you need them.

First Attraction: Make yourself joyful and contented

The basic rule: to be happy, keep a positive attitude. Positive attitude generates vital energy. Positive mental attitude means that you see the benefits in everything. You do not notice the dirt or the trouble.

The current word for vital energy is "HOT," as in "he is hot." Positive attitude helps you expect to find the best woman and lets you recognize her when she shows up. Positive attitude helps you solve the problems of dating. The inflow of positive energy can make you a treasure all by itself. When you have a positive attitude, you relax into easy power over women. All people, of whom half are women, are attracted to a positive attitude.

Now for a thought experiment: Pretend you have tried one of the methods advised in this book with five different women and it did not work. Positive attitude will give you the energy to realize that you learned something with each woman. It is easier to realize this if you write down your experiences. Your positive attitude will remind you that you are learning more each time you try.

Soon you will be good at the method of learning. You can say to yourself, "I am good. I am going to get the outcome I want. I will persist." Say this out loud. Say it with feeling when you awake in the morning. Say it several times each day.

Get the book *Success through a Positive Mental Attitude* by Napoleon Hill and W. Clement Stone. It has been a best seller since 1960. And *The Power of Positive Thinking* by Norman Vincent Peale. It brought the concept of positive thinking into the American mainstream in 1952. These books are listed at the end of this book.

Second attraction: Express yourself with words, vocal expressions and body movements

When you express more, you reduce stress. Men who stifle their feelings are making a potentially fatal mistake. Expressing emotions during arguments actually helps people live longer. This means showing your feelings. It does not mean screaming and swearing. Married men who had the habit of shutting up defined as " bottling up their feelings to avoid conflict" with their wives, were more than four times more likely to die of all causes during the 10-year study than those who showed their feelings in family discussions.

Ironically, clamming up may have helped preserve the men's relationships, but it definitely didn't preserve their lives. Men were actually more likely than women to keep quiet during disputes. But what we do know is that men and women are physiologically stressed by different aspects of marriage, so we need to dig deeper to find out why.

When you are angry, you tend toward depression, which only makes marital problems worse. So express whatever negative emotions are coming up. Women understand the language of emotions better than men. Your woman friend just may surprise you and let you know that she understands. What you think is only part of the message. The other part is what you feel. More communication is better than less.

There is a relief in expressing your feelings. There is no relief when you are insulting or trying to wound your wife or lover. If you are mean to her, you will get the payback later. If you do not get it today.

Third attraction: express your feelings to let your woman understand you

Memorize the formula below. Start practicing it today and every day. Practice it with every one; not just your girlfriend. Here is the formula:

"I FEEL (SAY A FEELING WORD) WHEN YOU (SAY HER ACTION) BECAUSE (SAY WHY YOU REACT TO HER ACTION)."
Examples:
"I FEEL ANGRY WHEN YOU CALL ME NAMES BECAUSE IT REMINDS ME OF SCHOOL DAYS."

"I FEEL JOYFUL WHEN YOU SMILE BECAUSE I KNOW YOU ARE SO LOVING AND BIG HEARTED."

Women want you to express certain feelings, like love, but not others, like rage.

You have feelings that help you survive and help you fit into a group. Get to know your feelings.

You have feelings that warn you something is wrong and that caution you to change your behavior. Become familiar with these.

You have feelings that you are surviving, that you are accepted by the group, and that you can enjoy life. Practice recognizing these.

You have pleasant feelings, painful feelings, and neither pleasant nor painful feelings.

Expressing your feelings is soothing to both your spirit and your achy joints. Because you feel the freedom to share what's in your heart and mind without worrying that your girlfriend might reject you. Later, you become so much more relaxed. And then you feel much less physical pain and sickness. There is a connection. Got it?

Fourth attraction: let pleasure lead your relationship into joy and contentment

Before you go on a date, make yourself feel pleasant. How can you truly enjoy pleasant occasions if you are in a rage or jealous? You can learn how to change your feelings. Then women will want to go out with you.

Ask for what you need from your lover. Whether it's a whole-body massage or an opportunity to complain. Having a great marriage or relationship makes a huge difference in how happy and healthy you feel.

Enjoyable experiences pump up your immune system, confirms Dr. Carl Charnetski, a professor of psychology at Wilkes University, in Pennsylvania, the co-author with Dr. Francis Brennan of *Feeling Good Is Good for You.*

And the most pleasurable way to protect yourself from colds and the flu is by having regular sexual play. In a recent study, men and women who made love once or twice a week had 30 percent higher levels of immunoglobulin A (a mucous membrane antibody that fights respiratory viruses and bacteria) than those who abstained.

However, Aristotle was right: All things in moderation—including sex. If more sex is not on your agenda, try listening to relaxing music, playing with pets, or even cultivating an optimistic attitude. Research shows these things increase the antibody, too.

We've known for a long time that stress is hard on the immune system. But what's new is finding out that pleasure makes you more immune. Anything enjoyable, from eating chocolate—or just smelling it—to making love has the potential to make you happy for your date.

Even anticipating something nice that's going to happen later in the week stimulates joy. It looks as though pleasure has the opposite cumulative effect that chronic tension does. Over time, injecting frequent small jolts of joy in your life starts you on an upward spiral to better health. And makes you a desirable date.

Fifth attraction: Joyful and contented people laugh more than angry and dissatisfied people

Have a chuckle and be a joyful date. Laughter has such a powerfully positive effect. You know your date goes better with laughter. Laughter acts on women like a sexual stimulant. Laughter may act on you like a sexual stimulant too.

Sixth attraction: Your best possible woman will be good company if she feels you love her. Then you will feel joyful inside yourself

Adoring your best possible woman or wife can help keep your heart healthy. A study found that men who rated their romantic relationship as highly satisfactory had fewer cardiovascular risk factors. Not only did the happily married men have lower cholesterol, but their blood pressure also was lower. This was in comparison with unattached men or unhappily married men.

Why would the state of your union have any effect on your cholesterol levels? First, a loving relationship means less stress, which means fewer hormones such as cortical, one of the chief culprits in weight gain.

Overweight men have fewer dates. Do you think huge fat men are in demand for dates? They are if they have become a treasure by following the advice in this book. Less weight gain helps decrease the threat of heart disease, the number one killer of American men. Indeed, the study tracked about 500 men ages 42 to 50 over a 13-year period. It found that happy husbands typically avoided weight gain, even during middle age, a time when men often pack on extra pounds. However, men who were unattached or unhappily married usually got heavier over the years. That's dangerous, because being overweight increases the risk for diabetes, cancer, and heart disease. So you need to feel love for someone, maybe your dog. Then you will lose weight and be more attractive and live longer. Fall in love right now. What a payoff! You have love, weight loss and better dates.

Support from your girlfriend or wife also can boost your motivation to ditch heart-harming habits, such as smoking or a high-fat diet. Consider John in California. Until his marriage, he was a confirmed couch potato whose only exercise was an occasional walk. Just before he married, he started a gym membership. Since then, he started working out three to five times a week. That means exercise machines, weights, and the treadmill. He was already slender, but his wife has commented on how much healthier he looks. His posture is better. He feels more confident

Seventh attraction: Confidence and erect posture make you attractive as a date

Confidence tends to show in your posture. A confident man is perceived as one who can support a woman.

Eighth attraction: The feelings of determination, ambition, and seeking to achieve a goal impress women

Those who express these symptoms of success are called "thrivers." They cultivate the seventh and eighth attractions. They embody the expression "when the going gets tough, the tough get going." It turns out those tough types, "thrivers" may boast better health than those who shrink from adversity. They also satisfy your date that she is with a supportive man. She may like it when other women are envious of her for having such a terrific date.

Literature is full of stories about people who make transcendent life changes after a tragedy. A professor of psychiatry and bio-behavioral sciences at UCLA evaluated the immune functions of men who had a relative die—usually their mother—due to breast cancer and. Those who placed the greatest importance on setting and achieving emotionally significant goals, such as improving relationships, had the highest level of activity in their "natural killer" cells in the blood. These cells are the immune-system in the blood that attack viruses and certain kinds of tumors.

Ninth attraction: You are as happy as you want to be

You decide how to feel about your life. You can learn how to call up happiness within yourself. Choose joy. This book hints about how to choose your feelings.

You cast your mental attitude over all your thoughts. What you dwell upon, and what you think about all day, creates your mental attitude.

You could examine your feelings and cultivate joy, compassion, and loving kindness. Then you would create the joy and contentment that make your life full of vitality.

Tenth attraction: The most attractive men have a healthy mind and healthy feelings in a healthy body.

Memorize this brief truth.

Women have a tendency to love healthy men.

Most women, but not all women, are in love with feeling love or knowing another person loves them. How do you define love?

This is an important question. If you ask anyone what love is, you will hear a different answer from each one. So what could be a general answer? People love what their senses tell them about another person. There may be many senses involved. Read *A Natural History of the Senses* by Diane Ackerman

<u>Visual appearance:</u> A woman may feel love for you because of appearance. Consider that men easily feel love for a woman who looks like their ideal, which is why women try to look their best.

<u>Sound</u>: A person may feel love for you because of the sound of your voice. Consider that a man can easily feel love for a woman with a sexy voice. This is why women study how to have a sexy voice. You could take speaking voice lessons for maximum effect.

<u>Smell</u>: A woman may feel love for a man just because he has a manly aroma or the right deodorant. Your perfume mixes with your bodily secretions to create your total fragrance or stink. The smell of what you eat and drink (like beer or fruit) will secrete from your skin. Women are involuntarily attracted to some of the sexual hormones that men exude. In plain talk, this means that women like some types of sweat. If you have an attractive, sexy smell, do not mask these hormones. If you eat more vegetables and herbs (not garlic and onions), and less red meat, your fragrance will signal that you are edible.

<u>Taste</u>: A woman may feel love because of the right taste of a kiss. Consider why breath mints are so popular. She may love you because of your cooking. Food is sensuous if it is delicious. It is the royal road to a woman's heart. Eating involves many senses: the visual beauty of the food, touch by the mouth, smell, taste, even sound.

<u>Touch</u>: A woman can immediately love you for the touch of your lips, or your strong hands. She may become addicted to your massage. There are obvious sexual touches in massage and many more subtle touches—maybe 1,000 touches.

You can invent non-sexual touches, sensual touches and sexual touches.

**Eleventh attraction: A woman's need for support can mean
she needs a powerful man, not just one who can support her**

<u>Gifts:</u> Women love to receive gifts like jewelry and chocolates. A woman may be deeply touched by something you give her. A gift can be touchable or it can be an experience.

<u>Security:</u> Many women need security above all else. A woman may love you because you will never leave her. Or because she is convinced that you will support her words, her opinion, her needs for food, warmth or for love.

Most women want power and money. Some women take notice of powerful men having fun. If you notice a woman who thinks you are powerful, be subtle about revealing the extent of you power and wealth. Reveal everything later. She will be more attracted because she will imagine you have exactly what she wants.

**Announcing eighteen more ways to attract that outstanding
woman who interests you and who you crave
Twelfth attraction: the basic requirement is that you
feel terrific and your body is in good shape.**

Would you know if a woman felt terrific? You probably would. Using the same intuition, women sense what you are feeling. When you feel joyful and energized, women are drawn to you. So that is how you start.

Thirteenth attraction: to meet a woman you do not know yet, say a neutral observation with a smile or a joke.

When you are in right place and you are magnetic because you feel terrific and your body is in good shape and you state almost any friendly and harmless observation, you will attract almost any person. The woman has already noticed you and wants to meet you so an observation is an invitation. Saying, "hello" does not engage her because it lacks imagination and does not suggest a reply.

Remember. What you say is not very important if she likes your looks, adores the sound of your voice, thinks you will spend lot of money on her, senses your power, and is drawn to your aroma. So do not yell or say obnoxious things. Say neutral things with a smile or a joke.

Example, "That shirt is my favorite color." She will reply to you. Then you can go from there.

Easy, is it not?

But she may walk off in five minutes. So you must have more than good looks, more than a sonorous voice, more than a powerful presence, more than a generous approach, and more that an aromatic after shave lotion. You need more than a friendly comment to continue attracting her tomorrow. Keep reading and find out how.

You need to ask her to write her phone number, name and email address and so on. You need to ask her to meet you tomorrow. If tomorrow is not possible, then persuade her to meet you another time. If you have what she needs, like a powerful support, she will meet you. Other qualities she may need are humor, loyalty, likability, and trustworthiness. So you need to find out what you have that she needs.

To complicate things, not all women are the same. Maybe she wants you to entertain her, to immediately buy her something or give her a valuable gift. You can ask bluntly about what she wants to do next.

You can experiment. Don't give up but sometimes you will never see her again.

Try again with another irresistible woman. You can learn everything you need to know. There is a lot to know.

The next time you meet, you must figure out what keeps attracting her so she will be your lover or friend.

See Chapter7. Skilled Speaking, Listening, and Acting. Adapt to the situation.

Remember, you can learn everything to attract many different kinds of women. How do you know you are learning? You will notice you have

- ✓ many new lovers and friends whom you feel good about,
- ✓ Engrossing conversations,
- ✓ Sexual seduction,
- ✓ improved etiquette in serious company,
- ✓ Confidence and mastery in groups,
- ✓ You know want to say.

Try reading, *Making Contact, by* V. Satir

It is described in the recommended books at the end of this book.

Fourteenth attraction: Engrossing conversation

Often, conversation is a major part of the date. Most of the first date is checking out the woman while she checks you out. She is watching your appearance, your movements, sensing your feelings, listening to your tone of voice, grasping what motivates you, getting your aroma. You are doing the same thing. About ten minutes out of the hour, she is listening to your speech, your words. For those ten minutes, what you say can make a big difference.

The exception is the mentally oriented woman. She likes to talk more than anything. She may even listen. A woman who likes to talk usually likes back-and-forth banter, like a tennis match. At that time, you want to learn magnetic conversation skills.

This is a skill that you can learn. This is not a skill you were born with. You can learn by reading one of the books listed at the bottom of appendix A. For example, try the books:

How to Talk to Anyone, Anytime, Anywhere: The Secrets of Good Communication by Larry King, the TV personality. Or

What Do I Say Next? Talking Your Way to Business and Social Success by Susan RoAne. Or try *Relationships for Dummies*. You cannot lose. Study them and memorize the methods. Practice this new skill. Sooner than you would imagine, you will be an interesting talker.

Fifteenth attraction: Listening

Think about how to listen so she knows you are focusing on her. Close your mouth and listen most of the time.

Second best is to have an agenda prepared so there is no embarrassing time when neither of you knows what to say.

Ponder *Men Are from Mars, Women Are from Venus* by John Gray, because women are really different from men. Then, you can talk about the book.

If you are interested in seducing her, sympathetic talk and listening are good moves toward intimacy. Would you like your new friend to lust for you again and again? The fastest way to attract your lover forever is to read the chapter below on How to Experience Sexual Thrills Beyond the Earthly Plane. It is just a tiny beginning. It will give you ideas to make sexual contact more thrilling. Get a partner and practice.

Another way to attract is to talk about commitment. To learn this, get the book, *The Power of Commitment. by* S. M. Stanley. Lead her carefully to the subject of commitment. Show how committed you are. Suggest it. It is amazing how attractive you become when you make a commitment. Some clues from you will help her volunteer to be committed.

Sixteenth attraction: Communicate what you want from her

Why should you care? Because you have to let women know. Some women like to please you. Some women want you to be predictable. A women has to know this to understand you.

Some women do not care at all what you want. Disappear from their lives.

Virtually all women assume you want to take them to bed right away. In any case, when a woman asks you, you better know the answer. The answer may help you to be satisfied with your life. She is asking you to make an offer to her. Then she will ask you for something in return. She may wait until she has given you her sexual attentions to ask for something. When you answer, it helps if you are confident, enthusiastic and grateful.

Then try reading, *La Vie En Rose* just before you go into a group or a serious affair. You will be in a tolerant mood.

It helps if you are confident, enthusiastic and grateful. To express these traits, cultivate a positive mental attitude. This is in addition to feeling good and having a body that is in good shape. To develop your attitude, read *How to Succeed With a Positive Mental Attitude* by Napoleon Hill and W. Clement Stone.

Also, before going to party, or on a date, read something you can bring up in conversation. What you read depends on the people at the party. Try *La Vie En Rose by* Glocheux listed at the end of this book. It will change your attitude so you can be more grateful. Also it will help you to invent interesting conversation.

What do you think most men want in addition to passionate sexual experience? For many men, the answer is men want a group of pals. Obviously, women do not want to hear this. If a woman gets in the way of this desire, a man usually wants to put her in the back seat. She will have less importance to him.

How do most men act in a group of pals? If you do not want a group of pals, this will help you to understand brotherhoods or gangs of men. Then you can react appropriately.

Consider this typical case of two men who have just come into a locker room. They are drenched with rain.

Lenny yells, "Hey you! Get out of here and lean against the wall outside until you shed that water."

"You shut up!" retorted Red. "We'll put you out there to catch the water we missed," he threatens as Pete rubs him down briskly to heat him up.

Just good natured harassment. Men want to have a group of men pals. They want to joke around and to open up by talking. Opening up means to talk about embarrassing things. They want to admit they do not know something and want someone to teach them without humiliating them or getting mad. They want to trust a group. A group that will not to gossip about them; about what they do not know; about embarrassing things.

Men feel alive when surrounded by their best friends, all laughing and contented, kidding each other, and exchanging insulting banter which does not sting. They engage in various tasks like playing cards or fixing things. One will sing while others laugh. This is the atmosphere they love. Sharing hard work and danger breeds fellowship. So no member of the group ever counts personal safety before duty to his companions. There is manhood for you; contempt for convention and danger. There is honor. There is unity of thought and purpose set in the rough speech. They are the dominating living forces. This is found in war.

You will find this camaraderie in groups of men everywhere in the world. Rejecting the men's group and complaining does not work. It is better to join in and accept this male bonding. Adapt to the situation. Don't expect. Just adjust.

What do men not want. Men do not want people who are hostile or angry toward them. This is true for about nine out of ten men and women.

You need to understand your feelings. If you feel hostile or angry (maybe she does not like your friends), convert your feelings to love, appreciation, gratitude, and acceptance before you meet your woman. You can learn how to make the conversion.

But what do you want. You may want something entirely different than this. What can you tell a new woman that you want? Most men want sexual contact.

If you can tell her this in a subtle way, about half the women will probably like it. Because she may want to please you. A woman has to know this to understand men. Even some men do not know the answer. Some men do not know what they want. The answer may help you to be satisfied with your relationship.

Seventeenth attraction: recognize that most women, not all, want to have a sexual event with you.

Learn the art of seducing women. Women look for many clues to excite them into willing sexual partners. Some women want power and money. Some want laughs. Some want mystery so they can pretend they have found the perfect man and that sexual contact is a good way to seal the deal. If this is a condition you are meting, do not reveal everything about yourself until later.

Who can sense what a woman is hiding behind her facade? You have to learn to see behind the mask. Here is a tip. Some women seem perfectly sexy but are hiding something. Just like you are. Watch for what is being hidden. The hidden things will bite you later.

Some women have a tough exterior. This is a mask hiding insecurity. Rough speech and a hard attitude hide a weak and easily hurt interior. Is it possible that the raunchy and randy women have weaknesses just like the delicate girls? Yes. How do you find out what she is hiding behind her mask? How do you recognize a mask? Give her a chance to soften up. You will be surprised. Even the tough women have a vulnerable spirit which you must respect. Show respect and kindness. The mask will come down for a gentleman who shows respect.

Women want you to show respect. Most women know all people want respect. Learn how to show respect. This will help you with men too. Part of respect means you are humble. You do not think you are more important or more powerful than the woman. This is very attractive for almost anyone, women or men.

Almost all women talk through their feelings. They expect you to understand their feelings. They want to talk about feelings. Women want you to express certain feelings, like love, but not others, like anger. Think about your feelings. Must you really be mindful of your feelings? Yes.

What are all the kinds of feelings you can have? Answer this question. And learn the names of your feelings. How can you change your feelings when you feel anger, rage, jealousy, fear and guilt? That is possible but difficult. Never, ever show up for a date with these feelings. Better not to show up.

Try to identify each individual woman's feelings and name them. Ask about their feelings to see if you have guessed right. You have feelings that help you survive and feelings that help you fit into a group. Feelings that you are accepted by the group You have feelings that warn you about some things that are wrong and that caution you to change your behavior. You have feelings that you are surviving in spite of trouble. YHou feel that you can enjoy life. You have pleasant feelings and painful feelings. Talk about your feelings.

Women are disarmed when you talk about their feelings. They usually will open up to you if you talk about feelings. Some women despise a man who exposes his feelings. Be careful.

If you fall for the trap of talking too much, she will resent you. If you do not ask her about herself she will scorn you. If you do not listen she will hate you.

If women like to talk so much, why do they ask so many questions and listen so much? They flatter the male ego as a way to attract you and to interview you. Do you want to learn how to listen to endear yourself to a woman? Ask about her interests and let her talk. She will stop when she is through. When she is talking, she thinks you are a wonderful conversationalist. An eager listener impresses a woman (and a man). You can talk after she sells herself on you.

For your own peace of mind, accept that women change their minds. So what they want changes. One day, a woman shows no interest and the next she shows focused attention.

Eighteenth attraction: your speech, your senses, and your body movements are in harmony with a particular woman

You have to figure out what each woman relates to. Give her what she wants. You relate to what she wants. If you cannot give her desired mode of experience, leave her alone. Go to the next woman.

Do not give up. Some women are focused on things they see. They like to talk and to think a lot. They like you to talk as fast as they talk and think. You do the same.

Women who get most of their information through seeing usually are mentally oriented. For example, they think about what it would be like to kiss you, or to make love to you. But they may wait to actually kiss you or jump in bed with you.

Some women are mostly interested in sounds, voices, music. Violent sounds, like a man yelling, may turn them off. Other women like loud music. A man screaming may be hell for them. They may like men with soft whispers for voices. They may have trained voices. Your voice may be the key to exciting them sexually. Find out what they want. You like the same things and relate through the channel of sound.

You would have more power to if you had the full use of your speaking voice. Learn to speak. Do you want to learn how to endear yourself to a woman? Go to acting school if necessary. Your voice is a potent tool. A kind voice with a deep tone will draw almost any women to you. How much of your body is included in your speaking voice? All of your body. You learn this in speaking voice class. You cannot learn to use your voice like a musical instrument by reading. Take lessons. I guarantee that the time and money will be worth it.

Some women like moving their bodies, perhaps in sports, or dancing. They are focused on their bodies. Their frame of reference is action, like war movies or TV football. They will move into your space and kiss or grab you. Some like to personally fight. They actually go to a bar and pick a fight. Some like luxurious beds or clothes on their bodies. With these women, you relate through touch, sports, and dancing.

Most women want to have a man induce particular feelings in them. Women are mostly attracted by the feeling they get from a man. Next in importance after feelings, most women want a man with a certain appearance. Yes, it is superficial and short-sighted. But it is true. Women are practical in the sense that they know they have to feel good around a man or there will not be any relationship. After they are attracted by their own feelings, they start looking for your other features.

They are also practical in wanting a man with money or other indications that he can support them. Good looks and money will not hold the interest of a woman if she feels bad around you. To hold a woman long enough to get a commitment even for sex, you must be magnetic. You must convince her that you can support her. She needs money but more than that, she needs sympathy, fun, respect, deference. She wants to feel romantic and removed from the pull of reality. This is not true for all women. These are all types of support that women want.

A particular woman may seem committed and even marry you. But if you are not able to support her, she will fade out of your life. Even if she still lives with you, she will fade out. Then you will have the same loneliness and heartbreak you had before you thought you were committed or married. Plan ahead to keep her interested.

Another case, when a woman has lost interest, she will cheat on you with other men, or you will notice a shift in attitude into boring sex and insincere seduction.

Study this book or one of the others recommended at the end with the woman who you want to become close to. Keep your focus and her focus on continuous and never-ending improvement of your relationship.

Your woman may focus on your commitment to her. Therefore, commit exclusively and forever. Therefore, learn the art sexual love as well as feeling love. The paradox is that the best seduction is to wait for sexual contact. Wait until she realizes that you are a whole person, not just a self-propelled sex organ. She will wait if you promise to be a powerful support.

On the other hand, you must realize she is the whole person, not just a sexual toy.

Nineteenth attraction: never have sexual contact with a woman on the first date

Face it. You will lose interest in her if you have a reckless or even a passionate lovemaking with her immediately. You may never want to see her again. You may be so inept that she will be embarrassed to see you again. Then you miss out on the payoff of a wonderful friend and lover. You can think of exceptions to this, but the rule holds true for most men. Men are fickle, even you may be ready to move on after the first fling in bed. In this birth control pill age, women will move on too. Most men just want a one-night stand.

Before going to bed with a woman, get your and her blood tests for sexually transmitted diseases. Do I have to tell you why? Be sure to use two contraceptives, the woman's and the man's. All contraception is less than 100 percent effective, but two contraceptives are about 99 percent effective. That means she gets pregnant or you become diseased once every 100 lays. That does not mean you get in trouble on lay 100. You could get a disease on the first try and not again for 99 times.

Have the courage to face the truth. Real sex is not like virtual TV. There are real consequences. Ask yourself, "Is 15 minutes of contact, during which the pleasure is small or uncertain, worth dying for? Or ask yourself, "Am I ready to pay for an abortion, or a legal paternity suit, and maybe never again have the ability to have a hard-on?" Is this 20 minutes of awkward fooling around, and the bragging rights, worth taking care of a baby for three years, a child for ten years and a teenager for ten years?

Twentieth attraction: Wait for sexual gratification and other more meaningful goals

Having had the courage to face the truth, the payoff is deeper attraction. Realize that the longer you go without sexual contact with a new woman, the better the relationship you will have. And the longer the relationship will last. And the more pleasure you will have during sex play. So how do you prolong her interest without using sexual favors?

Twenty-first attraction: indirect seduction

The most seductive men are powerful supporting images who do not actually emphasize sex. They suggest sexual contact under the right conditions. They make indirect jokes about sexual escapades that are possible. They emphasize their desire to enjoy a multitude of diverse sexual pastimes. They create an undertone of intimacy. This is the definition of "sexy."

Read in the chapters above about making yourself a powerful support. Women love mystery. Make them work for everything. Women value what they work for just as men do. They do not consider a man to be valuable if he is easy to date or easy to seduce. Give up your secrets a little at a time. Invent a mask and use it for a while. Who can sense what you are hiding behind your facade? Then give the carefully selected stunning lady the privilege of knowing who is behind the mask. She will be grateful.

**Twenty-second attraction: when you are on a first
date, complain about small defects in the woman.
In particular, complain about her not giving you anything
in exchange for all the money you spent, all your time,
and all your entertaining company. When she is defensive,
let her promise to give you something in return**

This sounds strange. However, it is proven to be very attractive.
You want her to be grateful and show it. Being grateful is the opposite
of taking you for granted. Do not let a woman assume anything about
you. Present a new challenge to your woman every day. You need fresh
proof of love every day. Does this sound strange? Most women love
small challenges. However, they will give up on impossible obstructions.
Most women love to work for a goal. But they want a guarantee that
they will achieve the goal after reasonable effort.

Almost all women love to give things to a man who is precious to
them. They feel grateful when a man accepts gifts and shows abundant
appreciation for their gifts. This includes sexual favors. Show lavish
praise for sex expertise. Show frequent and enthusiastic approval.
Remember, no appreciation and no grace equals no more gifts.

**Twenty-third attraction: withhold information about your past,
your assets, your experiences, especially about other women**

Almost all women want to know everything about you. Therefore,
put up a lot of barriers. Wear a lot of clothes. Let her take some of your
clothes off, but not all. Assume a mask, a pose. Then her take it off.
Then she will dig find more of your education, sports awards, travel,
or high income. But never, ever, talk about your past experience with
other women. That is poison.

In any case, when you meet her, wear high quality clothes in the trendy fashion. If possible and appropriate, wear a suit. Many people are intimidated by a suit lately. Some women actually think a suit is a bad sign. But they are sill impressed. On the second date you can dress in an entirely different trend. Decide whether the woman is attracted to your body. If so, wear clothes that show off your buttocks or other outstanding feature. No, I am not kidding. For body oriented women, these are the marks of the elegant man who has class, and high value. The first date sets the stage for her later attitude toward you. You never get a second chance to make a first impression.

Remember, you hold back or even wear a mask on your first date. But you look, speak and behave like a prince. Allow her to discover how valuable you are.

Twenty-fourth attraction: This is the opposite of the last attraction. This is her being attracted to you because you want to know everything about her

Just as you wear a mask, so does she. Identify her mask. An example is a woman who has particularly sexy clothes. She speaks about sexual acts, flirts with her skin, and tells sexy jokes. This may be the teasing mask hiding her fear of sex. Of the women who are very sexually suggestive, maybe 4 of 5 usually express themselves by talking, not by going to bed. Some women seem perfectly sexy or even sly. They seem to be hiding something. Just as you are.

Some women have a tough exterior. This is a mask hiding insecurity or her lack of confidence in her social value. Rough speech and hard attitude hide a weak and easily hurt emotional ego. Is it possible that the raunchy and randy women have weaknesses just like the sensitive guys? Yes. Even the tough women have a vulnerable spirit that you must respect. Note, here are two undesirable features here, unpreventable toughness and weak feelings that are too easy to hurt.

How do you find out what she is hiding behind her mask? How do you recognize a mask? Give her a chance to soften up. You will be surprised. Show respect, appreciation and admiration. Women love these responses. Some masks will come down for a man who shows respect. The mask may seem to come off but there is another mask behind it. Some masks never come down. Watch for what is being hidden. The hidden things will bite you later.

Twenty-fifth attraction: show impeccable respect, appreciation, and admiration

Women want you to show respect, appreciation, and admiration, just as men want. Most women care very much that you love and admire them. But all people want respect. Learn how to show respect. This will help you with men, too. Part of respect means you are humble. You do not think you are more important or more powerful than the woman. This is very attractive for almost all women. Women thrive on appreciation; on gratitude. Women will go to extreme lengths to draw admiration from a powerful and wealthy man. There are legends about women who are famous for gaining the admiration and support of a powerful and rich man. If you are not rich, show how powerful you are.

Then you can expect something in return for admiring her.

Twenty-sixth attraction: Always be aware of your feelings and always control them

To be most attractive, you have a healthy mind and healthy feelings in a healthy body. Think about your feelings. Must you really be mindful of your feelings? Yes.

Women respect control of feelings. They usually have trouble controlling their own emotions. Women are afraid of men who fly into anger, who drag on them with fawning like a calf for its mother. They perceive control as the ability to support them and to protect them. Learn to examine you self at all times and to be able to name your feelings.

Name all the kinds of feelings you can have. Write them down. Research the names of emotions. And learn the names of your feelings. You need to learn the vocabulary and the conversation about feelings. If you are a man who can talk about feelings, you are a superior communicator. Most men and women have to learn to talk about feelings.

Look in Appendix C: Feelings and Feeling Words for the formula to state feelings to another person. Learn to use it and then you will be way ahead of almost anyone in having close friends.

How can you change your feelings when you feel rage, jealousy, fear, anger, hostility, and guilt? The iron law of dealing with women is "never communicate with a woman when you feel poison emotions."

Indeed, it is possible to recognize your feelings and cause yourself to feel differently. But difficult. Start now. It will take months or years to master this part of communications with women.

Never, ever show up for a date with these negative feelings. It's better not to show up.

Men and women cope with feelings differently. Unlike women, almost all men have difficulty talking through their feelings. You may make the mistake of expecting women to ignore your feelings or to understand and accept your feelings. You may be absurd enough to expect women to ignore their feelings. This will never happen. If you insist on her ignoring feelings then do not try to do anything with women. Stay with men. Forget this book; give it to a man who is flexible.

You may not want to talk about feelings. However, women want to express certain feelings, like love and joy, but not others, like hate or irritation. This is one of the ways men and women are very different.

When you talk about feelings, use the exact names of the feelings. Say, "I feel irritable." Don't say, "I am upset." The meaning is too uncertain. Say, "I feel joyful." Do not say, "I am happy." Happy could be anything.

You still have to know what your woman is feeling. Because feelings are the basis of action and communication. Try to identify each individual woman's feelings and name them. You can name feelings, yours and hers silently. Do this constantly.

Ask about a woman's feelings. Be gentle about how you ask if she seems to be in extreme emotion, sad or angry. Then you will know if you have guessed the right feelings.

You have feelings that help you survive, and feelings that help you fit into a group. Feelings that you are accepted by the group. You have feelings that warn you about some things that are wrong and that caution you to change your behavior. You have feelings that tell you, that you are surviving in spite of trouble, and that you can enjoy life. You have pleasant feelings and painful feelings. Talk carefully about your feelings.

Use this form

"I feel (name of feeling) when you (name of action) because (your memories are the reason).

Now and then, ask her to talk about her feelings.

Twenty-seventh attraction: Listen

Your voice can become a seductive tool. After she notices you and likes your voice, she may want to talk all night. So listen. You can ask her about herself to find out if she fits your standards. You could think of it as interviewing her for a position in your life. She will answer your questions because she thinks you care about her and she feels an ego boost. On the other hand, women will listen to boost your ego.

You can imagine how you would feel if she does all the talking. So do less talking. If you can, let her know she talk as much as she wants. If she hogs the conversation, you will resent her. But you will also know she thinks mostly about herself, not you. If you do not ask her about herself, she will talk anyway. Usually about her daily life, maybe about her career. If you do ask her about herself but do not listen, she will think you are selfish and leave you. Experiment with various listening styles.

A few women do not like to talk. They want to move, to dance. So dance. Others want to listen to music. So make your voice like music. Listen to her choice of music.

Women like to talk more than men do. Why do women ask so many questions and hear so little? Is that your style? You can flatter the girl's ego as a way to attract her and to interview her.

Do you want to learn how to listen to endear yourself to a woman? Ask about her interests and let her talk. She will stop when she is through. When she is talking, she thinks you are a wonderful conversationalist. An eager listener impresses a woman.

Remember to talk about yourself a little, your desires, your enjoyments, your power. Because you do not want her to go home and suddenly realize she knows nothing about you. For example, you can talk after she finishes her standard first impression speech, her sales presentation, on you.

Twenty-eighth attraction: use the full range of your speaking voice to sooth her or to excite her

You would have more power to if you had the full use of your speaking voice. Learn to speak. Do you want to learn how to endear yourself to a woman? Go to acting school if necessary. Your voice is a potent tool.

You can cultivate a calming voice or an exciting voice. A confident voice with a deep tone will draw almost any woman to you. However, some women like a small voice, even a whisper. Most women recoil from a high-pitched voice. Experiment with your tone and notice the reactions you get from people.

How much of your body is included in your speaking voice? All of your body.

You learn this in speaking voice class. You cannot learn to use your voice like a musical instrument by reading. Take lessons. I guarantee that the time and money will be worth it.

Twenty-ninth attraction: Look behind her mask to have a heart to heart communication

Almost all women wear masks. So do men. So do you. These are their roles, their secrets are hidden behind the masks. They pretend to be the person you experience but there is another person they do not want to let you know. Note these masks when you see them. You may like them and they may or may not work for you. Please note that women cannot wear a mask forever neither can you. The mask will come down. Or they will feel stress because they are such phonies. Experiment with recognizing these masks. Watch for other masks. Be wary of the unexpected consequences.

If you can convince the woman that you can be trusted she will let her mask fall away. That is because you are so very attractive.

There are at least five qualities expressed by masks that most men fall for every single time. Men tend to be helplessly attracted to the following masks. That is why women use them. Which ones do you prefer?

Women Who Don't Take Themselves – or Life – Too Seriously

Who doesn't like someone who can see the humor in life? Do you like your women to have feminine requirements, like long nails? That's what makes them different from you. After all, you're not going to have a fun first date at the mini golf course if she is bitching over broken nails.

Women Who Can Play With the Boys

Are you a sucker for a girl who can explain the infield fly rule in baseball, drink a good draft beer, and shoot a mean game of pool? And if she does it in a short skirt and heels, all the better. Right?

Women Who Have Their Own Lives

There is a reason all those dating books advise women to play hard to get—it works. The same goes for you. It is far better to be busy with your own life. A guy knows that a woman with a full life that doesn't revolve around him won't get needy and possessive. She is also more likely to be stimulating because of her stories about her career. She will have something to say other than, "what are you thinking?"

Women Who Know They Are Sex Goddesses

Are you only attracted to stunning women? She does not have to have a perfect figure to dress like a lingerie model. She may just have a healthy appetite for sex and no inhibitions about making her desires known. Sexual spontaneity, variety, and enthusiasm get men every time.

This extroverted, even loud, approach can be centered on non-sexual interests, too. Spontaneity, variety, and enthusiasm always sell her goods.

Women Who Make You Feel Good

Do you want what most want in a partner, stimulation and rapport? Men feel good for many reasons. If you are in harmony and you two resonate, you will feel good. If she finds out what you believe in and reinforces your beliefs, you feel good. You feel good about who you are. What man isn't a sucker for admiration, respect, and frequent satisfying backrubs?

These masks are more than attractive. Masks help her actively pursue new men. They help you decide which woman you want in the crowd.

You are making progress

Where can you learn the subtle art of pursuing a woman? Now you are reading this book. You are a powerful support. You have memorized the way to attract a woman. Read the chapter later on Sexual Thrills. Your eyes will open to the real meaning of pursuit, of making love.

When you have mastered the art of attraction, you can assertively pursue new opportunities. You can pursue any woman you want. The next chapter teaches you this art.

Chapter 4
How to pursue her

- You will learn ten dating skills to catch up with the best possible woman
- Four mental tricks to keep yourself excited
- Fifteen tools for winning the woman you want

You will soon experience the kind of dates you want with the woman you want.

To pursue her means to take active measures to make friends with a desirable woman.

To pursue effectively, speak, think, and act as advised in this chapter. Pursuit is the opposite of attraction. Attraction is passive, like waiting for action while presenting yourself as a powerful support. This chapter will enable you to learn how to hunt for the best possible woman and how to connect with her.

Decide where your best possible woman can be found and pursue her. This does not mean sitting around waiting for her to come to you.

After you take this chapter to heart, memorize it and practice it all the time, locate your friend, lover, the best possible woman. You are encouraged to pursue a woman, to avoid loneliness, and to pursue a woman successfully.

Decide on the kind of women you want. Then convince her you are the best possible friend or lover for her.

You will need to assess your compatibility with her. Then you may make a lasting and satisfying connection.

You may take the inventory of gifts your new friend has for you. You will transform a stranger into a lover.

After you have read this book and practiced the suggestions, you will learn to convince that woman to accept, appreciate, and admire you.

Ten skills you must have to enjoy the dates you want

You will soon learn these 10 skills. Practice the skills over and over to master them. Then you will master the art of dating

Dating skill one: how to ask for a date

You can ask a woman to go out on a date. Men are usually the aggressive party. Men need to take the initiative and get the ball rolling.

If you are too shy to ask for a date, suggest to a woman where you will be, the time and date, what you will be wearing and tell her you will be delighted if she shows up. Women expect you to ask. They may object a little to show that they are not hard up for a date. Women want to go on dates so they will agree almost always. Especially if you appear energetic, powerful, wealthy and have a sense of humor.

A date begins when you have become valuable to a woman. Do you understand? Why would she date you if you have nothing to offer? Your playmate has to want you for a benefit. So clearly offer that benefit.

Please accept this: people take action to get a benefit or to avoid losing something they already have. The woman who you want to be your friend wants what you have or wants to avoid not having what you have. To have a date, present yourself as a benefactor; someone who gives benefits. You must appear to be kind and powerful enough to take care of the treasures she carries with her. Consider yourself to be the keeper of her treasure.

After you have learned everything in this chapter, go back and read again the chapter You Are The Powerful Support. When you are a powerful support, ask anyone to do anything. She will help you.

Dating skill two: Planning a date to get results

Consider the results of not planning a date.

a. You do not know the street directions to get where you meet your companion.
b. You do not have enough money.
c. You did not dress appropriately.
d. You have no list of conversations for the embarrassing silences.
e. You did not remember to listen (so your companion thinks you are boring and selfish).

Since you are awake and improving yourself, you will plan to avoid a, b, c, d, and e. Write down the results you want on the next date. Write down all the things you must do to get the results you want.

When you know what you want, you are more likely to get it. Write down what you want to help focus your attention, so you can interview your consort.

When you interview, ask clearly for what you want to know. You will avoid confusion.

Dating skill three: getting your desired results

What results do you want? Do you want to laugh? Do you want a woman who understands your feelings and sympathizes with you?

Men usually want sex. Is that what you want? You may want other things, too. Maybe you want acceptance. Maybe you want the date to be the beginning of a long-term relationship. You may want to talk to someone who cares deeply what you say, to be accepted as you are for a long-term relationship.

Plan your questions ahead in detail and listen for what your date wants. If you do not want to give her what she wants, expect to get fewer results. To get results, you must give the results your lady is asking for. She may ask for too much. Then you have to say "goodbye." Have the courage to face the truth. Not all women are going to fit into your life.

When you know what you want, you are more likely to get it. Write down what you want to help focus your attention. Then you can interview your prospect.

Dating skill 4: Choose an appropriate place to enjoy your date

This is difficult. However, if your companion is sold on you, the place does not matter much.

You have to listen to find out if she is sold. Listen to your acquaintance to find out her minimum requirements. Then exceed the requirements. Listen to what your woman avoids and avoid that. If you go to a place that bums you out, what feelings are you going to express? You will express negative feelings and therefore you will be a negative man. Your companion does not want negativity. Therefore, go places where you feel delight, excitement, or love.

If you like to think more than talk, go where your mind is stimulated. Go where you have comfortable feelings. Your woman may feel the same comfortable feelings. So both of you will feel positive.

Attention! Here is the punch line. If you remember this, you will get what you want and you will establish a good foundation for love and friendship. Remember that your girlfriend's feelings and desires are more important than yours.

Dating Skill 5: exciting talk

Have you ever been on a date with the perfect woman and you could not think of a thing to talk about? Plan what to talk about before meeting your date. Depending on what you are doing, dinner for example, talking on a date may be the main event.

You will learn faster if you study one or more of the recommended books. A stimulating book is *Healing Conversations by* N. Guilmartin.

Grit your teeth and face reality. Most women want to talk about appearances, money, and jokes. Others want to talk about their career or their vacation. Or women want to talk about beauty, face, hair, nails. They want to discuss celebrity gossip.

Many women like to talk about marriage. Maybe 9 of 10 women want to get married and have a baby. If you want excited and focused conversation, talk about marriage, babies and beauty.

So look in the newspaper or on the internet about money and jokes. Memorize it.

Not all women like to talk about how beautiful they are or gossip or joke around. So while you are looking for sports, find some other unusual news. Bring it up during the lull.

Avoid some topics. Most women do not want to talk about sports or computers or gadgets. Avoid these unless women bring them up. Also avoid politics, religion, and strong opinions. These give rise to flaming emotions that can easily get out of control.

Do not cause an argument. These negative subjects get associated with you. Then she remembers you as a flaming argument.

At the back of your mind, you know you want to get committed. Or married or have a baby. Maybe you are afraid because of past horrors with unfair women. More than half of women want to get married and have a baby. Almost all women want to be in a committed relationship. These are normal desires. Still, do not bring up these goals until you have interviewed your woman to find out what she wants.

When she is in love with you, talk about marriage and babies. Interview her about her related desires. Is she lonely? Who is she going to leave her wealth to? What are her attitudes about married people? What is her income?

What is her relationship with her father? The way she treats her father is the way she will treat you.

Write down all the questions related to commitment, marriage, and babies. Then you can glance at your list. Ask her the questions on your list. This is a subtle way of seducing her into a long term relationship.

You want excited and focused conversation. This is a mark of an excellent date. First joke around and find out what she likes to talk about. Listen well.

Dating skill 6: showing respect, and admiration and expressing feelings

Please note this fundamental reality. Few women will see you again if you are disrespectful or if you show no interest or if you do not show admiration. Unless they are totally sold on you.

Another fundamental reality: Everyone has feelings, even you. Four out of five men do not recognize their own feelings. They may repress feelings.

One out of five women do not know what they are feeling. Every man expresses feelings even if he tries to hide them. You do too. It is strange that men are out of touch with their feelings, but it is true. It is up to you to detect your feelings and your woman's feelings. Then ask her what she feels. She will usually say, "Nothing," or some similar blank answer. Try to verify that you have guessed her feelings accurately.

Assume for a moment that you are not mindful of your feelings. So you do not explain your feeling state to your companion. If you do not express feelings, your date will try to guess your feelings. And she will be wrong. She will mess up by guessing the wrong feelings. To prevent this discord, note your emotional condition and reveal it from time to time.

So when you plan your date, plan how to show respect, admiration, and your feelings.

You need a book to study on this communication skill. Treat yourself to *Older Couples, New Romances by* Kemp. and Kemp. It is much more valuable than the title suggests, even if you are young.

Dating skill 7: listening to get results

Consider this fact: You will communicate more by pressing your lips together and listening with your whole body and mind than you can possibly disclose by talking. That does not sound right, does it? You can prove it yourself by trying it out.

Learning to listen is as difficult as learning to talk. You really need listening lessons to know what it means.

Try this. Fake it till you make it.

Pretend you are in love with your companion. Then lean toward her and focus. Feel sympathetic joy for what gives her joy. Take notice of how this affects your own attitude toward her. Also notice how this affects her.

You can teach yourself with Be Your Own Dating Coach, for which there is a review at the end of this book.

Dating skill 8: wear appropriate clothes and appear irresistible

You already knew your clothes and appearance speak for you, did you not?

Your clothes can say "impoverished" or "boring" or "sexy" or anything you want. What do your clothes say? There are easily 1,000 books on this subject. I am not going into this because 1,000 pages are not enough to cover it. There are 1,000 seminars on clothes. Start studying.

You can learn from *The Unofficial Guide to Dating Again, by* Tessina listed in Appendix A the end of this book.

If you want a fast lay, stay close to your woman. Wear tight clothes to show off your best bodily features. Put your hands all over her. Kiss her a lot. Tell her, "I love you." Say "Yes" to everything. If she responds in a loving and sexy way, you are going to get lucky. If she rejects you, it's probably your last date.

If you want your woman to like you as a person, not a sex object, wear trendy clothes appropriate to the kind of date. Reveal your best features in subtle ways.

Dating skill 9: coping with your feelings

Ponder this thought experiment. You are on a date. You are falling madly in love with this woman who has all the advantages. So obviously you grab her and kiss all over her face and neck and your hands are... STOP!

You are not coping with your feelings.

How do you know what she likes? She may be disgusted by aggressive seduction. Or she may go along with your aggressive groping. Because it is new and flatters her ego. You may end up in bed tonight.

It will seem like a good start with this woman. But chances are you will never see her again. Most women do not like this aggressive approach unless you are like a famous actor. Some women like this passion and crave it. A few women do indeed want a lay. However, if she wanted sexual excitement and you gave it to her, then she got everything and she is through with you. This is what men do. Now women are doing the same one night stand.

Try this thought experiment again. Somehow you have managed to be on another date. She is "buying" you, touching you lightly, and looking into your eyes with focused lust. You are feeling like you are no longer pursuing her but she is pursuing you aggressively. You may even feel fear. You remember the last disaster when this happened. But you also want to connect with her in every way. You are confused. You retreat. You go home alone.

You do not know how to cope with success because you are unable to cope with conflicting feelings.

Learn to let your emotions "speak" for you.

Read about emotions in the chapter, How to Attract Her earlier in this book.

Dating skill 10: communication through touching

Do you think you know all about this? How long did it take you to learn to talk magnetically so people were drawn to your voice? How many years did you struggle to express your feelings accurately? Did it take many years? Therefore, it will take a while to learn to express yourself with touch.

Massage is a fitting way to "talk" to your lover with your hands. You can also touch with your whole body massage.

There is kissing. Kissing is not as simple as you think. Invent new kisses. Experiment with them.

A classical book is *Kama Sutra*. There are about 100 versions of this instruction manual. The translation of the title means, Lectures about Lust. It was written hundreds of years ago. It remains the best book on sexual technique. Several versions are recommended at the end of this book. Reading it will infinitely improve your originality when touching women with all the parts of your body.

When was the last time you had a perfect date? Can you say what you need to know to have a perfect date?

Invest in your dating satisfaction. Try *Dating for Dummies by* Silverstein and Lasky a truly educational work. Please be ready to learn unusual dating behavior. This is a huge study and you deserve a Bachelor of Arts degree if you learn successfully. Consider the skills discussed.

- ✓ Do you want to learn how to successfully ask for a date?
- ✓ How should you plan a date for maximum benefit?
- ✓ How do you keep the conversation going?
- ✓ What results can you expect on various dates?
- ✓ Why is listening so important?
- ✓ Do you want to know how to recover from mistakes?
- ✓ What are you communicating when you touch different places on your date's body?

Remember the perfection of a date depends on your feelings and on her feelings. Your feelings and her feelings depend on the way you think.

Mental tricks to arouse your excitement

You benefit by learning mental tricks and methods of thinking. This book is full of mental tools. The following are some complex mental tricks you can use to change your mind. If they are too abstract, skip them.

The **first trick** is thinking of the results of a date as a profit or a loss. You want a profit. Yet thinking only of profit is not enough to keep up your enthusiasm when you have had several losses. All people who now have profitable dates experienced losses at first. So focusing on profit may actually cause more losses. How can that be?

A single-minded desire for profit magnifies the feeling of loss when a date does not meet expectations. The feeling of loss results in disappointment. The disappointment unleashes a host of destructive emotions. The solution is in how you handle the loss and not in the fact of the loss.

The solution is to focus on profit plus the possibility of loss. By removing the addiction—the obsession with profit—you are prepared for a loss without the amplification of negative attitude.

The **second trick** is detachment from the feelings that go with profit and loss. Think of profit or zero or loss. Convert a loss date into one that does not achieve the desired outcome. Convert a date that does not have the desired outcome into a zero, neither a profit nor a loss. Convert it by thinking of what you did that you could improve. not what your date did wrong. Maybe next time ask your date to go home early. A zero is better than a loss. Since you learned to be better next time, it was a profit.

The **third trick** is conversion of the negative mental attitude into a positive mental attitude. Look at the zero date as a way to improve yourself for the next date. How can you improve your way of speaking, of feeling, of behaving? How can you be positive, encouraging, joyful?

You can be grateful for the zero date because now you are ready to have a better date next time.

What is so great about a zero date? You have energy to go on another date. You have ambition to try out new behavior. You are eager to try out new stories or a speaking voice. You have self-esteem to tell friends how you are getting better. Then your friends will praise you. Do your friends praise you when you tell them about a boring date? They praise your positive attitude.

The **fourth trick** is to view the dating scene as a magnificently complex game full of opportunity. The game gives you interest, boring and exciting times. You learn to recognize the winning patterns. You get ego satisfaction out of watching yourself go from loss to zero to profit. You transform and evolve.

What does it mean when you ask your date to go home early several times? You pick the wrong women. An amateur analyst might ask, "Are you afraid of a loss? Maybe you are overwhelmed by your own destructive emotions, anxiety, fear, shame."

Men pick the wrong women all the time. Stop focusing on profit. Use the tools.

Sixteen mental tools for winning the best possible woman

Make these tools a part of your social events.

**The first winning tool: men are different
from women in almost everything**

Is that obvious? Okay, now let's have some fun. Let's discuss sex. Let's discuss women. This lesson is worth the price of this book because you will avoid so much pain.

This may seem obvious. Please note, it is worth a fortune in avoiding pain.

Get the book *Men Are From Mars, Women Are From Venus* by John Gray. Read a chapter a day and let it sink in. It explains the details of the difference between men and women.

What do women want? You have a notion, but basically you are confused, are you not? Even Sigmund Freud, the great psychiatrist, did not know what women want. Here is the answer. Women want a whole lot of people to talk to. Please memorize this.

Why should you care? You are a man. You care because you have to please a woman. If you do not agree that women need lots of people to talk to, what do they want? Ask the next 20 women you meet. Learn from them. Then give it to them.

Let's pretend you have asked 20 women and they affirm that they want to talk. What do women want to talk about? Women want to talk about everything. Therefore you will listen because you want to please them. Women love it when you just listen.

The second winning tool: listen

Answer this question. What do women want to talk about? That is the key question when pursuing women. Women want to talk about everything. To pursue a woman, ask her a question so she can talk. Do not interrupt.

Men cannot help themselves. They are constructed to give everything to women. Why would men like to give things? Because women will give you something in return. You can think of exceptions, can't you? Dump the exceptions. If she doesn't give you something in return, get a normal woman.

The third winning tool: the principle of give and take

What do men want (besides sex, which you think about every 10 seconds)?

You have some inkling, don't you? But you are not sure. Memorize this answer. Men want pals and they wish people would not get so mad at them.

Is that true for you? Read the locker room scene in Chapter 3. How to Attract Her.

Some women can be a pal. Most women cannot be a pal to a man. If your girlfriend cannot, then do not ask her. Keep her out of the locker room. Ask her to be more of a woman; to be feminine. Her value lies in her womanliness. When you pursue a woman, draw out all her soft and receptive woman's instincts. This causes her to feel needed and to open up to you. A man gives to a woman who is soft and feminine. This makes you a magnet because you are a powerful support.

The fourth winning tool: learn to be a magnet

Start with two skills. Learn Networking and Schmoozing. But what do these terms mean? Networking means to make contact with everyone. Get their name, phone, email, and other information to contact them again. Become close to them. Exchange favors. Even strangers can fit into your network. Everyone in your network started as a stranger. Add more people to your network. Even though this advice is simple, it is valuable. Now memorize this and use it today.

The fifth winning tool: start a conversation
with a stunning or an ordinary woman

Schmoozing is defined as circulating in a group and chatting with everyone. Sit or stand inside a group and listen. Schmooze until a stranger seems interested and then ask name, e-mail, phone and so on. Ask to meet somewhere specific another time. If this seems too abrupt, then suggest where you will be on a certain date and time. She will volunteer to come and meet you.

The 'icebreaker' is a method of starting a conversation with someone you have not met. Your best friends started as someone whom you had not to met. Just make a comment about something nearby. If thewoman you want meet also wants to meet you, she will reply. Then you can get to know each other.

Learn to project a positive mental attitude. Your positive or negative mental attitude casts a shadow on all information.

The way to start schmoozing is to comment on something, anything, around you: colors, someone's speech, a changing surrounding. Do not comment on a person's clothing or looks because she may be insulted or have hurt feeling. You can not know how a woman feels about his looks.

Do not say, "hi" or "hello." Do not comment on the weather or the time. These topics tend to receive nothing or a negative reply because they sound empty. Like saying, "Good Morning." People do not think they have to respond.

Make a comment which stimulates her (Not a sex comment or an aggressive comment). Then press your lips together. Listen and nod your head. Do not feel lust and aggression. Within yourself, feel kindness, gentleness and love. Women know when you are feeling these emotions. They like men who feel kind, gentle and loving. Please memorize that.

If you do this you will soon have lots of women saying, "Yes" when you ask for a date. Also, women will start talking to you energetically. And also, this method will start a stimulating conversation with your date. This knowledge is worth a great deal to you

If you ask a woman this question, "What do men want?" What will she answer? "Sex" Then ask her, "What else do men want besides sex which men think about every 10 seconds?" She will not know. Or you may not agree. You need to tell her the answer. Then she will understand you a lot more. Here is the answer for you to tell her. "Men want pals and they wish people would not get so mad at them." This will disarm her and open her curiosity. You can go on from there.

If you have made yourself into a powerful support, almost any woman will reply to your neutral comment. Ask her about her interests. "What do you like to do the most?" Look into her eyes and listen. Schmooze until the strange woman seems interested and then ask for her name, email, phone and so on. Write it down. Give her your name, email, and phone in writing. Ask to meet somewhere specific another time. Sounds easy, does it not? It is easy. Try it! Do it with the next person you see, man or woman.

Indeed, people want to talk. Speaking about neutral subjects is a way to say hello. If a person does not reply, go listen to some other group. Listen carefully to a group to feel when you can contribute a comment. Remember, most people are lonely and want to have more friends. You will seldom be rejected.

Get the book *How to Work a Room* by Susan RoAne, and *Power Schmoozing: The New Etiquette for Social and Business Success*, by Terri Mandell.

They teach you all the details of schmoozing. Sounds easy, does it not? It is easy. Try it! Do it with the next person you see.

Schmoozing and networking, talking to anybody about anything will connect you with the community. People will help you make your life what you want it to be. For example, your life will be full of dates with your choice of women. Also, you can help new friends improve their lives.

The sixth winning tool: tell the truth about yourself

Live your life so you can be transparent. Then you will not be caught in the web of lies. Do not tell "white lies." They grow into black lies. A comment that cannot be based on fact is an opinion. But opinions are not truth. Opinions can turn off communication because they may oppose the listener's opinion. Women do not want to hear a direct contradiction to their opinions. If you must state an opinion, say that it's what your buddy thinks.

Tell the truth about yourself. Gossip is worse than an opinion. Gossip will always cause you trouble. Speaking about someone who is not listening is gossip. You have gossiped, haven't you? Maybe you love to gossip. Do not do it again. Follow this rule and you will not have to go through the pain of learning why not to gossip. The pain is caused by losing friends or worse. Follow these rules and you will not have to go thru the pain of learning them by losing friends.

The seventh winning tool: Your pursuit of woman will not pay off unless she notices you

Obvious isn't it? How do you get people to notice you? To talk to you? To like you? Read the book.

Power Schmoozing: The New Etiquette For Social And Business Success by Terri Mandell

All the methods on this book have been researched. I have followed the instructions. You must also follow instructions. The results are guaranteed to be better than you are getting now. If you read the books and follow instructions and if you still do not get what you want, all the misery you had before will be refunded.

The eighth winning tool: talk to strangers

Your parents told you not to talk to strangers. It is not helpful advice. That was when you were a child. Now you are an adult so you need to start a conversation with as many strangers as you can. Get their names and a way to contact them again. There are very few weirdos and you can usually spot them. Do not go where there are people who you do not want to know. Go where you will like people. All the best friends you ever wanted to know started as strangers. A stranger is one of your good friends whom you have not met.

The ninth winning tool: do not set your standards for an impossible woman who you will never meet

If you insist on waiting for a perfect woman, you are going to very lonely. If you only want people exactly like you, you are going to be bored. Some people will not like you. Accept this.

Still, talking to strangers or those who are less familiar is more exciting. Outside your safety zone is where you discover excitement, lovers, and friends. Discovery expands your life.

On the other hand analyze what kind of woman you want. This is difficult. Do it in stages. First, write down everything you want in a woman. Then try to find this woman. As you look around, your list of what you want will change. So rewrite it. Some of the features are less important. Be flexible about the less important items. Be rigid about matters of principle.

The tenth winning tool: look for a woman who meets your reasonable standard

You can offer some benefits to a woman. Not all women want what you offer. Some women want much, much more than you can offer. Set a reasonable standard. If a woman meets most of your standards, give her an interview. That makes sense doesn't it? Avoid the superficial standards. You can relax your desire for the perfect looking woman and explore one who is plain, overweight and older than you thought at first.

The main standards are listed below, after the suggested rewards to offer her
The eleventh winning tool: offer rewards to persuade her to be close to you

This is complex motivation. You need to practice this persuading method on several women to make a smooth delivery. So go and try it out on 10 or 20 acquaintances.

To learn efficiently, write down your test cases. Keep a journal of your progress. After you finish this book, read your journal. You will realize how much you have improved.

You may be asking, "How do I persuade? How do I motivate her?" There are four basic ways to motivate a woman.

1. Reincarnation

Let her know that if she has you, she will live forever.

Let her discover that if she mothers your children, she will live through them.

Let her believe that whatever she does for you will not be forgotten in her next life.

Let her know that she will go to heaven if she is an angel to you.

Inspire her with lofty aims.

2. Romance

Help her to feel pleasant, or even intensely thrilled and looking forward to sex play. Sex is an obvious motivator. Experiment with more refined sex, or sophisticated sex, or pleasant sex, or sex that makes her believe she will live forever. These are highly motivating.

Reading this book, you will learn how to use romance as a motivator.

See Chapter 19. Mastery of Communication on All Levels Adds to the Marriage.

Offer her what she wants to get what you want in return. Some women want gentle moments, comfortable events, companionship in the nest, and tenderness in sex. Find out want she wants.

You can understand and motivate thru her drive better. Women are motivated by romance more than sex; the thoughts and feelings of sex more than the physical sex.

3. Recognition

Women need respect and admiration, appreciation and approval; just as men do. Women are often motivated more by respect and admiration, appreciation and approval, especially if it is awarded by a certain group of people whom she respects.

You may be a man who also is motivated by these recognitions. Give that same kind of recognition that you want for yourself. See what happens. Most women need these motivations, too.

4. Reward

Motivate thru rewards: money, sex, prestige, fame, ostentatious luxury, relief from worry. You can approve of her going out with the girls shopping. Women will work toward these rewards doing things that please you. Men are motivated similarly in some of these rewards. Project your enthusiasm for having these rewards.

Remember to be enthusiastic. You are persuasive when you are enthusiastic. Watch her reactions to know what rewards motivate her.

Motivating, persuading, and flirting are so interesting that you should read about them. There are hundreds of books. Romance novels ponder flirting. You can take courses in flirting. Flirting and attracting are a kind of sales presentation. You could say they are even careers in sales. Look at the recommended book list at the end of this book. Now invest in a book on the selling profession.

Discover whether your desires and her desires are matched

You can only achieve the ultimate connection if your main desires in life and her life desires are matched. You live at certain levels of desire. She lives at her chosen levels of desire.

Consider the eleven levels of desire.

1. Air, food, water
2. Rest, making babies and sexual relief
3. Shelter

4. Safety
5. Acceptance and approval by your family and groups
6. Giving and receiving love
7. Independence
8. Status and function in a group
9. Understanding and controlling perceptions of reality
10. Achieving highest dreams
11. Spiritual enlightenment

Consider that you are at levels 1 and 2, so you want babies and sexual relief. You also are considering levels 3, 4, and 5. Then you will have difficulty learning to give and receive love at level 6. But it is possible. You may have a problem becoming independent and gaining status and function, levels 7 and 8. But these levels will require concentration and effort over a along time. Levels 9 and 10 may be out of your reach even if you make an effort for years.

Now consider your sexual partner. She must also be at a level of desire near yours. Think about what would result if you are at level 6, Giving and Receiving Love, and your partner is at level 2, Resting, making babies, and sexual relief. She may reject levels 3, 4, 5, and 6 because she cannot comprehend them. This will work for a while. You could relate on the physical level and have great orgasms and babies. You could even relate on a high emotional level. But your partner could not learn the mental perceptions or the spiritual sensibility necessary for higher connection. This may not matter to you if you are satisfied with the physical and emotional gratifications. But you may want more after you master the physical and emotional methods.

You may want to find a more evolved partner. There may not be such a partner within your commuting area. You may never find the partner you dream about. You have to decide to be happy with what you find.

The opposite case also may cause friction. You are level 2 and your partner is at level 8, Desire for status and function in a group. You will be satisfied by physical and emotional gratification. But your partner may want to relate to her employer's group where you do not fit in. There will be conflict about where to make the effort: work or sex play.

So think about the consequences and the payoffs. You may have more than enough achievement using the improvements taught in this book. The search for the perfect match may be exhausting and it may not pay off. You have to decide. No one else can do this for you.

This book is attempting to inspire you to achieve goals on the higher levels of desire.

The twelfthth winning tool: go where can you find a woman who meets your standards

You can find women everywhere. But you want women who also want you. Go there. Also try new places where you guess there are people who would make good friends. Where would people go who are at the same desire level you are? Try places where you do not usually go: charity banquets, ceremonies like store openings, professional association meetings, school events, parents meeting children after school. Look in local magazines for events. Go there and stand next to people you do not know. Listen to them. Comment on the topic of conversation. Get their phone numbers and e-mail addresses.

You can meet hundreds of people on the bus, the train the airplane. Almost anyone will talk to you on the bus, train or airplane. Use the travel time to practice your lessons that you are learning in this book.

The thirteenth winning tool: it is easy
to make new acquaintances

Almost everyone has a need for new friends and lovers. They will give you a chance to connect with them. Sometimes they like you and you become close. Other times, you do not hit it off. Keep trying. You will get better after a while. You will become expert if you read this whole book and invest your time and effort in the recommended books.

The fourteenth winning tool: list all the possessions you want.
Many women also want similar things with variations

Even though they are different in most ways men and women want much the same things. You may want a red Corvette and she wants a blue truck. There are similarities and differences in transportation. Some women like what you like. Others like different things. Ask a woman why she wants her car. Listen to why she wants a different type of transportation than you want. You may learn something. Be curious. Enjoy the differences. Most men like women because they are different. Is that true for you?

In any case, when you listen, your woman will think you are a good conversationalist. One thing about people that is similar: They want to talk and to have someone listen. Welcome the differences. Differences make women interesting.

The fifteenth winning tool: The seven
basic needs of a sane person

You want to have friends but do you need friends? A need results in a stronger drive for satisfaction than a want. The following needs are deep within your mind. You could call them psychological needs.

Talking about these needs with your woman leads to intense conversation. Note however, if your woman is at these levels of desire:

Air, food, water,
Rest, making babies, and sexual relief,
Shelter,
Safety,

And no higher, she will not want to talk about the following six needs.

She will consider the six basic needs to be meaningless. She still has them. She pursues them. But she will not want to talk about them. If you can actively pursue these needs with your woman, you will connect deeply.

The seven basic needs of a sane person

These needs were distilled out of studies of human nature after removing cultural distortions by Erich Fromm in *The Sane Society*. The definition of normal human nature or common sense is vague. Also, humans can put up with horrible conditions and survive. Many horrible cultures are sick and still cause conformity to this sickness. For example, a culture where people are all obsessed with guilt and shame is a sick culture.

But if you know what basic needs motivate all people, you can be in harmony with the needs. You can remember not to obstruct people's satisfaction of their needs. The following are the threads of similarity for most people's psychological needs in all cultures regardless of gender.

1. Need to love and be loved, to relate to other people; relatedness not narcissism is a basic human need

You need to relate to other people and to other living beings. The necessity to unite with other living beings is a need on which sanity depends. You need a sense of integrity and individuality. You need to be an individual and you need to be connected to other people. There is only one passion which satisfies your need to unite and to be an individual. That passion is love. This love results in a creative orientation. This love is not restricted to one person. It includes everyone. You are convinced that you are separate from other living things but you need to be a member of the group. In the experience of love, lies sanity.

There are contradictions in this need. The opposite of this all embracing love is narcissism. This is a failure to have the capacity to love. For the narcissist, reality is his own thoughts, feelings and needs. This mentally disordered person has lost touch with other people. Sanity lies in relatedness. The productive type of relatedness is love.

2. Basic need for identity of ego; effectiveness and individuality not herd conformity

You need to own your personal experience of your surroundings. You need a sense of identity, "I am I." The identity is vital. You cannot remain sane without it.

Those in a clan may say, "I am we." Losing your clan, you ask, "Who am I? Am I the one who thinks? The one who feels? The one who creates? The one who relates to others?" You could identify yourself as belonging to a group, a herd, "I am an American, a Christian, a business owner." Then you are what the crowd or the herd wants us to be. You conform to the herd to feel a sense of identity.

Or you may be non-conforming. You may need to have a secret experience. You may need to have privacy, to be alone. Still, you need to be with other people. You need to love others and, loving them, to blend into their experience of the world outside their bodies.

More contradictions are hidden in this need.

3. Basic need for transcendence, mastery, effectiveness; and creativeness not destructiveness

You need to transcend your limited existence. You need to transcend being a passive creature. Your needs stem from the conditions of your existence. To simplify this, consider that you are sick. You want to be well. If you are a poor baseball player, you want to learn to be a good one. If you are lonely, you want a friend. This is called transcending the moment.

To transcend, you create or you destroy. You create babies, for instance, to escape death and to escape loneliness. You create buildings to escape the weather.

However, if you cannot create, we destroy. You destroy forests. You destroy other cultures. You make war. You even destroy what you love. Destructiveness is rooted in your being human. It has the same intensity and power as any passion. But it is only an alternative to creativeness. If you cannot create, your second choice is to destroy.

There are more contradictions in this need.

4. Need for rootedness in a place and culture; and clearly related to all people as one unified being, not the concept of always churning a limited number of ideas

You need to have roots. You have the root of being. The root is completely convinced that you are inherently real. Your root perceives events affecting "me, myself, and I." The elementary root is the tie of the child to its mother.

You and your parents are rooted in your families, your parents, your shelter, your street, your customary clothes, your nearby plants and animals, your culture, and your spiritual conceptions of the non-material. Sometimes this is called "ego." You cling to your ego and try to keep it the same.

The contradiction is that you are also trying to change and to grow. Also the root changes whether you want it to or not. It changes due to your stage in life and or hormones. The word root is so important for sanity.

The severance of you from the root is frightening. If you lose your roots, who are you? You would become insane. There is a deep craving not to sever the roots.

5. Need for a worldview, a frame of orientation, and an object of devotion not merely a drive for material things. Reason not irrationality.

You need to make sense of the world outside your body. You need an orientation. Although you can never completely know what is outside because you cannot sense everything, you still want to make up mental pictures and explanations.

This is another contradiction.

You need a rational explanation that is constructed by your intellect. But this mental construction is irrational because you are limited to your puny human mind.

"Irrational" means the emotional or other unknown drives that explain your life. For example, you can only see to the horizon but you can not see x-rays. Your eyes are limited. In a roller coaster, you yell and feel fear. Your control of your feelings is limited.

You do not want to admit, even to yourself, that you are acting out of jealousy or some other rotten emotion. And you can only hear a sound closer than 100 feet away. You cannot hear high-pitched sounds. You can only taste a little of what is in your mouth. All your senses are limited.

You cannot comprehend complicated phenomena because of your limited mind. You may learn a profession but you will never know all the ways to make a living. You will never know what everyone in the world is doing each day. You need to have a rational orientation in spite of the fact that it is an irrational approximation to what is outside your skin. Your mind is limited.

You have a body, a mind, and a spirit. Thus your worldview is contained in your thinking, in your bodily reactions, in your feelings, and in your devotion to a Higher Power. The Higher Power may be almost anything, an entity, a religion, a philosophy, a corporation, a brand of beer. The object of devotion gives meaning to your existence. The Higher Power gives credibility to your worldview of orientation. You are devoted to your Higher Power. In spite of your limitations, you need an explanation, an orientation on the world.

You know that your mental pictures, songs of love, and mental construction of the world are rough guesses. You still want to believe that your orientation is absolutely true. You are convinced your orientation is fixed and true.

But you know you have to change your beliefs. You change your mind constantly. You change your feelings about the world rapidly. You are on both sides of the fence, reason on one side and chaos on the other.

You are moved to figure out the contradictions.

6. Need for excitation and stimulation; resolving contradictions not boredom and not chronic depression

Read *The Sane Society*, by Erich Fromm to understand these ideas.

Resolving contradictions drives you to act. You could claim it is the spark of the willpower.

You may be one of the few who have the need to find ever new solutions for the contradictions in your existence. You may need to find ever higher forms of unity between yourself and nature, plants, animals, and other people. This may be the source of all psychic forces that motivate many people. This need to find new solutions is the source of many people's passions; the source of all feelings; the source of all anxieties. Are you one of these who have this need?

You may have an inner dialog that tries to sort out the contradictions between the rules, the sense of yourself, your ego and the root, I. Can you identify your instincts, your intuition, your feelings, your logical reasoning, the forces external to your body, and your unknown impulses. For example, you may want to let your instincts drive your behavior, but if you kill someone in a fit of anger, you have major trouble. You want to have lusty sexual experiences whenever you are taken with desire, but your conscience tells you not to.

You have contradictions because you are aware of your surroundings but you do not want to take the time to ponder why laws of nature exist. You want to know the laws of nature but you do not want to make an difficult and lengthy effort to discover the laws.

Your ground of existence is a calm center. While calm, you activate your will to move and run. But you cannot have both the peaceful calm and the excited running. This is another contradiction.

7. Character structure to organize human energy toward goals

Another contradiction is the desire to be lazy and enjoy life, but this bumps against the desire to learn and achieve. This is your problem in studying this book. How can you be lazy, enjoy life and also make a huge effort to learn for months at a time. You need this internal contradiction to move you to resolve contradictions.

Working out the contradictions results in activating the "willpower"— the volition to act. This willpower is the source of all thoughts, actions, and speech. This is the source of feelings that arise from the mental processes.

The forgoing are the needs that define a normal and sane person. A person who does not have these needs, or has no intention to pursue them, is abnormal, more or less disordered. These needs exist in all places, in all times, in all cultures. You can use these needs to relate to anyone, even if they have a different language and orientation.

When you meet a woman, you can always remember that she has these needs. If you relate to her needs and compare them to your needs, you may find yourselves to be in harmony and friendship.

What if a new acquaintance is missing one of these needs?

If a woman (or a man) does not pursue these needs, be cautious. Maybe you should move on to a normal woman; someone who fits into the social order.

The sixteenth winning tool: expend the time and effort to ask questions and answer them

Write down your questions and answers. Read your answers again after you have studied this book. Read your answers after you have tried out some of the advice. Then you will know how much you have learned.

Who is your true love? Or maybe what is your true love, if you like things more than people? How do you pursue love, or help?

Do you know people who are charismatic, or magnetic? You can learn from them.

Are you ready to learn how to pursue the friends you want?

What are the places to locate the best possible woman, friend or lover?

How can you pursue the best possible woman successfully?

How does pursuing women help you avoid loneliness?

What transforms strangers into lovers?

What is your inventory of gifts that make you a treasure for your new friends?

When are you going to make the effort to learn to convince people to accept, appreciate and admire you?

What standard do you use to decide on the kind of woman you want?

Do you know how to convince her you are the best possible friend?

How do you consciously assess your compatibility with her?

Describe how you make a lasting and satisfying connection with a desirable woman?

What do you say so she will go out with you?

How do you move to take control of the situation?

How can you persuade her that you are a treasure not to be missed?

Do you want to learn how to discover if she is compatible with you in a relationship?

Is she clinging to you, harmonious with you, learning what you are like?

Think of what you value most; does she also think it is important?

What do you offer her to connect with you?

What does she have to give you so you will commit to a lasting connection?

Do you run from one woman to another? You may be addicted to the chase.

If so, get the book on Addiction to Love, listed below.

Addiction to Love, by Susan Peabody, Suzy Allegra, and Karen Adler.

Now write the answers to these questions. If you want to answer briefly, do so. If you want to write several pages for each answer, do that.

Your good luck is the combination of your preparation and your opportunity.

The seventeenth winning tool: hunting for the best woman and connecting with her

You have to learn how to chase women. Do you think you can stay the way you are and get awesome dates with the best possible woman? You have to put out the effort, the time and the practice to get the dates you want. You will be a master of the hunt after you experiment with the lessons in this book.

After you practice the lessons over and over with different women even when you do not get what you want right away, then you will get what you want.

Yes, it is humiliating and frustrating to try out the lessons and get nothing. However, that is how you learn. How many times did you date between age 10 and now? How many times did you change something and try again? Many times, right? You figured out that you could not become good without this book. You bought this book because you could not figure it out for yourself.

Now you are going to get some results. Keep practicing the lessons. Get the other books and study them. Practice what you learn. You will get results. That is a promise.

Why is it so important for you to write down answers to the questions in this book?

Because the effort to answer will give you clues about what you need to learn. When you come back and read the answers in a month or a year, the answers will show you how much you have learned.

For your own peace of mind, accept that people change their minds. One day she shows no interest and the next shows riveting attention.

What are the feelings you cannot have when you are with a woman because they will ruin your friendship with the woman?

What are all the kinds of feelings you can have that will help you to make a friend?

How can you truly enjoy pleasant occasions?

How do you find out what she is hiding behind her mask? How do you recognize a mask?

Can anyone sense what you are hiding behind your façade; your mask?

Where in this book can you learn the subtle art of seduction?

How do you greet a woman you do not know yet?

Here are some more questions to help you discover the answers that suit you.

Is it possible that the raunchy and randy women have weaknesses just like the delicate and politically correct girls?

Hint: Even the tough women have a vulnerable spirit which you must respect.

Do you want to learn how to listen to endear yourself to a woman?

How much of your body is included in your speaking voice?

If women like to talk so much why do they ask so many questions and listen so much?

Must you really be mindful of your feelings?

How can you change your feelings when you feel rage, jealousy, fear and guilt? These are the feelings that women cannot bear.

All these questions are answered in this chapter and the chapters before this one.

If you have gotten this far, you are doing well. This is a difficult book because the lessons are so demanding. This book will work for you if you are willing to change your thinking, speaking, and moving.

If you can keep interested in improving, then you will never experience the following situations.

You see a woman you really find attractive, but are too afraid to talk to her.

You go up to a woman to meet her, but can't think of anything to say, and end up feeling like you "blew it."

You think a girl might like you, but you're not sure, so the opportunity slips away before you can take advantage of it.

Thoughts of ridicule and rejection keep you from having any real success with women.

You feel shy and want to meet mature women with class, but you don't know how.

You befriend a woman in the hopes of turning it into a relationship, but then you get stuck and don't know where to go from there.

You fall for a woman who has a boyfriend, and you don't know how to get around her boyfriend to let her like you.

You meet a girl who seems to really like you, and then when you call her for a date, she acts like she doesn't know you or doesn't seem as interested as she used to be or worse yet, doesn't return your calls at all!

You think you're not good looking enough to attract women, so you don't even try.

You've gotten rejected by so many women, that you think there's something wrong with you and you end up resenting women, and stop trying to meet more of them because you think you'll just get rejected even more.

You are able to meet a woman and attract her to you, but you don't know where to take it from there, so things fizzle out and she moves on to another guy.

You see one jerk after another walk off with the women you want, while you're stuck being the "nice guy."

Are you ready to avoid thee nightmares? Most of them will never happen because you will know how to think; because you think you are a treasure, because you attract like a magnet, because you know the rules, and because you know how to attract, and how to pursue.

Chapter 5

Now You Are Ready to Learn the Art and Science of Dating

You ask, "What were the last 4 chapters about if not dating?" That was preparation in the fundamental science. There are solid rules in science.

Now you are going to learn how to get results. This is more of an art. The specific speech and actions you take depend on what you think. What each man thinks is different. Each man's approach is different.

Let's review, please.

Did you study and experiment with the introduction and the first four chapters?

Did you try out everything that was suggested?

Did you experiment with several women?

When you did not succeed, did you try again with a different woman until you achieved the goal?

If you did not take the time and effort to do these actions, you are not ready to read the next chapters. You cannot expect to succeed in this difficult learning career. Now is the time to learn the first chapters.

If you have done the work, you are ready to learn about dating. If you have gone through the experiments to improve yourself, you can now read the rest of this book. If you have convinced yourself that you can attract women, go and do it. If you have experimented with pursuing women, continue studying this book.

You should be able to answer these questions.

What are the skills you need to have mastered to have a perfect date?

How do you successfully ask for a date?

How should you plan a date for maximum benefit?

How do you keep the conversation going?

What results can you expect on various dates?

Why is listening so important?

What winning tools can you used?

If you could answer the questions, you are ready to learn more.

Again focus on what results you want on a date.

What exact results do you want? Usually, men want sex. Then they want other things; maybe acceptance, maybe a long term relationship.

What do women want? Women want to laugh, to talk to someone who cares deeply what she says. Most women want to feel like their man supports them and accepts them.

Your date is checking you out for a long term relationship. A woman wants to know her man is in control and capable to handling events.

Some women only want a man who they can control.

You want results. She wants results. To get your results, you must give her the results she is seeking. You get when you give. To get results, plan ahead in detail and listen for what your date wants.

I made this book to give you most of the methods you need

I am realistic enough to know that only a few readers will actually practice all the lessons. I would just like to know that I have helped you to avoid pain. I want the satisfaction of knowing I have opened the door to pleasure for you.

By now, you should realize that this book discloses important avenues to successful dating that you cannot read elsewhere. More of the same vital information fills the remaining chapters.

I have made a huge effort to write this book. I have done it to enlarge my love for everyone. Now you can get into the exciting subject of dating. Thinking out the date before you start will result in a much more satisfying adventure.

Planning is covered in the next chapter. A smooth date is lubricated by planning. Time is so much more delicious when there are no glitches. A well-timed adventure is worth a hundred plans.

Read the easy lessons in Chapter 6. How to Plan Ahead for a Perfect Date.

You may have noticed all the advice on speaking and listening. A common mistake is to assume you know ordinary speaking and listening. If you took speaking and listening classes, you would agree right away that there is a lot to learn. A brief hint about these skills is in Chapter7. Skilled Speaking, Listening, and Acting

Always consider her needs and feelings

You will suffer damage if you do not pay attention to a woman's immediate needs and especially her feelings. You must also pay attention to men but in this book you will focus on women.

Many men intend to go on a date and end up the day in bed. This end to a date has become more common practice since the birth control pill in 1962. As people get older, most of them realize that this is not satisfactory. In addition to disease and pregnancy, there is often deep emotional damage. There is a lot of hurt when the one-night stand does not bloom into anything of value.

The intent to use women for sex and discard them leads to karmic payback later. In other words, if you hurt a woman by being selfish, then you will be hurt by selfish women.

Large groups of people, societies, have always developed rules and laws of behavior for dating and marriage. These rules, customs, and laws are very similar to one another, regardless of the place on earth. This leads us to the conclusion that there are good reasons for the rules. Some of the rules even become laws that punish violations. Please consider why these rules have come about. Then do not violate them with your sexual behavior.

There are books on all types of etiquette for social behavior. Other rules have become formalized into etiquette. There are books on all types of etiquette for social behavior. You will profit by reading at least one of these books.

An underlying principle is that people are valuable and they do not want to be hurt, slighted, or neglected. People do not want to witness disrespect to themselves or others.

The details of the rules do not matter as much as the three principles:

1. Be considerate
2. Be respectful
3. Be honest

Women need to feel important. They need to witness that you are considerate of them. They need to feel love within themselves. They want to know you love them. They need to know you are honest.

An underlying principle is that women are valuable and they do not want to be hurt or slighted. They need to have proof that you respect them.

Get the etiquette books listed at the end of this book. Memorize the rules. You will agree it is worth your time and money.

Be a woman's friend before you are her lover or husband

Friends are so important to her. They make her life meaningful.

An excellent principle is to learn how to be a friend. Then after you know how to be a friend, you can establish a friendship with another person before any sexual event occurs.

Our society has become so loose that this principle is being lost. For the protection of your own emotional state, learn to be a friend.

Women do not want to witness disrespect to themselves or others. You will understand this clearly if you violate someone and they stomp you or you lose all your friends.

For the protection of your own emotional state, study Chapter 8. How to Be a Good Friend before Being a Lover.

Love is discussed and written about everywhere. There are love songs and movies. The meaning of love is usually lost. Perhaps 9 out of 10 people have never experienced love of any kind neither a feeling nor a moral principle.

There is a cult of people who speak of "falling in love" as though it were a new religion. Maybe it is. Love is a spiritual experience even at the rudimentary level. There are many types of love. You will find it valuable to make the effort to bring love into your life. Bring love in at all levels.

There are few places to learn about love. Or perhaps there are no schools of love. Today you can start to feel love.

To comprehend the range of love, read Erich Fromm's book, *The Art of Loving.*

You can immediately read Chapter 9. The Seven Heights of Love

There are ways to express love through touch

Take some time right now to think of all the ways there are to touch another person or several people. Touching can be gentle, or rough. It can be any part of your body touching any part of another person's body. There is the touch between parents and children, between lovers, between the police and rioters. Just the touch of the lips on another person is explored in romantic novels in great detail.

The full science of loving touch is massage. There may be a million ways to touch.

Erotic touching and caressing, however, are poorly understood. There may not be any schools to teach the caresses for lovers. There are many books on the subject of touching.

The point is, what do you know about touching? This is another vast subject like speaking, listening, and other communicating methods. Chapter 10 opens up your options for touching on a date. It does not cover much territory because the subject is too great. You will find it worthwhile to read other books about it and put into practice what you have learned. Get a book on massage from **Appendix A: References in the Text and Recommended Books to Study** and experiment with your friends.

You can read Chapter 10. You Can Give and Receive Hundreds of Caresses.

Parties and dating go together. Take your new friend to a party. Or invite couples to your party. Or go to a party to meet a new woman. Parties have their own etiquette. They have their own anxiety and excitement. There are so many kinds of parties. They are a separate culture. There are books on party etiquette that are recommended at the end of this book. A brief description of some basics of parties is in Chapter 11. How to Be in Demand at Parties.

At the other extreme from parties are serious events. Serious ceremonies and dating do not go together. When we think of weddings, we do not usually plan to take a new acquaintance. Of course, you could meet a new woman at a wedding or a funeral. In fact, serious events may even be better venues than bars or parties to meet. Women will behave in a mature and responsible way. Weddings and even office parties have their own etiquette books. Follow the same procedures explained in this book at serious events. Plan them. Dress appropriately. Prepare to meet people by opening your heart. There is another requirement: get an etiquette book. An outline for how to survive by not making serious blunders is in this book, Chapter 12. How to Survive Serious Events

Try *Dating for Dummies by* Silverstein and Lasky a truly educational work. Do the words, "educational" and "dummies" turn you off? Pretend "educational" means advice from your best friend. And interpret "dummies" to mean you are so smart that you are willing to read a book to have a thrilling date. In fact, most people who read the "for Dummies" books are well educated. We know the value of books.

The following chapters outline the many faces of dating and courtship leading to marriage. Do you agree that there is more to dating, to finding the best possible woman, and checking a prospective wife than you have ever imagined?

If you ever doubt that this effort is worth something, just remember all the horrible dates you had. Remember all the money and time you spent on boring dates. Remember how mad, disgusted, and disappointed you were after some of those embarrassing dates. Remember when she told you to get lost.

When you use the methods suggested herein, you will have a payoff: great times and a great marriage. You will feel confident. You may become famous as the best date in your town or your neighborhood. You may become the one who many women seek out to marry. Your best friend may become your wife. In that case, you will be part of a tight couple whom other people look up to as the perfect match. You will be the inspiration to other people.

Is that worth working toward? Keep reading. And do your homework. Keep your cool because you have a lot to learn. Before you meet your life's companion, you have a lot to do. You must make yourself absolutely sure of your success.

The next step is to plan the date in detail.

Chapter 6
How to Plan Ahead for a Perfect Date

Eight step plan for peak performance

1. Briefly stated, plan to know where, when, who, what, how, why.
2. Plan ahead if you want the date to flow effortlessly for a spontaneous and fun time.
3. Be prepared to handle unexpected inconveniences like travel, unacceptable behavior, cost, and disagreements.
4. Rehearse for unexpected pleasure, romance, and good luck.
5. Plan to show up as a happy man, a powerful support for your woman.
6. Watch and listen for your woman's problems and deal with them immediately.
7. Watch and listen for your date's pleasure and help to improve the wave of happiness.
8. Discuss the date in detail with your woman and all other people whom you will meet.

Daydreaming about your date will not substitute for good planning. A lovely daydream follows.

Your bodies and spirits are joined in one breathing center about which the earth and stars revolve. You lovers know the whole truth. It is great fun indeed for you lighthearted people. It's solemn and emotionally edifying at the same time.

Most of your fear has gone out of the uncertainty of the date. There is mystic union! An end to loneliness! Exaltation! A moment compared to which all other moments are tedious and unbearable. You are convinced that sexual love is the greatest gratification. You seek more happiness in sexual relations. You want to make erotic pleasure the focus of your life.

You know there are no restrictions on your instincts. You will never again exchange this happiness for security. You are manic. It is like a movie when the hero beds the heroine.

That sounds like a romance novel. There is something remarkably exciting about the sex lives of fictional characters. It is not confused and clumsy. Voyeurs imagine movie lovers with more excitement than when they are in the real thing. However, fantasy is not reality. Consider a more realistic experience that you may have: a nightmare.

You have just said goodbye to your date. Something has magically deepened between you in spite of the awkwardness of the lovemaking. In spite of the beauty of the act, the union was not well made. Even in a daydream, there are frictions between two people who are not yet attuned to one another. Her hands are rough but sensitive, and what about the hair on her legs?. You have always detested hair on the legs. You, the hero have a short penis and. it takes forever to get hard. You knew she was faking her orgasm. You were overly excited by the novelty and the danger of what you were doing. Fears and inadequacies rose up into your fantasies. In spite of all this, you feel light and heavenly.

Have you ever felt these uncertainties, these anxieties? At the same time, have you forgiven the imperfections and boo-boos? Did you blame yourself or did you blame the discord on her?

You can have much more harmony. You can imagine everything can go off almost perfectly next time. For example, you can force a smile. You can look at the sunset. You can believe in a perfect future. After all, your ignorance of women is gone because you have this book. You will try some of the suggested experiments and have some adventures. You will get better everyday. You will have much more harmony. Soon you will be a master of the art and science of dating.

Good planning will help to turn fear of friction and clumsiness into cozy feelings

Get out your dating journal if you have one. If you don't have a dating journal yet, stop now. Go and get one; a big one about 8" by 11" bound in cloth. It will be your master piece and a comfort in your old age.

You have a journal now. You will write about each date beginning with your plan. Write down the answers to the questions on this page for each date. Then you will think more about the payoff from each date. Another day, you can read about your progress. The answers to the following questions will help you to have a better date. That's right, every date will be better. You keep track of your triumphs. You write the occasions when you did not get what you wanted. Figure what to change next time to succeed. The answers will help you to have a better date next time. What's so great is that you get to go on lots of dates with lots of different women to get better. Then you will have more dates with the best possible woman.

Think about what was so great about your last date. Think about what feelings you had when there was a moment when you were lost. What are you going to do differently next time? You can improve your looks, acting, behavior, speech, conversation, and touching. Everything is an experiment.

Where are you going?

What are you going to do when you get there?

Where are you going later?

Who else will you meet or who will be there who you do not know?

What can you read so you can discuss it with a new woman?

How much does it cost and how are you going to pay for it?

What exact time, date, and exact location are you meeting?

Do you have to reconfirm the time and place?

What do you wear?

What do you want your friend to wear?

Have you discussed every detail with each other?

There is another kind of planning. You need to plan your skills of speaking, listening, and acting. You will grow better every time you practice speaking, listening and acting with people. You could try it with your trusted friends.

Chapter 7
Skilled Speaking, Listening, and Acting

You know your lover, friend, or companion because you communicate in many ways. Without skilled speaking, listening and acting, you will never have a close friend. This chapter will focus your skills on some of the ways to communicate.

Note that the improvements listed work for men friends as well as women friends.

Twelve ways to improve your speaking, listening, and acting

When you wake up each day, think "continuous improvement."

Do you believe you need to learn a lot? If you can be honest with yourself and admit you need to learn a lot, you are on the way to great dates with women. You will need to learn a lot to have the kind of dates you want. After you improve in many parts of your life, you will find the best possible woman.

Improvement one: Communicate in every possible way

Communicating totally, you deepen your friendship. You communicate information when you talk, move your hands, choose your clothes, or drive a particular car. Examine every communication and improve things to better represent what you intend to communicate. If necessary, change your body posture, make a facial expression, change your tone of voice, loudness of voice, change clothes, move furniture in your space, change car ownership, change living space. Where you take a vacation expresses something. Some women can sense your emotion.

When you mindfully transmit and receive information from all your communications, you have a richer relationship.

Improvement two: Speak clearly

When you are speaking clearly, you connect. If you mumble, or have sentence fragments, or yell so no one can understand, or speak a foreign language, or invent words, then you damage your communications.

Improvement three: Control your voice

When you are mindful of your breath, upper body, face, hands, and feelings, you can control your voice. If you were formally trained in speaking voice or singing voice, you would know all the parts of your body that make up your speaking voice. You can consciously control all your body parts to make clear speech. Clear communication helps your relationship.

Improvement four: Communicate by touching

What are you saying when you touch different places on your date's body? You can read a whole chapter in this book about this: Chapter 10. You Can Give and Receive Hundreds of Caresses.

Some touching improves your relationship. Unskilled touches ruin the chances of having your future together. Some women like to be touched a lot and others want to be touched only in certain ways. Find out what she wants by experimenting. Touch her arm. Watch what she does. Let your leg touch her leg. Listen to what she says. Look lovingly into her eyes and move your lips toward her. Does she move toward you or does she seem shocked? When you kiss her, try it very gently at first. Does she come on aggressively? Or does she smile with approval? Accidentally let your arm brush her breast area. How does she react? Respond to her reactions. You and she will introduce each other to the limits of touching. Caresses are like talking. You and she will invent the speech of many different touches and their meanings.

Some men like to display touching, hugging, and holding hands in public. Do you? It tells other men that she is your property. Other men and women refuse public displays of affection.

What if she is grabbing you aggressively? What do you do? You may like it. So you grab back. You and she make up the rules as you go along. If she feels threatened, she will push you back and say something like, "No. No." firmly. If you keep it up and she is offended, she may give you a good shove away from her and raise her voice a little.

She may be too aggressive. Then you can say "Please, don't do that in public." Or if she is disappointing, say, "When I am ready, I will be passionate in private." Be careful because women want to feel needed. If you reject her touch, that may be the end of your chance to be intimate. She is testing you too. Get the limits to acceptable physical communications understood immediately.

Improvement five: Listen completely

Listening completely, you communicate more than speech. You can communicate love better with listening than with talking. As you listen, watch her body language, clothes language, hands, and face. Then, you will hear the whole message.

Try this experiment. Look into her eyes while calling up all the feelings of love you can. She may sense your love. She may think you are weird.

Four out of five women are good at knowing what you feel. But only a few men can read a woman's feelings. Changing your facial expression to match her words is part of listening. For example, she may talk about how she hit a home run at her baseball game. You look surprised and then smile in approval. Use your imagination on how to show your feelings on your face. Take acting lessons.

No, I am not joking. You are reading this book to succeed. Do what is necessary to succeed. The easiest lessons are the Dale Carnegie Course. A few acting lessons will give you the point of view of other people watching you. Then you can express yourself more effectively.

Improvement six: Read body language, clothes language, and face expressions

Her body, her clothes, and her face movements communicate too. If you learn to watch body language, clothes language, hand movements, and facial expressions, then you read the whole message.

Remember that you are also expressing yourself with vocal tone, clothes, words, face movements, and body motions. Be sure you are expressing what you want. If you see certain expressions on television, that does not mean they are appropriate for you.

Let us assume you are reading her whole message. Respond to her whole expression. Reply to her body motion. For example, if she raises her hand to give you a "high five" then you raise your hand to reply.

Improvement seven: Learn to speak the same language that she speaks

How do you respond to her language? If she uses street talk, so do you. If she uses polysyllabic college talk, so do you. When she whispers, answer in a whisper. When she talks fast and loudly, you respond in kind. Understand?

Improvement eight: Show integrity

When your speech and body actions are in harmony with your words, you demonstrate integrity. What does integrity mean? It means integral, or one intact person. If you are angrily yelling, "I love you," does it make sense? It is confusing. What if you are running out the door and saying, "I want to be with you all night?" That is like two people. One wants to stay and one wants to leave. Your vocal tone and your acts must say the same as the content of your words. It is called congruent; one fits the other. Practice making your words say the same thing that your body, hands, and face are saying.

Improvement nine: Use skilled methods of thinking and feeling

Feeling love within herself and observing loving intent within you are the main events for a woman. This is true for 9 of ten women.

Whether it is within you or her, hate, anger, irritation, and bitchiness will end your date and you future friendship.

Tell the truth and seek the truth. The opposite, doubting her truth will not bring you closer. Believing her lies is a skilled means of being in rapport.

Work hard and pursue your goals ambitiously. She will notice. Laziness, sloth, and doing nothing will not get you anything from her.

Be generous with her.

Greed, jealousy, and lust may feel good but ruin your relations with your friends.

Learn to be content. Teach yourself to be happy. A woman will easily love a happy man but she will reject a man who complains and whines.

Hurrying her up, worrying about your lover, staying too busy to see her? You lose!

Improvement ten: Use the skills of communicating through the channel of clothes and appearance

Your clothes say something about you. If you are in jeans and a T-shirt, you may think your clothes say, "I am relaxed." But she may read your clothes as, "I don't care enough about you to dress up." What do you tell her if you pick her up wearing jeans and a torn T-shirt and she is in a suit and pearls?

If this happened, you change to a suit and tie immediately. These communications help you to be in rapport, in close harmony.

Which is better for you to fall in love, an argument or sweet harmony? Are you thinking harmony? That is the right answer. The same style of clothing shows harmony.

You already knew your clothes and appearance speak for you, did you not? Your clothes can say, "Impoverished" or "boring" or "wealthy" or "sexy."

When you dress for a date, ask yourself, "What do my clothes say?" There are 1,000 books on this. Read one. There are 1,000 seminars on this. Go to one. You could try reading *The Unofficial Guide to Dating Again,* by Tessina.

Improvement eleven: Control your feelings

This means you are mindful of your feelings. You are examining you feelings. Notice what you are feeling. You name your feelings. If your feelings are inappropriate for the occasion, change them. It is difficult but possible. You are going to learn how to express your emotions. Most communications have emotional undertones. So you cannot ignore your feelings.

Nor can you ignore her feelings. To start, make a list of all the feelings you can think of. You can use the dictionary or the thesaurus to find the words. Start using feeling words. Practice changing your feelings. See **Appendix C: Feelings and Feeling Words**

Every single woman cannot bear to be near a man who has outbursts of feelings such as anger, yelling rages, crying, pouting, and boisterous laughing, and so on.

But almost all women admire a man who hides his feelings when he is humiliated or has lost something or is exhausted and so on. This shows strength of character. It shows that he will support her when she feels terrible or weak.

Go back to Chapter 2. You are the powerful support: How to make yourself a major attraction. Memorize the method.

Again, here is an example of how to disclose your feelings. Say this exact sentence:

"I FEEL
(feeling word like, EXCITED)
WHEN YOU
(act or words by woman such as, TOUCH ME ON THE LEG)
BECAUSE
(memory of this act or words such as MY SISTER USED TO DO THAT)"
Again:
The formula is, "I feel _____ when you _____
because _____."

Why is this repeated? Because men do not want to experiment with this effective expression.

Improvement twelve: Learn to give and to take information

You give and take information by speaking, wearing specific clothes, listening, touching, asking questions, and so on.

The following ideas are useful mental tools for giving and taking information.

Have you mastered speech? The value of speech is so huge that it is worth the investment in time and money to get trained in speaking voice.

Are you afraid to speak in front of a crowd of strangers? You probably said yes. Very few people like to speak in front of a group. This skill can be learned. After you learn this, you will have self-confidence. You will not be stuck by shyness or embarrassment in groups.

Why would you want to learn how to say you are sorry? Most of us have made a mistake in our dealings with another person. Some of us knowingly insulted another person or something worse. Could this be true about you? Saying, "I am sorry." will remove the load of guilt and shame. You may even have your friend back on your side. Get the book about apologizing listed at the end of this book.

Can you calm down your spouse or playmate by speaking or by listening? Consider how you could do this. Calming down your friend is a valuable service. Especially if your friend is yelling at you. This communication is special and usually is done by a professional. If you can learn how to do it, you are doing well.

Can you disagree without raising your voice? This is another communication skill that you can practice until you get it right. When you are getting stressed out or arguing, be alert to keep your voice down and keep your feelings out. Raising your voice usually starts more trouble. It does not solve the disagreement. You have to say, "I'm sorry." This is called, "agreeing to disagree."

Listen intently so your friend tells the whole truth. Look in her eyes. Keep calm. When you have a chance, tell her how you feel. For example, you could say, "I love you a lot. So I am listening to get the whole truth. I trust you. You want me to trust you, don't you?" Experiment with various words and body language to convince her that telling you the truth will be more pleasant than lying. You could say, "If I ever find out you are lying to me, I will never talk to you again." You could make a more serious threat. Or you could point out the pleasure she will have after she tells the truth.

Prepare an agenda for any possible embarrassing silence. For example, write down the issues that you need to discuss. Talk about them when there is a lull in your banter.

What does your voice itself, not the words, communicate? Become conscious of your speaking voice at all times. Your voice is composed of breath, tone, loudness, pronunciation, emotion. It comes from all parts of your body, not just your mouth. Convince yourself that you should you take speaking voice lessons. Your trained voice communicates much more than the words you say.

A woman can hear your emotions in your voice.

Speaking in a group, or in a bar, is totally different from whispering into her ear. Do you agree? Research what you need to know about speaking within a group of friends.

The following are some stimulating ideas about voice. Listening, asking, and remembering everything about your woman are the most effective means to communicate. When you remember what she said last week or last month, she knows you care about her.

How can you learn to listen? This is easy. Press your lips together and look into her face. Mirror her body posture. Express in your face some feeling that shows you are listening.

Why should you listen carefully? You will get to know her. You will ask relevant questions. Hold up your hand or touch her arm now and then to make her stop talking so you can express yourself. Comment on what she is saying. Talk about similar experiences you have had. Ask questions.

Here is how to ask the questions you need to ask. Listen to her and ask about whatever she is talking about. Or get out your agenda and read a problem you want to solve with her.

Another kind of information is about future dates. Interview your best possible wife or lover to screen her for future events. You cannot go everywhere with everyone you know. Do not burden your possible wife by forcing her to go everywhere with you. Take people with you to events that they enjoy.

If you take your best woman to events that she enjoys, then she knows that she will enjoy herself with you every time. Interview your best possible woman to discover compatible interests or causes of discord. Find out ideas you agree on. Dig up events you both like to go to. There are some habits she may have that are completely different from yours. If she does the wrong things or has friends that are discordant, which drives you crazy, do not do those things with her.

Demonstrating your respect, admiration, and appreciation is giving information. Without showing respect, admiration, and appreciation for a particular woman, there is no future with her. Always show respect and admiration to everyone you are with. If you cannot do this, get some new friends whom you respect and admire.

What do you think would happen if you were always disrespectful of your friend or lover? She might refuse to see you. You might argue a lot. She may force you to be respectful. Show respect.

Show love and other feelings. Few women will believe you if you say, "I love you." You must also show that you love her. Ask her how she knows if someone loves her. Reflect her answers back to her.

How do you ask her? Example, "How would I have to talk so you would know I love you?"

"How would I dress so you would know I love you?"

"How can I touch you so you will know I love you?" Try it out.

Be careful when communicating through touch. There is more meaning than you think. What are the many ways to touch, and what do they mean? A caress is more loving than a touch. A kiss is more intimate than a caress. Touching her breast is loaded with meaning. Touching her arm has less meaning.

How would you prepare for the moment when the conversation stops? Make up an agenda of news stories and problems you are having. Write them down and carry them with you. Then you always have an intriguing conversation. You are exciting, not boring.

How can you change the topic when there is argument or questions you do not want to answer? Get out your agenda and say, "I am going to change the subject." Then change it. Do not go back to the argument or the discord. Be firm that you are not going to argue.

Next are some more questions to stimulate your mind.

Have you mastered speech?

Why would you want to learn how to say you are sorry?

Can you calm down your spouse by speaking or by listening?

Can you disagree without raising your voice?

Do you want to learn how to listen intently so your friend tells the whole truth?

Can you read body language, clothes language, face language?

Do your words say the same thing as your body, hands and face?

Do you believe you need to learn a lot?

What do you need to learn about expressing admiration, love, and other feelings?

Read this book again after you finish it the first time. By then you will find the answers to these questions.

If you have experimented with the suggestions in this chapter, you have already improved. You may have been able to start a close relationship of a sexual adventure.

Jumping into sexual events is usually a source of pain. Have you begun sexual advances without knowing the woman well or feeling friendly with her?

In the next chapter, you will learn why this beckons disaster. You will learn how to be a close friend before being intimate.

Chapter 8
How to Be a Good Friend before Being a Lover

The sexual act exists for making babies. So the outlook is long-term for raising children. Ignoring this part of human instinct could lead you into an alienated feeling. You could be alienated from yourself and your natural intuition. After recreational sex, you cannot feel closeness with any woman. Hard-hearted life is lonely and leads to emotional trouble and isolation. You lose your ability to read woman's thoughts and feelings, if you ever had such a rare ability.

I have known women who have not really liked their sexual partners, maybe hated the sexual act, and who were deeply disturbed over it. Based on my opinion (which is not fact), I recommend that you become a friend first and feel free to open your heart and receive your woman. This leads to sexual adventures ten times more fulfilling.

I know you can think of exceptions to this opinion. However, after observing the impact on men, including myself, who have not really liked their sexual partners, I recommend that you become a friend first.

How can you compare friendship, respect, admiration and feelings of love with a passionate drunken orgy? The probability of an orgy leading to lasting love and family is almost zero.

Can you imagine sex without friendship or love?

I have met women who just want a temporary sexual romp. So there are women who like sex as recreation just like men like this. You may be experimenting with this non-loving sex, too. My opinion is that sex without love leads to hardening of the heart, distrust, and lack of respect for the opposite sex.

A description of love is an opening of the heart. Love is relating on a deep emotional level when you feel identified with a woman. However, love has many definitions. Love is a temporary emotional state. This is a current way love is defined by many people.

To understand love in a broad sense, read Chapter 9. The Seven Heights of Love.

Friendship is a relationship based on knowing a lot about each other. Respect is based on esteem for each other. Respect means that the other person's goals, morals, and inner character are admirable and approved. Admiration is a kind of devotion or appreciation of another person based on anything, such as appearance, wealth, education, etc. Friendship, respect, and admiration are based on concrete qualities that have been uncovered through meaningful communicating and doing thing together. This approach could be called 'rising in love.' This is much more valuable than the purely emotional state of 'falling in love.'

Falling in love has become a sought-after experience. It is a rush. It can be addictive in the sense that you want it over and over. This emotional state cannot be sustained. It is a wonderful feeling. But it leads to disappointment because you will lose the feeling. You can never repeat the first experience of falling in love.

When you find you cannot fall in love again, then you will think there is something wrong with the woman because you do not feel the same love. So you go looking for another "hit" of the love chemical. Falling in love is not a deep connection. The deep connection that can be sustained is based on respect, admiration, and friendship. The intoxicated state of falling in love cannot survive the first conflict.

To rise to a higher view of love read, *The Art of Loving,* by Erich Fromm. After you read *The Art of loving,* then you can read another chapter of this book. You will rise into a higher understanding of love.

Interview your woman and observe her in several surroundings to get to know her and develop friendship. Let love permeate you toward your best friend.

What does it mean to be a best friend? Best friends are in rapport, a close harmony. Harmony is based on shared principles, morals, politics, spiritual life, and other important aspects of life. Best friends are not based on having the same brand of cosmetics or cell phone. You are lucky to have one best friend. Sometimes you might go for years without a best friend.

If your woman is your best friend, invest yourself in the friendship. Give a lot. Accept your friend. Give approval and appreciation. Give a favor before you take a favor. Make time for her. Share your deepest secrets. Tolerate conflict and stay until the conflict is resolved. Never, ever treat your best friend disrespectfully. She is one of the treasures of your life. Develop a meaningful sexual life with her.

You can create the foundation to have a best possible friend

Buildings have foundations; so do relationships. You give her what she needs. She gives you what you need. You and she need acceptance, approval, appreciation, respect, admiration, integrity. So give these and ask for them in return. You want relief from trouble. So contribute to respect, admiration, harmony, empathy, fun, stress relief, discretion, and loyalty. Respect and admiration were suggested in previous chapters. So we will move on.

What is the difference between sympathy and empathy? This is a difficult question so you need a little help. Sympathy means that you feel the same way as your woman feels. You are on the same frequency. If she feels glad, so do you. This is a kind of communication through feeling. The problem with sympathy is that you can feel lousy if your woman feels lousy. But you do not want to feel bad. You have enough trouble. So you burn out and do not want to be around her anymore.

To avoid rejecting her because of sympathy, you decide whether to feel sympathetic to what your friend feels. You decide to reject her feelings, not reject her.

The alternative is empathy. It is also a kind of communication. Empathy is mirroring back the woman's feeling or attitude without feeling it yourself. The objective is to give her feedback so she can see or hear what she is feeling or doing. You could talk about how she is affecting you. You could show an exaggerated version of what she is feeling. You hope she would like to change her feelings. If she is fun, then you feed back the fun. For example you could act out her behavior with your body language. There are many books on these subjects that you can get. Sympathy and empathy are valuable expressions between friends. Sympathy and empathy are so valuable that psychologists and doctors provide them for a fee.

Do you prefer harmony or discord, coziness or combat? This is not a clumsy and facetious question. I have dated women who liked to argue, who always took the opposite view from mine, and who were physically aggressive. Friction was fun once, but easy to grow tired of. Make an effort to be in harmony and to create cozy feelings with your friend. Even though you have seen women who communicate through discord, making trouble for their men friends, do not do it. In spite of your seeing women on television creating discord, it does not work in real life. On television, they are puppets, making believe they are superior or something. You may have witnessed verbal combat between a man and woman. Did you wonder why they were together? You may find it hard to believe they are lovers if they hit each other. If you find you relate to a woman through combat and discord, you may like it for a while. You will soon look for another woman. You need harmony and coziness.

Arguing and differences of opinion are part of almost all relationships

This does not mean that you never argue, that you never assert your side of an opinion. You must bring up difficult subjects. You must feel open enough with your friend that you can negotiate or make a deal. If you are afraid or refuse to discuss difficult topics, you have a big problem in your relationship. To prepare yourself, study a book on negotiating. This will get you through an argument or an impossible demand.

Remember giving in exchange for getting

Can you ask for a favor without giving one in return? All successful cultures are based on giving something in exchange for receiving something. If you give without getting anything in return, you lose interest in the taker. You feel the taker is selfish. You do not want to give anything else. Take a favor, then give a favor.

If you take without giving anything in return, the circle of community and caring breaks down. There is nothing free. Do not pretend that you are worth the gift and do not have to return something. Do not believe in the delusion that you can take favors or things and not return the favor or gift. The connection with the giver will break.

There is friendship if there is integrity; otherwise not. The concept of integrity means a consistent, whole, honest, truthful personality. What are integrity, honesty, consistent behavior, sincerity, truth, and other character traits that enable friendship? Look these words up in the dictionary. Discuss them with your woman. Now we are in the deep questions. You must answer these questions. You cannot have a lasting friendship unless you have these traits. Work on these character traits.

You lack integrity if you make love to a woman but are not also a friend. Is it good for you to dislike a woman and still go to bed with her? Correct this lack of integrity. How do you feel the next day or the next week if you violate your feelings just for sexual contact? This lack of integrity is not a way to feel good.

Remind yourself of these traits. Maybe remind her, too. Mind your thoughts and speech. If you notice you are not holding up these standards, try harder.

Does everyone want approval, appreciation, and acceptance? Yes, everyone does. Animals want these, too. This is where we are all alike. To learn how to give them, you become mindful of approval, appreciation and acceptance whenever you are with a woman. Dwell on how you can show approval, appreciation, and acceptance. Practice these over and over until they are automatic.

Do you want a friend and lover or do you only want a sexual thrill with many partners? You need to answer this for yourself. The answer changes your behavior. It changes what you get out of a date. It changes your sex life and your long-term relationships. Here is a hint: your best friend is not a one night sexual encounter partner. Think about it in detail.

You can be the best friend. You can have a best friend. But, a best friend is not a one night sexual partner.

How well do you know her? How would you describe your best possible woman now that you have met her? What is she really like?

You interview her to answer this question. You check her out in various situations. Here are sample of questions to ask.

Would you make a good wife?

Are we compatible or we causing each other trouble?

Make up your own relevant questions.

What do you value the most; what does your friend value most? Ask her.

Few women have all the character traits that you want. She is missing a few. Some of her behavior might disgust you. Or you may have some other negative reactions.

What excellent traits does she have that make up for the missing traits or the ones that you dislike?

Is there something you really loathe about her that you cannot put up with in spite of all the other perfect features and benefits that she has? If yes, walk away and find another woman. Are you able to walk away and start searching for another woman again?

If you want to have children, does she? Ask about this and ask about raising children.

What are the parts of your friend's life that are exciting, surprising, and outstanding?

How do you ask questions or lead the conversation without being rude or raising a barrier to open a flow of ideas?

You can ask the question that most men want to know: how much money does she make? Is she willing to give her money to you?

What do you listen for in her answers? How can you verify that she is telling you sincere answers?

What mask does she wear? A way to get behind her mask is to pick an argument. Make a contrary statement about religion or politics. How does she handle her anger around you? Does she come out from behind her mask?

When you ask her to consider what you want in a woman, and what she wants in you, dwell on love. Love means a lot to almost any woman. It may not mean that much to you. What kind of love does she need? But do either of you have any idea what love is? Ask her. Has she ever felt a higher form of love?

In the next chapter, you can learn a little about love. You can get the answers to vital questions about love.

Chapter 9
The Seven Heights of Love

Love is one of many pleasant feelings. You want to experience pleasant, not painful feelings. You can learn to have pleasant and useful feelings.

If you love your sexual partner, you will connect on the emotional level in addition to the physical level. Prepare yourself to rise in love consciously. This is in contrast to "falling in love" by accident.

There are many definitions of love. One definition is that love is a productive orientation toward other people. There is a paradox when two people become one couple. Those who master the art of love become one with many people. To the enlightened,. love is never restricted to one other person. Because if you can only love one other person, you become more alienated from all the other people.

You can say, "I love you." You can say "I love in you all of humanity, all that is alive. I love in you also my self." Then love will make you more independent because it will make you stronger. Love makes you integrated with loved people so that your individuality seems to be extinguished at least for a while. Then you could say, "I am you." If you can rise in love to integrate with other people or animals or any living beings, then you have reach a higher view of love.

If you can conceive of a higher love, and believe it, you can achieve it. When you believe in love, when you believe you can rise to its full spiritual potential, you can do it.

There are at least seven levels of love.

You may rise to a high level of love with your best possible wife.

122

First level of love: Attraction

This is the power to draw other people's consciousness toward oneself: to charm, to fascinate, to captivate, or to enchant. The positive attracts the negative. The yin (female) has allure for the yang (male). The authentic is attractive. The natural person is charming.

Opposites attract. The profane people are fascinated by the sacred people. The forbidden draws the pure. You have positive qualities and negative qualities. In some things you are strong. This attracts someone who is weak in the same things. Whatever you are, radiate that. This is called the natural man. The deeply human man wears no false mask. He is attractive. Learn to be attractive. It is an art.

Many attractive people are not selective in giving love. They can smile at a stranger or help another man's child. Many attractive people are not looking for approval. Looking for approval is a sign of fear of inadequacy. Fear can lead to jealousy. Women are wary of jealous men. Many attractive people do not compare themselves with others (especially movie stars or weightlifters) so they can respond with enthusiasm.

You may want to be attractive: content with yourself, your excellence and your weakness. This is a way to express love.

Second level of love: Infatuation

When your feeling of attraction is intense, then the door of perception may open into the magical vision of women. The distance to the object of your love is never long. She cannot be far because you have an unbounded connection.

The break through into infatuation is a shift of perception. The shift is from being a separate person to being blended with another person. The infatuated lover perceives the world as holy. In particular, the body of the beloved is holy.

You are in a magic make believe world. To emphasize this world you have invented, you may find out that other people perceive you lovers as silly or even repulsive.

You lovers can perceive the extraordinary in the ordinary. You can see the appearances beyond the ordinary in the magical world of your imagination. In this condition, you feel the peace beyond understanding even in the middle of chaos.

Third level of love: Communion

The sharing of spirit, a spiritual connection of souls called rapport or communion. You, the lover, cannot imagine you are a different person from the beloved. To experience communion, both lovers must drop their defenses. They must abandon their illusion of separateness. This can be a threat if a person has an investment in the notion of individuality.

Many different barriers arise to deny communion depending on a lover's attachment to being different. To pass the barrier, communion is assisted through ceremonies such as Christian communion or Buddhist tea ceremony or the world wide marriage ceremony. After the ceremony, you lovers express a deeper communication.

Communion is the sharing of spirit, the joining of the non-material psychic vitality. It is based on trust. In trust the lovers move into the unknown blending of two people into one entity. The I becomes the WE. Each of the two people drops the delusion of separateness and allows the other into personal space and time.

Trusting the unknown prevents the rebuilding of the ego defenses.

The loss of communion is threatened by the notion that the thoughts and feelings of the other person are picked up through intuition. The symptom is trying to finish the sentences of another person. Another threat is the belief that, since two people are in communion, then there can be no difference of opinion. Another threat is transferring another person who one can remember onto the beloved; believing the lover has the same personality as someone in the past.

Projecting your own feelings or thoughts onto the beloved destroys communion. Projecting is the belief that the beloved is the one with your thoughts or feelings. Not realizing that she is not your thoughts or feelings, you believe the delusion that what you think or feel is transferred to you from your beloved. This disordered thinking can cause enormous discord and emotional pain.

The opposite is when you reclaim your own thoughts and feelings as your own. Then you will feel liberated enough to feel the communion.

Fourth level of love: Intimacy

Intimacy is close association, familiarity, or contact of a private nature. Sexual orgasm becomes a communal act. The human mental energy fields blend together. The psychic part of the spirit comes alive with sensations.

You realize that sexual vitality or sexual will power is the creator of all living things. You lovers perceive that sexual vitality is inherent in passion, inspiration, mental alertness, excitement, and long life.

Interconnected lovers are on the way to freedom from insecurity, from loneliness, from need, and from conflict. Note that intimate physical contact follows emotional and mental blending of the lovers. If the lovers are spiritually advanced, sexual contact follows the spiritual contact.

Intimate sexual play is more than just sex play. It is sex experience without emotional or mental boundaries. Intimacy cannot happen when one or both lovers insist on their boundaries, their shields, or their masks. When the trust is high and the boundaries come down, then orgasm explodes physically, emotionally, and mentally: three levels. The lovers sense one another's feelings, maybe their thoughts. The state of intimacy reveals to lovers that sexual play is sacred and divine.

Sexual behavior, like flirting, and dating, is driven by instinctual feelings to make babies. You may be convinced that sexual drive is for the purpose of enjoying pleasure. You may conceive that sexual play is the avenue to feeling pleasant feelings and that having babies is an annoyance. Sexual events are attractive to people for many reasons that you may not have thought of yet. You desire sexual contact for your own reasons not someone else's reasons.

In any case, the sexual vitality you feel is the creative energy of all living things. It can be felt as arousal, lust, awakening, passion, inspiration, excitement or enthusiasm. When lovers feel these emotions, the key is to experience it with joy and keep it alive.

You can expand your sexual life. You can go beyond your expectations. Expectations are fixed thinking from your past which inhibits your experience of the here and now. If you forget our expectations, you can forget to compare yourself with the performance of movie screen lovers for example. You can stop wondering if you are feeling love. Sex is often tied up with love. You can stop trying to feel whatever you expect to feel. Be mindful of what you actually feel. Be thankful for what you really feel.

You can stop selling your sexual ability to your lover and stop asking for approval. Sex may become a meditation of the infinite for you. Experiment by expecting the infinite. You have this book to learn about sex. You have thousands of books, movies, songs to expand your love making. Open your heart and mind to the possibilities

Fifth level of love: Surrender and non-attachment

The kind of surrender in this case is the act of giving up your ego's last claims to being separate. You are no longer attached to the delusion of being a separate person disconnected from other people. The act of giving up oneself to another person is also the act of releasing obstructions created in your mind.

You can dissociate your essence, which you may call the witness of your thinking and feeling, from the ego (your thoughts of I, me, and mine). Then you can attain a higher plane of existence. The dissociation is the entry into the non-attached existence, where love has no bounds. Then you can love all living things. All your fears are diminished: fear of loss, fear of abandonment, fear of poverty, fear of rejection, fear of breaking the rules, and so on. Surrender is the opposite of attachment which is sometimes mistaken for love.

Attachment is based on fear of loss, fear of abandonment, insecurity, belief in the delusion of an unchanging world. Attachment results in acts to control. When you are attached, you ask, "What can I get from this lover?" Or "What's in it for me?" Attachment is the impulse to possess. It is based on the fear lf loss.

The level of love that is surrender and non-attachment is the opposite of fear. Attachment leads to bondage but love leads to freedom.

When you surrender, you never feel the need to control, to beg or to convince. In trusting your lover, you do not feel anger. You can meditate together to become inner peace. When you surrender your spirit to your lover, then you avoid the conflict of two egos. Your innermost self, the silent witness becomes united with your lover's silent witness. This kind of surrender makes you into a holy person.

This kind of love is available to you when you are not attached.

Sixth level of love: Passion

Passion is a strong emotion, not a logical state of mind. Passion is a focused mental, emotional and physical state. The object of a strong affection or enthusiasm is also called a passion. In this book, the object of passion for the man is the woman and the object of passion for that woman is that man.

Each lover senses a higher reality. The reality is the experience of the merging of yin, feminine vitality, and yang, masculine vitality. The reality is the merging life and love. In the higher reality, events unfold as passion creates them. This is different from events unfolding out of the control of the lovers.

Passion seems to be the work of a divine higher power. Hindus consider it to be the energy of creation, the energy of masculine creation, interacting with the energy of feminine creation. This is the merging of opposites. Loss and gain are merged. Creation and destruction merge.

Passion is not just hunger for someone else. It is real power. It is the power to create. The Hindus call this power in women, Shakti. When you are in communion with the passion of a woman, she transmits Shakti to you. It is the inspiration to accomplish the impossible dream. The mystery of passion is that it is spiritual not material. And yet it can conquer the material world.

The play of the divine is what the Christians call "God's will." Other people call it by various names. The play of the divine consists of five facets: creation, protection, destruction, concealment, and revelation. You can conceive of God, or some other source of the underlying reality, constantly creating something, protecting someone, destroying what is there, concealing the weak creatures, and revealing truth. When you are awakened to the merging of your mind, your emotion and the Divine will in your state of passion, then you perceive these five facets of the play. Your passion keeps these five Divine energies alive in your life and in your love.

Seventh level of love: Ecstasy

Ecstasy is intoxication of extreme emotional excitement. There are no words to express this ineffable state of being. Perhaps ecstasy is the merging of the lovers with the collective consciousness. Hindus mean this when they say, "You are That." That is not expressible. Does this sound like a kind of sexual bliss you would like to experience?

Ecstasy is the final state of sexual connection. Your spiritual basis flows through love. This is the objective of all your effort and longing. This is could be called Tantric connection, your final completion by connecting with another person. This is not just physical ecstasy stimulated by the senses, the couch, the sight, the sound, the smell the taste of your beloved. Your inner vision of what is possible opens to the ineluctable, indefinable. It has been called awakening to the God and Goddess within. Your heroic striving for the highest human achievement, like a God or Goddess or butterfly emerging from your unknown self, or your cocoon is gloriously breaking through the clouds of ordinary consciousness. These are meaningless words unless you have experienced this ecstasy

It is said by those who have experienced this ecstasy, that there is a merging of the silent witness behind the ego with the collective consciousness. This is contact with spiritual ecstasy.

Those who have experienced ecstasy praise it as entry into the Garden of Eden, the state of grace to which we will one day return. Words such as exuberance and delight are poor descriptions of the state of complete sexual awakening. Perhaps it is a master vibration that everything in nature is expressing. Perhaps ecstasy is when there is a mixture of the human experiences of mind, emotion, physical copulation, and spiritual awakening, mixed with the unknown unconscious, mixed with the unknowable Spirit often called God or Buddha nature. The science of this ecstasy is the Tantric Way.

Perhaps you are ready for the Tantric Way. How high do you want to go? What level of love can you achieve? Write down the levels of love you want with your best possible woman.

Look up the books on Tantra the end of this book. Read *Kama Sutra including the Seven Spiritual Laws of Love* by Deepak Chopra.

They will help you raise your mental picture of your sexual life.

There are hundreds of other feelings besides love. See The Appendix at the end of this book.

You want to be free of pain and suffering; therefore your emotions are a major influence in your life. You have control over most of your feelings.

These ideas about emotions are obvious to me but they may be controversial to you. Each person has an opinion about what his world is made of. Some people think it is sounds, others think sights, others smells, or taste of food, or people, for others thinking is the main world. Your world maybe composed of several of these. If you sit quietly and examine yourself, you will notice that you always have some feelings even though they are barely noticeable. Go to Appendix C: Feelings and Feeling Words

A major part of your experience is emotion; feelings. Your pain, suffering, relief and pleasure register in your perception as feelings. Feeling good is one of the goals for most of what you do. Do you ever feel that feeling good is a matter of life and death? Some people do.

(See *Animals in Translation*, Scribner, New York (2005) page 198ff by Temple Grandin and Catherine Johnson)

Staying alive is a goal. Emotions help you survive. Emotion is so important that if you had to choose between having an intact emotional system or an intact thinking system, the right choice would be emotional system. Your perception and intellectual functions would collapse if emotional value systems were destroyed. This has been tested. It has been observed.

You have been taught that the main thing that makes you so superior is your ability to think. This is an arrogant and inaccurate notion. You may have been taught that emotions are dangerous or irrelevant. This is an ignorant opinion. You may think that emotions are best hidden and kept under control. These are beliefs that undermine your successful attainment of feeling good.

Not only do you need to know what you are feeling, you communicate with your best possible wife when you know her feelings. People and even animals have feelings. You cope better when you gain the skill of identifying other people's feelings. Think about this: you see a huge dog lunging at you with an evil face. Do you think about how to survive?

In the brain, logic and reason are never separate from emotion. Even nonsense syllables have an emotional charge. Nothing is emotionally neutral. Learn to believe this now. Use the beliefs in this book. You will move toward feeling good and avoiding pain.

Learn the connection between thinking and feeling. If you are unconscious of your feelings, especially when you are frantically reacting and not thinking something through, are your conclusions reasonable? In this condition, you think you are using logic but you are really using reflex guided by emotion.

In fact, this is how salesmen sell you. They stir up your emotion which guides your thinking. Then you think up reasons to buy. Especially if you have learned the habit of ignoring emotion. Later, you wonder why you bought that useless gadget.

Sometimes, when you are aware of your feelings because you're passionate about a woman, you make bad decisions. You blame feelings for the bad decision. Because you are unskilled at using your own feelings.

Is it possible that you think other people's emotions are getting in the way of your making useful decisions? On the other point of view, have you ever decided other people's emotion based decisions are destructive?

Some decisions are destructive. However, the problem is not the emotion. Everyone uses emotion to make decisions. The problem is that you do not know how call up the useful emotions for a given decision to help you. Or you do not know how to calm down and sit quietly for a count of ten or a hundred so your logical parts of your brain start working. Once you cultivate the habit of calling up your reasonable part of your mind, you will use the logic tool not the frantic, immature emotion tool. Even when you are concentrating on thinking clearly, there are emotions coloring the process. Use the right tool, not the wrong tool.

Read *Descartes' Error* by Demasio. This book explains observations of people who did not have your normal ability to use feeling to make decisions.

You may have thought you could live your life without feelings. In fact, you cannot make any decisions without feelings. You would not respond to life. You would have no gut feeling. And other people would sense that you were empty and totally in uninteresting. Without your emotional tone, you would be an empty shell.

You use your feelings to guess the immediate future

People and animals use feelings to predict the future. That's how you make decisions. You may think endlessly about what would happen in the future based on a decision. But you wouldn't ever be able to base a decision on thinking alone. And to make it worse, without using your feelings to guide your thinking about decisions, you would mostly make the wrong decisions. Emotions help you to invent hunches, intuitions, or what ever you want to call it. When you are in a threatening situation or with a dangerous person, your feelings inform you to run. They help you survive.

Your feelings predict the future. You do not wait until you're weak from hunger to eat. Your feelings inform you way ahead that you need to eat or the future will be starvation. Your feelings move you to take action to survive. If you waited until a sleazy bar maid was yanking your wallet from your pocket, you would not survive. You take action in time to prevent trouble because your feelings inform you of the threat.

An exercise when you can feel anything you want

Here is a suggestion to learn to use your feelings to make your life better. Every day, sit quietly alone for 5 to 20 minutes in a secluded place like the toilet or a church. Close your eyes and focus on your heart for a while. Notice your feelings. Try to change your feelings by remembering your past life. To feel joy, remember a joyful time. Next focus behind your eyes. Notice your feelings. Change your feelings by making an effort to feel what you want.

If you do this little exercise every day. You will realize you are becoming a master of your feelings. This is an accomplishment. Few people can do it.

**Your feelings send you information on the
threats and opportunities near you**

This information from feelings is called "street wise." Your sense of smell informs you when a predator is near. Some people know the smell of dangerous people and animals. You may not know consciously, but perhaps non-consciously on a deep level. You may have an emotional reaction to the smell even though you many not be aware of it. In New York City for example, you even react to the powerful smell of predator people and animals who have left their smell behind and will come back later. If you are street wise, you leave that location.

Your smelling sense may also inform you about women who are in heat or able to conceive babies. Women give off certain odors when they are fertile. It is unlikely that you are consciously aware of the smell but you may move toward it. You feel lust and you begin to protect the woman from other competing men. It is not just the way she looks. Some women use so much perfume you cannot pick up their natural aroma. If a woman has not washed for 20 to 40 hours when she is fertile, she is particularly attractive. Remember the lusty women volleyball players at the beach in the evening? They were so magnetic because they were spraying the signals to you all day and they had not washed off the scent. Your feelings helped you predict that they would succumb to your persuasion. Part of your persuasion was your own scent which was maddening to a woman who consciously wants to have a baby. Based on other more certain information such as her staring at you, a decision to take action favors a successful bid for a new friend or lover.

This is just an example for you to use when you are acting crazy about a woman or when you are terrified for no obvious reason. Notice your feelings and guess what smells, or invisible sights or tiny sounds are causing you to react. When you are suddenly overcome by the willpower to take a dangerous chance, sit down for a few minutes and wait to identify the source of the madness.

Another exercise when you can feel anything you want

Here is another procedure you must learn to feel good and to have your feelings work for you. You want to avoid jumping into situations. You want to be the one with the cool head who does not take serious losses.

This will take time to change our instincts. You must do this every day just as you have to do the other one above every day. You will slowly change into a more mature man.

Go to Appendix C: Feelings and Feeling Words

1. Learn the names of most of your feelings You could start by memorizing 5 feelings. Later, you can add 20 to 30 names.
2. Be mindful of what you feel all the time. This is like hunting the ox when you will go hungry if you do not pay attention. If you slip and do not pay attention, you will be hunted by the lion.
3. Learn to call your feelings by name.
4. Pick an emotion you want to feel.
5. Practice starting that feeling to replace whatever you were feeling before. This is difficult, maybe impossible for you.
6. Tell other people what you are feeling.

It takes lots of practice, but you can learn it if you persist every day.

Feelings are part of your major environment. They are not obvious all the time but they are inside you. You have to learn the skills to know your feelings. Concentrate on feeling pleasure.

Pain and suffering are in the realm of emotion. You are interested in feeling alive, excited, and pleasant.

Touching your woman is a way to feel better. Read the next chapter after you have practiced being aware of your feelings for a week.

Chapter 10
You Can Give and Receive Hundreds of Caresses

Each time you touch another person, it has a meaning. Find out what each touch means. Find out her boundaries and ask permission to touch her secret places. What do accidental touches mean? Are they really an accident?

Awaken to the touching in sports and dancing. Can you find the thrill in touching hands and arms?

There are 100 different kisses. Experiment to find out how many you can discover. Can you invest an hour in touching only legs and torsos? Do not limit yourself to the touch of sexual organs.

Touching one another is part of dating. It is part of marriage. But you can make big trouble if you touch a person at the wrong time or on the wrong place. That is why you are going to study touching.

Answer these questions in detail before your next date.

What do you know about touching?

How many ways can you kiss?

What parts of your body can you use to touch her body?

There are hundreds of massage books. Get a massage book and try out all the ways of energizing another person. They are at the library for free. Look at *The Book of Massage* by Lidell or the one by Downing.

Touching can be much more fun than you ever thought. Concentrate on how much better it can be. There are hundreds of movements in sexual copulation. They all mean different things if you are mindful enough to be conscious of them. Practice being mindful.

You can focus you attention on massage by answering these questions.

Do you flinch when a person who you loathe touches you?

If you touch 100 people on the arm, does it mean the same to them all?

If you touch your lover when she is sexually aroused, does it mean the same as when your lover is enraged?

Are you aware of what all your movements mean during sexual copulation?

Are you mindful of your body, feelings, mental state, and thoughts when making love?

Which people could be turned off when you touch them on the legs intentionally?

What if you touch someone's leg accidentally?

How many hundreds of ways can you touch a person's hands and arms?

What does it mean to hold hands: does it depend on the person and on how you hold?

Did you ever ask your friend what it means when you touch parts of her body?

Do you ever feel fear when someone touches you?

How many ways can you kiss her lips?

Her neck?

Her back?

If you write the answers to these questions, you will learn faster. You cannot expect to have great thrills without learning from people who are trained in massage. Follow the directions in this chapter.

Touching is so important that people make their living touching others. There is massage that heals. Therefore I am not going to try to tell you very much more. You have to get the books and you have to experiment with touching.

Until you pore over a massage book, and experiment by actually doing the massage, you will never know anything about the magic of touching. And try out the ideas you get from all this reading. You will enjoy touching. You can be sure of that.

Have you ever experimented with touching lots of people at a party? Touching at parties can result in extreme success or failure. There is much to know about party behavior. Do not try out touching people at parties until you have gained some distinct skills.

Since you have learned so much by now, it is time to learn the many tips about parties in the next chapter.

Chapter 11
How to Be in Demand at Parties

Next is some information about parties.

How to get invited.

How do you know what to wear?

How to remember all those names when you arrive.

How to make them remember you.

How to meet people and make them like you in 90 seconds.

How do you take part in activities?

Are you afraid you will not have anything to say?

What if you think you cannot dance?

What about eating?

Do you want to get over stage fright?

What to do if you are consumed by lust for someone?

What about drugs like alcohol, legal prescriptions, and illegal drugs?

How do you leave the party so you are invited again?

The fundamentals of partying have been known for hundreds of years. There are no really modern party rules. Although people think the rules change, the basic rules remain constant. They are attitudes of respect, admiration, helping the other person feel important, don't get drunk or socially destructive. There are many books on this.

The contemporary standard of behavior is *Miss Manners' Guide to Excruciatingly Correct Behavior* by Judith Martin. A simpler book is *Miss Manners' Basic Training*, also by Judith Martin.

These books are about how to communicate.

Five ways to be invited to lots of parties

First Invitation: Find someone who gives parties.

Second Invitation: Get ready. Do not just go. Plan it out to have the best possible outcome.

Third Invitation: Arrive at the best times and join the party. Make friends. That should be easy.

Fourth Invitation: Be a part of all activities. But do not act stupid even if others are rude and ignorant.

Fifth Invitation: Say goodbye and thank everyone. Get addresses, e-mail, and phone numbers. Plan to meet again.

These are spelled out in detail.

First Way to Get Invited: find someone who gives parties

People have parties for many reasons: to meet people, have fun, get drunk, and so on. Find the people who give parties.

Or give one yourself. Then you find out who is going to give a party from your guests. You have to be the kind of person who others want at their parties. Act as follows wherever you are. Then people will want you at their parties.

A. Be sociable and reach out to people.
B. Talk about what others want to talk about. Do not talk about yourself unless asked. Turn the attention on others after you have answered a question about yourself.
C. Laugh, especially when someone jokes.
D. Ask people about themselves. Listen eagerly to the answers.
E. Hold your own party. Invite the people who throw parties to your parties and events.

Guests will then invite you to their parties.

F. Be at ease. Do not get upset, outrageous, irritable, or anti-social.

G. Be friendly with those around you: at work, school, classes, bars, church, seminars and so on.

H. Unless you are close with someone, don't ask if you can go to a party that you've heard mentioned. You will be invited if they want you. You can also get someone else, other than the host, to ask if you can come as his or her guest.

Second Way to Get Invited: Get ready:

A. Ask the host about the party.

1. Ask if you should bring anything. Even if the hosts say no, always bring something. Bring something that will enhance the party. For example, music, games, food, drink. Or bring something just for the host, a gift. For example, candle, potted plant, fancy soap.

2. Ask the host what to wear. This is often difficult to get a useful response to. In case of the typical, "Oh, just whatever you want," or the dreaded, "dress casual," jovially ask the host what he or she is wearing to the party.

3. Ask what kind of people will be attending.

4. Ask if there a theme (and what is it?)

5. Ask what is the purpose of the party.

6. Ask if it is alright to bring a guest (make sure the guest is appropriate, fitting with the type of party and the party attendees)?

B. Dressing

1. Dress according to how the host advised.
   Take into account the theme of the party: birthday? Bring a gift. Reunion? Prepare to greet old friends.

2. Find out who the other people are will be attending. Find out what the host is wearing, the location of the party, the purpose of the party, the season, the time of day the party will be taking place.

3. Dress comfortably. Your clothes affect your feelings and the feelings of others. A party is not the right time to try to wear an untried outfit; always wear an outfit that you've worn before. If your pants are too tight, or your shoes pinch, it will be hard to be a good partier. Be able to move freely in your clothes. You don't want to be left out of dancing with a sparkly new acquaintance because your shirt gets caught on things! Or your pants are so tight they might tear when moving briskly. Wear an outfit in which you feel good. You must feel comfortable, sexy, handsome, powerful, and friendly in your outfit.

4. Approve of the makeup, hair, accessories, perfume, and accoutrements of the hostess. Make sure your accessories work with your attire. Make sure your hair is cut or managed easily. You don't want your hat, or hair being the first concern, even more important than relating. You should be more concerned with who you are talking to, or kissing, than keeping your clothes straight. When you sweat, your hair gel should not run into your eyes, or your dance partner's eyes.

Your cologne or aftershave, must be subtle; you should not be able to smell it. It is meant to be only a faint hint of an essence.

Third Way to Get Invited: Arrive at a reasonable time.
Get Integrated into the Party

You can read about all this in more detail in etiquette books.

Arrival Time is flexible: As long as you get there before the party is over, you are on time. Three hours late may be too late.

Your role at the party will differ depending on when you arrive. You could arrive right when the host says the party starts. You can not arrive early. You can arrive early only with the host's permission. Then your role will be helping to set up. You will be involved in greeting the guests. You will take on part of the host's role. This can be great because you will meet the attendees as they arrive. But it also can put more responsibility on you regarding the way the party runs. If you jazz up the guests as they arrive, you will find gratitude. If you put guests on the defensive or anger them, you will never see the host again.

A. People often are shy when they first arrive at a party, especially early arrivals. This means that they are more open to meeting new, different people. If you are greeting people at the door, help by introducing them to someone else. If you arrive early, take advantage of the shyness of other guests by becoming instant-friends with the other early arrivals

You could arrive, "Fashionably Late." This elusive term means arriving when you think the party is about to reach its peak. If you arrive when the majority of the guests are in attendance, you will enter into noise, commotion, laughter, and friendliness. People will have established groups and new acquaintances. There will, therefore, be a lot of conversations and communication taking place. This can be easier for you because you don't have to start conversations or experience people's awkwardness. But it can be difficult to break into a group that was formed without you.

B. Meeting people for the first time at a party

Start by introducing yourself. Most people at parties know few, or none, of the other partiers. When they arrive, this means that they are all eager to talk to someone. They want to feel like they are part of a group. Introduce yourself! Ask their names. Remember their names.

Now you want to know how to remember names. You can write them down on your business card or something. Or you can repeat their names several times as soon as you can. Make up some flattering compliments with their names. People love to hear their names. Make it a point to introduce yourself to as many people as possible at the party.

Next, get in rapport. This means a close or sympathetic relationship, a harmonious, agreeable conversation. You can easily get into rapport with people by following their lead. Take on their physical stance, or a similar variation. Hold your arms and legs the same way. Pay attention to their vocal tone and speed. Use the same tone and speaking speed. Pretend, to yourself, that they are an old friend. Open your heart and allow him or her in. Your new acquaintance will pick up on this vibe and feel like he or she has known you for much longer. You will both feel warmer and more at ease. After you are in rapport, you can become closer if you move your body a little away from the identical position. He or she will follow your body movement.

Then, find out about your new acquaintance to create a friend. Ask questions: How did you hear about the party? What do you do for a living? What do you enjoy the most? Why are you at the party? Lean forward and listen intently. Reply to the subjects they talk about. Ask more about general topics they bring up. Try to find common ground.

Find ways to relate to what they say. What do you have in common? Have a short opening conversation. This can consist of just the above or more.

Then, move around and meet everyone. Remember to keep the first conversation short. You want to keep moving around, meeting all the different people at the party. You do not want to become attached to anyone too early on. Even if there aren't any new people to talk to, when you've had a sufficient opening conversation, get away to do something else for a bit. You want to stay interesting, not allowing the conversation to get tedious, boring, invasive, or slow. You can come back to this new friend in a little while.

C. Be mindful of making lots of friends. Instant friends. Networking.

Take on the attitude that since you've spoken to someone once at a party, their friends are your friends. Assume that you love everyone. Include everybody. Do not irk someone or exclude anyone. Now that you've established acquaintances around the party room, you can go back to them. Meet the people that they are talking to. You can just walk up to the group that they are conversing with and say hi to the person you've met. He or she will usually introduce you to the others in the group. If not, introduce yourself. Make sure when someone does introduce you, that you also introduce whomever you are speaking with to whom ever has just arrived in the group. You do not need to remember both people's names to do this, though it helps. You can ask "Have you met?" Then if they haven't, they will introduce themselves to one another. Or say the name of the one you do remember, "I want you to meet Bob." The other person will say his or her own name.

Fourth Way to Get Invited: Participating in Party Activities

Dance.

You don't need to know the details of how to ballroom dance. In the last 40 years, a much more informal dance style has come into being. The new style allows everyone to take part. It is better to dance than to watch. By participating, people get to know you. There is a lot of communication in dance. Others pick up your dance communication. Some of the guests are interested in knowing you better. They will watch your dance communication. Everyone appreciates when someone dances. If you are the first to dance, you will receive gratitude. Most people will not have the confidence to be the first one on the dance floor. When the dance starts, things are more interesting. Imagine that by dancing you are helping everyone have a better time, especially yourself!

If you are afraid because you do not know how to dance, you can follow the lead of other dancers. Mimic how they move to the music. No one will reject you if you dance. Some may reject you if you do not dance. Most dancing nowadays is not complex; it is just some bopping up and down to the music. It is actually called "hip-hop." That should tell you about the movement. Add in some hip movements, or some butt shaking, and you're hot stuff! Add arm or hand movements and you are a dance god! The more energy you put into the dance, the more space people will give you on the dance floor.

Networking.

Often people attend a party to network. It may be the main reason to go to a party. At parties, you can make friends and business contacts.

You may see these people again outside of parties, or they may be your doorway into more parties. Practice asking leading questions with open-ended answers, answers that require a story or instruction.

Listening.

After the party, think about your questions and listening. How can you improve them? Get books on networking. There must be 100 of these books. Learn this tool.

Eating

Eating is a type of communication. People watch you eat. They can tell your social class and your economic class by the way you eat. Think about the analogies used to describe the way a person eats: pig, bird, wolf, or slob. Eating may be the most transparent revelation of yourself. Learn to eat properly. It is dealt with in etiquette books. Watch others eat and you will realize that you read a lot into their habits. Therefore, please note that, although party food is a delight, you shouldn't go to a party ravenous. You may communicate that you are a food addict.

It is important to focus on the other aspects of the party more than the food. You don't want to hover around the food table, if you can help it. Take other people's lead, especially the host and the host's closest acquaintances, as to how much to eat and in what manner to eat. For example, with fingers, using chopsticks, or from plates.

Drinking.

Alcohol is an integral part of most parties, but never, ever, get incredibly drunk!

You should never go to a party just to get shit-faced drunk Make sure you know how much alcohol you can handle and remain a coherent and calm individual. You can get falling down drunk after you leave the party. Stating the obvious, if you hang out around the liquor and drink without mixing and talking, most everyone will notice. The result is that you will likely never go to a party with any of the guests again unless they are drunks. Because you will expose your alcohol addiction.

The problem with alcohol is that it is legal. So you think it is alright to use it. It is still a dangerous drug. You can still die from alcohol or end up in the hospital. One of the tendencies of drinkers is that one drink is not enough. They keep drinking until drunk.

Probably you are like this since most people are. If you cannot stop at one drink, do not drink. If you have to drive, don't drink. If you have to go where there are muggers, don't drink. If you want to have friends, to keep your job at a company party, to impress a lover, do not drink at all. No, this is not a joke.

Get drunk with friends who also get drunk and who do not care if you are stupid when drunk. Did I really write that? Yes, almost everyone gets stupid when drunk. That is why you do not get drunk with strangers or at a party where you want to make new friends.

The main thing to know about alcohol is that your behavior is worse after three drinks. You cannot dance as well, talk as well, or drive as well. When you are drinking, your judgment is poor. This means that you will do things, say things, and think things that will get you in trouble. For example, after three drinks, you think your jokes are funny. No one else will think they are funny unless they are drunker than you. In short, you get stupid when you are drinking. The more you drink, the stupider you get.

Sometimes, you can get drunk with small losses. Such as when you are with the guys only watching football. Or when you are with the girls who would never gossip about you, if that is ever possible. And then only if they will forgive you for being stupid. Remember you can ruin a love life, or a career, in one drunk. People often invite you to a party to see you drop your defenses when drunk. The rule is that people will forgive you for many things you do at a party. But never, ever, drink to black out. Never drink when you may get belligerent.

For example, if you show up at a party when you are already furious, absolutely do not drink. You will lose control of your fury. You may also lose your friends. Unless you are looking for punishment, the rule is never get drunk.

If you can have one to three drinks and stop, then you could drink if you are in a good mood. Do not drink in company when you start out angry or depressed, or some of those extreme feelings. The feelings will be amplified. Getting tipsy is a better alternative. However, not being inebriated at all will lead to more contacts and more invitations. Be cautious, even reserved. Again, gauge the party. Especially by what the host and those close to the host do.

Drugs and Drugging.

Alcohol is a dangerous drug. Illegal drugs may be dangerous too. Advice similar to the above alcohol advice is applicable to drugs. There are serious legal consequences related to drugs. With prescription drugs, take them as directed by the doctor. It is best to hold the written prescription with you or on the bottle in case the police stop you. It is illegal for you to have prescription drugs if they are not prescribed for you. That means that you can go to jail or pay several thousand dollars to a lawyer for legal drugs.

For illegal drugs, it is best not to carry them on your body. Stash them somewhere in case of being of being stopped by the police. There exists a book listing 5,000 drugs, legal and illegal. No one knows all the ways to alter your consciousness or your mood. There are uppers that make you feel energetic, like cocaine. There are probably 100 new uppers that you have never heard of. You can take too much and go to the hospital or you may die. Uppers can make you too aggressive or obnoxious, like alcohol. So you could not realize how unacceptable or anti-social you are. Yes, it is true. You might think you are just having a good time. But everyone else hates you and wants you to get out. In fact, they may throw you out. Any type of drug, including alcohol, can destroy your judgment, so you think you are amusing when you are destroying everyone's party. Many drugs make you anti-social. Anti-social means criminal acts like rape or destruction of property. Take one hit of your dope and stop. Do not mix dope with alcohol because you can easily overdose and either die or get very sick at the hospital emergency room. The same rules apply as for alcohol.

There are downers that make you feel tired, like heroin or sleeping pills. These are life-threatening when mixed with alcohol. Do you want to sleep through the party? Why go? Do you want to be with a date who is groggy and helpless? Your date may then be an easy lay. Remember it is a felony to drug your date or to take sexual advantage of an unconscious date.

Women consider the consequences of being raped and impregnated with HIV while sleeping on a downer. So do not take downers at a party. Do not take a date who is on downers to a party. If you do either of these, the host will know. You will never get invited back. That is assuming you are not in jail. The host or someone may call the police. You may end up in prison.

Sex and Sexual Behavior.

Not drinking or drugging will help you avoid awkward situations regarding sexuality at parties. It is fine to meet attractive people at parties and to express your attraction. Show good taste if you want results like necking or intimate touching. But don't be tacky, crude, rude, or insulting about it. Some flirting and suggestive talk is expected, even welcomed. However, participate in other activities as well. Everyone present will take note if you focus only on flirting sexually or trying to make sexual contact with several women. Women loathe a man who is going from one woman to the next making sexual talk. You will acquire an instant reputation as a whore. Yes, even men become known as womanizers or whores.

Sexual behavior must be the result of mutual attraction. That means you cannot force yourself on a woman. Most women, not all women, are turned off by men who pursue them intensely. Some women love an intense game of pursuit.

Therefore, you can open up the flirting with a neutral comment or a witty sexual innuendo. If your target is attracted, she will respond in a way that is clearly welcoming you. Any comment in good taste will do. The exact words do not matter much because it is just a gambit to probe for interest. You could make a statement about a color or a smell or a texture. If your desired stranger does not answer or turns you down, even with a look, go elsewhere. If you perceive that you are welcome, talk about the surroundings or a neutral topic. Listen. Assess the instant relations that are happening, the chemistry. If you seem to connect, bring up a topic you are interested in.

If you are making friends with a man, you should talk about sports until another subject comes up. Why? Because the majority of men and many women relate to sports.

If you are starting up a connection with a woman, compliment her clothes. Another subject is TV shows. Ninety-eight percent of people have favorite TV shows. Do not talk about politics or religion, or gossip about other people. These subjects will bring you rancor, abuse, and criticism, maybe a fistfight. An easy preparation is to read the newspaper or look at the latest news on TV or internet. This gives you information which you can comment on with strangers.

Do not kiss, or have sex play or intimate touching with *multiple* women at the party. Unless it is one of *those* kind of parties, like a swingers' club or something crazy like that. You will look like an ass, a womanizer. Have you ever seen a man doing this? Were you turned off? That is how people will feel about you. Most people have negative feelings when a man or is aggressively sexual. It will be obvious, no matter how stealthy you think you are. Hint: virtually no one likes a whore.

Word gets around about sexual activity. Even before the party is over. Actually, don't have sex of any kind while *at a party*, period. It is disrespectful to the host and the other party attendees. There is no secret sexual act.

Both men and women start talking about their sexual adventure to whomever will listen. Learn this now. So you do not have to learn it the hard way. To the contrary, do not talk about anyone who is not listening. This is called gossip. It is addictive, like tobacco. This will cause you deep suffering. The people to whom you are gossiping will then tell others that you gossip. So no one will want to deal with you. No one will want to have sex with you because you talk too much. You have shown a lack of integrity.

Some people will test your gossiping by telling you a confidence and listening for others to tell them about it. You told someone. Someone told the tester. Then you are the subject of gossip. You are someone who gossips. Gossiping shows a mean streak. Do not experiment with this; just accept it. Keep your mouth shut.

If it is a company party or a professional conference, do not make any public displays of affection. You could ruin your professional reputation in five minutes. In professional life or most kinds of career situations, your reputation is one of your foundation stones. If you lose it, you will have a difficult time getting it back.

It is normal to feel lust for some hot woman. If you are helplessly in love, discreetly suggest meeting your target outside. If you must do sexual things, or even excessively kiss, grab your lusty partner and leave the party!

Games.

Whenever the host offers games, participate. The host will love it, and you *will* be invited to more parties. Games can open different kinds of communication, and can be fun.

Fifth Way to Get Invited: Say goodbye to the host and thank her.

Get addresses, e-mail, phone numbers and so on. Plan to meet again. This is when the host remembers who will be invited to the next party.

Say, "Thank You" to the host. Compliment the host on specific elements of the party, like the decorations, or the food. Show gratitude.

If you stay to the end of the party, or near the end, always offer to help clean up, or do whatever is needed. This is a sure way to get an invitation to another party. Other guests also will note this. It is unusual and shows good, humble sincerity. These are prized qualities, because they are rare.

Say goodbye to those you've met throughout the party. Ask for contact info, or give out contact info at this point, if you haven't previously. You can ask for e-mail, phone, or address. Most people will give them to you. Here is the critical moment. Ask each person to meet you at a specific time and place. Try to establish a next meeting with that woman in whom you are particularly interested. See if they know of any other parties or events going on soon. This will cement acquaintances into friends.

The end of the party is the beginning of the next party

Thank the host a few days later, again. Contact each person soon, like the next day. This firms you up as a real sincere person. Not a party person, not a virtual reality.

P.S. Aside: Most people do not know the simple ideas in this chapter. So if you practice them, you will seem very mature, maybe elegant or grand. Practicing these few good communications gives you the air of integrity.

This chapter is only a short summary of a few simple ideas. However, parties are a fact of town, country and city life. Parties are a means of communication used all over the world to accelerate people meeting people.

Please get these books and study them.

How to Make People Like You in 90 Seconds or Less by Nicholas Boothman

What Do I Say Next? Talking Your Way to Business and Social Success by Susan RoAne

How to Work a Room. A Guide to Successfully Managing the Mingling by Susan RoAne

You've Only Got Three Seconds How to Make the Right Impression in Your Business and Social Life by Camille Lavington

How to Talk to Anyone, Anywhere. The Secrets of Good Communication by Larry King

Now you have read the books. You are a treasure. You have memorized the way to attract a woman. You know how to pursue that special woman. You are smooth at parties. You know a lot. And you have practiced enough to feel confident that the methods work.

You are ready to try out your skills at a serious event. Read the next chapter. Your eyes will open to the real meaning of all you have learned.

Chapter 12
How to Survive Serious Events

"Serious events" sounds so formal and forbidding. For the past 50 years, the preferred description of a social event is "casual." Even today in this casual age, there are ceremonies and graduations, meeting your lover's parents, and company parties. After all the training you have achieved in the last weeks and months of studying this book, you are ready to show your mastery of social skills in a serious event.

If you have eagerly pursued the questions and answers of the previous chapters. You can feel comfortable at occasions such as, weddings, affairs with your friend's family, church and religious gatherings with your lover, business meetings with your favorite associate, and a company party with the top managers.

You may like to know how to enjoy your best possible woman's family. You need to learn about wedding etiquette quickly. You can get started gaining these behaviors in this chapter.

There is so much to learn that you will find you learn a great deal more from the recommended etiquette books at the end of this book.

The term, "etiquette" is a set of rules which are part of your culture. In America, there are about one hundred cultures based on various groups of foreign immigrants and on various classes. They are based on long experience by large groups of people. There is a general set of behaviors that make your life easier with almost anyone. Most people prefer to act in accord with the rules because they have less pain and more satisfaction.

Three basic rules of etiquette

1. Be considerate of the feelings and needs of other people.

2. Be respectful.
3. Be honest but do not say harsh truths.

Why are these rules mentioned? Because etiquette is almost lost in America. Part of the reason is that are so many different cultures. Part of the reason is that many people that in America think they can say anything and be as vicious as they want because, "It is a free country." Among certain classes, there is a pervasive rotten attitude that people can say and do anything they please. This is a perverted notion of freedom and democracy. Do not believe this perversion. Believe this book. Follow the three basic rules.

Are you ready to learn what is necessary about your woman's religion? See the several books at the last chapter. Ask her about her religion. This will erase future friction.

Use the rules of etiquette to earn friends at work

Use them to attract that special someone at work. Use them to rapidly advance within your company as a result of your astute and mature party personality?

In America, there are about 200 different immigrant groups and about 50 different economic and social classes

Wherever you go, you will find people different from you. This has been the environment in America for over 200 years. And you have to fit in to serious events in all the different groups. These serious events are widespread. They are everywhere in the world. They have happened for the past 1000 years in Europe. Serious events began to be formal in China 3000 years ago. They take on the form of a ceremony.

Correct behavior is codified and taught in most cultures. Unfortunately, most of the world's population does not know the rules in other cultures. The upper classes often teach their children how to behave by the rules. The rest of us can take courses in the details of correct protocol. Do not complain; just adjust.

The answers have been developed in detail. Look through the recommended books at the end of this book. Use the Internet or the library to find the answers. You could find them free at the library. You could go online to find the titles of the books to answer your questions. There are endless books. Books and recorded materials help a lot. Some of the books on these questions are hundreds of pages long. You have to do research. Your study will pay off right away as soon as you are in a strikingly different culture and you know how to avoid trouble and to make friends.

Lately, books have taken a lighthearted writing style to these ceremonies. So they are easier to read. Some of the books are even fun and entertaining.

I cannot summarize the behavior for 200 cultures. There is too much to write. The rules for serious events are very clear. But the rules are separated by culture. Ask older people at work and your mature friends about books to read. Ask them how to behave. You could even ask your parents.

No, I am not making empty excuses. Research is your best source of information about serious gatherings.

Here are some etiquette books with detailed answers to your questions. The Miss Manners books go way beyond your questions.

Dazzled, Frazzled & Back Again: The Bride's Survival Guide by Ginger Kolbaba

Emily Post's Etiquette:The American classic.

The Groom Book: A Survival Guide for Men by Shelly Hagen

Miss Manners' Basic Training on Communication by Judith Martin

Miss Manners' Guide to Excruciatingly Correct Behavior by Judith Martin

Miss Manners on Weddings by Judith Martin

Priceless Weddings for Under $5000 by Kathleen Kennedy

Are you are getting tired of these lessons because they are the preliminaries to sex? The next chapter has the hints to the main questions you have about extremely thrilling sexual escapades.

You may be asking, "What is the secret ultimate sexual experience?"

Or, "How do I fulfill my sexual fantasies?"

Or, "Where can I learn the subtle art of seduction?"

Now you have read this book and other books. You are a treasure; a powerful support for a woman. You have memorized the way to attract a woman. You know how to pursue that special woman. You are famous at parties. You can impress anyone with your excruciatingly correct behavior at formal events. You have earned the right to be proud.

You have practiced enough to feel confident that the methods work. Sometimes you have sexual opportunities during these social adventures. You have succeeded because you have learned the vast wisdom of this book.

Now you are ready to read the next chapter on Sexual Thrills. Your eyes will open to the real meaning of seduction, of sex, of making love.

Chapter 13
How to Experience Sexual Thrills beyond the Earthly Existence

If you are looking for an explicit description of your possible sexual thrills, read the rest of this chapter. A hint of the sexual thrills beyond he earthly existence is given in this chapter. This book teaches you how to connect with your best possible woman on four levels simultaneously. It's true! You can have four times the rapture and enjoyment that you felt before now.

One of the many priceless information gifts in the book is an eleven-week course in joining your every part of your personality to that of your best possible woman. You and your lover teach yourselves this course. The course could be called, "How to Rise in Love." This course teaches you what to do during eleven weeks of continuously improved attachment. You will have constant improvement in your sex life, your emotional life, your physical life and your spiritual life.

If you follow the step-by-step guidance, then your relationship with your best possible woman will grow in ways you have never considered. It is possible that you have never even heard of most of the ways you could have an excellent relationship.

As you and your woman study and practice the ways of living described in this book, experiment with the daily step by step activities. You will experience thrills beyond your imagination. Do you imagine you have had thrilling sexual events?

This book will be an awakening. After you have read it, you will think you have been asleep all these years.

How a man and woman connect in every possible way

This life of living with complete absorption with your woman is called Tantric Sexual Practice. It comes from ancient India.

Begin by improving your way of thinking about relating to your woman. You experience the rapture after you study and prepare, not before. Study your internal body, with hatha yoga for example, to have the best experiences. Look at anatomy books with pictures of the inside of your body. Doesn't sound like fun? When you know what you are made of, you will take better care of yourself. You are much more delicate and sensitive than you thought. Also you are tougher and able to survive types of torment than you realize. Exercise to get the feel of your movements, to get in touch with your body.

Sexual contact helps your relationship be more intimate. Sexual play allows you to have fun. Learn to master your feelings to feel the whole orgasm. Learn to master your mind to think of the preparation for prolonged lovemaking. Find all the clues about lovemaking that lasts for 5 to 12 hours while you have multiple orgasms.

When you achieve the master in this seven week course, you and your lover will able to rise in love over and over again.

This chapter is just a suggestion and a guidance. You will need other books and plenty of practice to gain the vitality that is waiting for you. Read the other books. Some are recommended at the end of this book.

Tantric Sexual Practice from ancient India

Even a tiny summary of the Tantric approach is a titillating tidbit from the sexual science called the Tantric Way. Some ideas you will need to learn a.) Definitions of some words

b.) Tantra for lovemaking couples

c.) Yoni Massage on the woman

d.) Lingam Massage on the gentleman

e.) Sacred Spot Massage on man's prostate

Imagine yourself being disrobed within the soft glow of scented candlelight and helped into a rose petal-covered bath. To relax in a place where your beloved partner will soothe and lavish the most careful attention upon every inch of your aching body; particularly those often neglected areas. Using a variety of soaps, scented oils, and sponges your body will be caressed and relaxed. Soft hands and adept fingers will move about and caress every minute part of your physical being, massaging your head and temples, neck, shoulders, ever further down to your most sensitive areas. Even your feet and toes will not escape attention. The warm water will melt away your stress and relieve your anxiety. In time, you will begin to think only of the sacred space you and your beloved are sharing. You will begin to feel reborn as your newly invigorated body is gently dried with fluffy warm towels. You will know that you are only beginning your adventure. This is not just a bath; this is a bath ceremony! And you have not even started the sexual part.

Interested yet? Does this sound like a sexual experience you have had?

Consider a class teaching you to perform these techniques with your partner. Does this sound like an experience you will never forget?

Tantric practice is the science of amplification of the sexual union of man and woman, raised to an art of pleasure and absorption.

When you get to the next chapter, persuade your woman to read the description of a sexual action she can perform. Then ask her to give you this pleasure that is described.

"Yoni is the Sanskrit word for the woman's sex organ, her sacred space or "Sacred Temple." In Tantra, the Yoni is seen from a perspective of love and respect. This is particularly important for men to learn because American men speak disdainfully about the yoni and call it disrespectful names.

You will get the books of Kama Sutra and Tantric practice. Then you will give her the yoni massage. Before beginning the Yoni massage, it is important to create a space for your woman, the receiver, in which to relax. From which she can more easily enter a state of high arousal. In which, she experiences the extreme reality of sexual experience.

If this beginning sounds like what you want, get the *Kama Sutra* books. There are many of them. Some are listed at the end.

You will give her the experience of pleasure she has never felt. You will experience the joy of giving pleasure

The next chapter describes a sexual act your woman will enable you to experience. Both giver and receiver witness the slow buildup of sexual energy, joined with emotional passion, inflamed by mental visions, raising their bodies to a massive peak of vitality that may last for hours.

The Sanskrit word for the male sexual organ is Lingam, Wand of Light. In Tantra or sacred sexuality, the Lingam is respectfully viewed and honored, as a Wand of Light that channels creative energy and pleasure. American women could learn to feel more delight in the Lingam by changing their way of thinking about it.

Orgasm is not the only goal of the Lingam massage, although it can be a pleasant and welcome side effect. The goal is to raise the man into a highly receptive state; a state of peak feelings, aided by studied mental perceptions, enabled by a fit body capable of aerobic exertion, leading to hours of sexual lust. By holding off the orgasm, the man can experience intense vitality, and superhuman powerful energy normally hidden from him.

The massage of the Lingam, the balls, the surrounding area, and sacred spot (prostate) externally, allows the man to surrender. Surrender is a form of pleasure he may not be accustomed to. Men need to learn to relax and receive. Traditional sexual conditioning has the man in a acting in a goal oriented mode. From the Tantric perspective, both receiver and giver relax into the massage. The Lingam massage allows the man to experience his softer, more receptive side and experience pleasure from a novel perspective.

Now that you have read about an evolved and exquisite sexual thrill, remember the function of this togetherness.

Remember that the purpose of sexual congress is to reproduce human beings

There are at least 23 ways to create a baby. Since about 1965, there has been a huge sexual revolution. But artificial insemination (mechanical fertilization within the womb) began in 1776. Sperm, eggs, and embryos (impregnated eggs) can be frozen until you want to make a baby. The egg and sperm can be joined in a test tube (in-vitro fertilization). The egg can be removed from Sue, fertilized in vitro, and transplanted into Jane, who is then pregnant and delivers the baby. Virgin birth can be observed by cloning in a virgin womb or by artificial insemination in a virgin womb. Jane and Sue and choose which gender the baby will be. Three women and their lovers can each make embryos, fuse the three embryos into a single embryo and make a baby with six parents. More ways of making babies are being invented.

Are these new concepts?

These complications of making babies evolved in such a short time for three main reasons

1.) A huge growth in science, technology, and medicine in the twentieth century. People started living longer due to medicine. They wanted to have more choice about their children or no children. They were living most of their lives after the children grew up and left home. They wanted to enjoy sex in middle age and old age.

2.) Women were liberated sexually. They could enjoy sex because the birth control pill and other contraceptives kept them from getting pregnant. Women were liberated to work and to have enough money to live independently. Women got the vote and equality at work and home.

3.) There was instantaneous communication of all these changes all over the world with TV, radio, phones, satellites, and news. So women all over the world made the decision to delay having children of to have no children.

A contemporary and embarrassing problem arose

Many men do not have the urge to make babies or even to make love to women. This is a radical change since men have always been crazy about finding women and copulating. In addition, in some countries, such as Japan and China, there is a trend for women not to want to make babies and not to make love. There are many reasons for these changes. For example, women in Japan and China are allowed to get a job or to practice a profession for the first time in 2000 years. A great many men cannot make an erect penis. Then there is the problem of homosexuality so many man and women do not have the opportunity to make babies.

Let's do a mind experiment. You are on a date. You are falling madly in love with this woman who has all the advantages. So obviously you grab her and kiss her all over her face and neck and your hands are buzzing around.

You suddenly realize. You are not coping with your feelings.

You are consumed with lust. You cannot control your actions; you want her now. To hell with tomorrow! You just want it now! You do not care if you ever see her again. But your penis does not rise up. You have to take a pill to erect your penis. You feel embarrassed and other feelings.

You hesitate and think, "How do I know what she likes? She may be disgusted by aggressive seduction. She may be lesbian. She may need a show of acceptance. She may need time to open her heart to me before she can get her juices flowing." Of course you do not think that your penis is your problem She has only a little influence on your becoming erect, especially after your lust erases your reasoning.

Did you ever think those topics? Since you were born after the sexual revolution in 1963, it is possible you need a pill to become erect. You may have thought about the woman's point of view. And because you found you needed more time and intimacy to get a hard penis and to "perform."

She may go along with your aggressive groping. Because you are a new lay. You flatter her ego.

You are expected to "perform." But there is a part of the younger cohort born after the sexual revolution that cannot get hard on demand. They are anxious. So what if they do end up in bed? Maybe you are one of them. Many contemporary men do not become hard on the spur of the moment. So you and she have an embarrassment.

166

She can not accommodate his non-sexual response. You go through the motions but it does not work. You have to stimulate her to orgasm but not in coitus. You both feel inadequate. You both are angry and frustrated. You have started something you cannot achieve well.

You need a better approach that will yield the desired results. You need to figure out what is necessary for you two to have a fulfilling sexual escapade.

Some changes in the American Society that have caused a few men to have sexual dysfunctions

The sexual revolution started early about 1942 when women went into war work and most men were gone to war. No one suspected the results. The twentieth century saw a revolution of both male and female roles.

For women, there was a revolution of female education. women went to college. The unexpected results were that women were liberated sexually. By 1963, they could enjoy sex because birth control pills and other contraceptives kept them from getting pregnant. Women were liberated to work and have enough money to live independently without marriage. Women got the vote and equality at work and home. Attitudes about sex outside marriage changed radically.

For men, there were effects on men's sexual role. The unexpected consequences of the sexual revolution are

1. The feminization of the American man (Other countries are also finding this)
2. Some percentage of women did not want men. Women were liberated sexually. They could enjoy sex with many men just as men had always had sexual contact with many women because of the contraceptives.

3.   The family was destroyed leaving women to raise boys into men without fathers. The feminization of the American man began in the school system about 70 years ago. It began in the home and family about 30 years ago affecting the mother-son-boy relationship.

About 1960, a peculiar lie began to overtake American society. The Feminist movement began perhaps in 1800 in Europe. Women invented the insanity that boys and girls are the same in most ways. This may be hard to believe, but it is true. You would never believe such obvious nonsense, but the news media and the schools taught this. Schools now treat boys and girls mostly the same. But the mental, physical, and social developments are different for each gender. This description is a general concept to get the idea across. You can think of exceptions. But for the majority of boys, since about 1970, this is the experience.

Boys are more aggressive and have much more energy than girls. However, they are expected to be like girls: passive, neat, quiet, mannerly, obedient, and emasculated. The boys evolved into sexual adults about age 13 to 18. But they are treated like children even they are allowed to die in war. Aggression is taught to be resolved through speech and passive-aggressive behavior. But boys like to show physical aggressiveness; they engage in rough sports, fight, push, and show how tough they are. They are expected to hold in their normal physical energy until sports after school. They need to burn off psychic energy that builds up in class. That energy has to release somehow. It often releases as vandalism, anti-social behavior, crime, homosexuality, and premarital sex. They use drugs like marijuana voluntarily to make themselves passive, because their superego rules will not allow instinctual behavior. Or they use alcohol to increase aggressive expressions. The normal reaction of males to being dominated by females is anger and hostility. It is normal.

Most of the staff in schools is women. Most women who do not understand nor approve of male energetic expression. When boys act normal, they are treated like criminals, even expelled from school. School teachers, and even single mothers, began to call normal boy behavior Attention Deficit Hyperactivity Syndrome (ADHS) and other psychobabble. About 1980, school women started giving boys drugs to contain their energy and make them passive. This builds up habitual behavior that is good for office work. The development of masculine traits is ignored. Again the boys feel hostile at being dominated by women. They feel anger at being herded into acting like girls, and not being guided into manhood. It is normal.

The contradiction between the school-accepted drugs and the police-prohibited drugs leads to a disrespect for authority. Other parts of our culture also cause disrespect for authority. The result for many men is destructive behavior, prison life, and a loss of constructive use of energy for society. This is only a few of the problems that evolved from feminization in the USA.

The traditional family consisting of mother, father, and children is destroyed. The number of divorces is about half the number of marriages in a given year. This has been going on since 1976.

So the USA has had 50 years of converting boys into girls in the family. Authority is held by the mother. The father is ejected from the home of half the boys. Since there are no adult masculine models at home or school, boys and young men bond to each other in gangs. They cannot learn to be men from their mothers. They learn how to be men from little boys. Obviously, this is impossible. The young men know they are being cheated out of a father by women. They feel anger and hostility toward women.

Anger and hostility toward women does not result in an erect penis. So dear reader, you have to find the warm, accepting, open-hearted woman to have a satisfying love life. You have to find the opposite of the women you have experienced in your life. Most of your women were not sex objects; they were trouble. You have to discover the sex goddess or some other type of woman you respond to.

The repulsion between the mother and son leaves the son in a vacuum about realistic feminine behavior. Often, there was no father to teach the son how to treat women in about half the homes in the USA. So men fantasized about women while they were growing up. They invented stereotype women. These women were not real. They were mental and emotional creations. So when such a son meets a flesh-and-blood woman, he does not relate very well. He is often angry and hostile, feelings that he was taught to represses because they are considered abnormal by women.

The following examples may not be true for you. However, they describe approximately half of American men.

One fantasy is the Super Bunny. *The playmate is liberated from pregnancy by contraceptives. She says "Yes" to anything, including sexual contact, ready for the sexual whims of men. She makes no demands nor does she discriminate between crappy boys and respectable men. The boy thinks that if a girl refuses, she is abnormal and needs to lose her virginity. The Super Bunny does not want to get married and tied down to love and commitment. She has her own contraception device and pays for her own abortion.*

The other side of this is that the Super Bunny thinks that all men can perform on demand. The irony is that men see so many women exposing bare skin around the breasts and upper thighs and are subjected to so much seductive clothing and see pictures of naked women on magazine covers and even billboard advertising, that they are no longer aroused by it. When faced with a naked and demanding Super Bunny, they are impotent.

Another fantasy is the Super Bitch. *She is super sexual, but in a way that aggressively threatens the sexual ability of men. This is called castrating or ball-busting. Sort of like the angry mother. A mother who changes from a warm, soft protector into a fierce demon is a nightmare that most men remember. She eats men. The Super Bitch abuses men sexually while taunting them to screw her. This leaves men crushed and flaccid. She is the spider to the male fly. Men's reaction is hate, hostility, and at least sexual insecurity about liberated women. When a man thinks of the Super Bitch his Lingam turns into a flaccid thing.*

Another popular stereotype is the Butch Lesbian. *These women have liberated themselves completely out of heterosexuality. They say, "Who needs a man?" Women can completely satisfy each other. This attitude undermines male confidence. She says, "No" to everything. The opposite of the Super Bunny. Men do not relate sexually to her.*

Perhaps another fantasy arises, the Grand Dame. *No one would call her a "girl." A woman who has finished her childbearing. She is a professional and has the means to discriminate toward the best men she can find. She is too mature to bother with women's liberation arguments. She is sexually adept from the start of flirting to the open-hearted acceptance of her man to the full vivacity of post-coital intimacy. Men are always potent with her. She makes dalliance into an art because she has studied the whole physical, mental, emotional, and spiritual levels of connection with a man. Her physical body is toned and ready for the demands of many hours of sexual acrobatics with her man. She is in control of her feelings. She is whole, combining the female anima and the male animus into a completely satisfied life.*

I confess that the Grand Dame is my ideal. I have the pleasure of enjoying her loyalty. Maybe you can appreciate this type of woman. Maybe you are ready for this Grand Dame.

Many men have sexual trouble, so do many women

An old and still a contemporary problem: many women cannot be interested in sexual activity. The simple summary of men's sexual troubles above hints that there may be reasons why women have sexual trouble. In older histories and novels, we read of "frigidity" and other resistance women have to sex. The pressure on women to perform sexually is an old story.

Just because there are many women who are freely sexual, especially since effective contraceptives in 1960, does not mean all women are comfortable with sex. Just because there are pictures of near naked women on television, magazine covers and billboards implies that all woman should be willing to play the sex game. But not all women want loose sex, or any kind of sex.

In spite of her seductive clothes and flirting eyes, do you want to risk a loss within a few minutes of the sex game? Let's consider an example of a woman who does not want to open up sexually, despite her sexy appearance.

Phoebe is over thirty years old and still a virgin. She has decided to encourage the passion of an old friend who she respects and feels close to. After a formal date, he is visiting her apartment expecting the intimacy he has waited for these many years. She has been ready, tense but still ready, even excited. Clad in a silk dressing gown, she submits to his lust. He is passionate, vigorous, forceful, but fast. He suddenly came, shot his load all over her gown, not inside her. This was the screeching anticlimax of a farce. But the farce was not as bad as his sobs, his excuses, and his threat of suicide. A contemporary man who could not perform. How did she contribute to this tragedy? This is a contemporary chapter of sexual frustration.

In the face of this weakness of her long standing man friend, she persuaded him that she was the one to blame. She panicked, the ancient panic she always felt of being touched. The dread of reaching hands and poking fingers could hardly have encouraged him. She told him what she believed. That if he would continue to be her friend, she would give him more than any lover. He would be all the man she would ever want.

She had made a place for herself in the godless male world. But she wanted to know why she could not feel any sexual desire. In psychoanalysis, she uncovered the impenetrable veil. Behind the veil, she recoiled in horror of the wiggling, writhing things that might lurk behind it. There lurked the fingers, the eels, and the tumbling mess of her phallic nightmares. There were the episodes of the milkman, the intrusions of older cousins, the hand of a close relation, and the dreams of sexual threat from which it was simpler to die than to dream. There was always lurking terror of having to speak about what was hidden behind the veil. The solution was to hold herself in reserve.

So you understand that both men and women have their demons called up by sexual activities. In spite of sex being thrown in your face on billboards and on TV, there is no promise that you can have a fulfilling sex life with your favorite partner. This is one of the barriers you must face as you learn this Tantric game.

When you meet up with your best possible woman's demons, loving kindness gentleness, compassion and true friendship are usually the antidotes. Accepting and appreciating your woman in spite of her sexual walls may help to remove the walls. Ask her what will remove the walls. But you must be ready to face the demon of inadequate sexual release.

A full sexual life with your best possible woman requires weeks or years of making the effort to connect on all levels as is being held up in this chapter.

**Are you willing to stick with this learning process
until you have made all the connections?**

Maybe you feel some of the same need to have time to open up your heart. You can learn to play with your companion over several weeks or what ever is required to come together in a meaningful sexual bonding. Yes, you can do it. Ecstatic love! Hours of intimacy and titillation. No more impotence.

It is worth it. Read the Tantric Way books recommended at the end. Take plenty of time to study. You can learn at home with your partner without going to school. Practice with one partner till you can do everything in the books. If your partner will not cooperate, get another partner.

Follow directions in this book!

In a few months of studying and experimenting with the methods of this chapter, you will the master of your many parts, your feelings, your communicating, your pursuing, your seducing, your sexual recreating. How do you plan to direct yourself, a rare treasure, a powerful support?

You are now ready to achieve the true connection of marriage.

Chapter 14
Mental Preparation: the Main Sexual Organ is Your Mind -Brain

The main aphrodisiac is your thinking.
You think yourself into lust and the reflexive sexual drive

The next four chapters guide you into four levels of connection with your best possible woman. The objective is for you to learn to come together with your lover on all levels. But especially come together as one being, perhaps as one consciousness. The total concentration of the couple amplifies thinking, feeling, sensing, and spiritual contact with the infinite. This is when the wonder and deep fulfillment of sexual oneness come from. Make your best effort to explore how close to this ideal you and your woman can come.

We assume that thinking happens in ours brains. Focus your thinking on your sex partner and feelings will arise in you. Feelings like admiration, love, gratitude and lust. These feelings especially, such as lust, give you the willpower to take action. Your sensations, the sight, the touch, the taste, the smell, and the sound of your lover, stimulate feelings. These senses trigger feelings. You might remember the sensations and the feelings you had at the time you met your best possible woman. When you remember the experience, you might remember the feelings. Then the feelings trigger more thoughts. Try it out, you will agree this happens. Your thinking starts the whole sexual process.

You can learn to use your feelings and your body to drive your sexual system. When you learn about your feelings and your sexual system you will be confidence to act on your feelings. Earning the love of your best woman helps you feel love. Teaching your best woman to wait for you with lust in her heart helps you feel lust also. Knowing that she is going to give you pleasure, as she has done in the past, stimulates your sexual desire. Thinking she is capable of giving you satisfaction stimulates you to take action to meet her as soon as possible. This thinking helps you to focus on the immediate sexual adventure. Thinking and knowing increases your sexual arousal.

You can read love stories aloud that encourage both of you to feel romantic. You can gain knowledge through books, TV, recordings, or other means. You can read aloud to your lover. You can look at pornography. You can watch movies about people in love. This is the thinking influence on making love.

Focus on the growth of your love and your sex life by gaining knowledge. When you focus on your rise in love and your sexual expression, the rendezvous is more titillating. The longer you think of loving relations with your best woman, the more electric energy you create when you meet. Practicing being attuned with your best woman will actually build up an attractive charge between you. The charge is released when you touch after being apart. Thinking is part of the charge generator.

Have you heard anyone say, "I get a charge out of you?" Now you know why.

Planning is a thinking process. Planning the sexual liaison removes mistakes and improves performance. Learn how to plan for dallying with your lover by reading this book as well as the books listed below.

Are you convinced that your thinking creates the mood for love?

Try a thought experiment. Think about someone you dislike intensely, or about slaughtered people or sewage. Think about being humiliated, about being insulted to the point of rage. Now are you sexually aroused? No, your mind has turned off your intimate and romantic feelings.

Somehow you learned that you are separate individual person

All people are convinced in their minds that they are separate and alone. This is part of the ego function, "I am an important separate person. My thoughts are mine alone." This leads to feelings of loneliness. As long as you believe you are alone, you will have tendency toward a mechanical or physical approach to other people. You will not be open to their feelings or their mental energy.

However, there are plenty of reasons to believe that we are connected and interdependent. Consider the thought of collective consciousness. Then you will be mindful of other people's mental states or their emotional condition, especially your best woman's condition. You will allow yourself to ask about her reaction to you.

Also, other people tune in on your feelings and mental attitude. Train yourself to perceive how you are interconnected with other people. Then you will be in harmony with your best woman.

When you are mentally connected to your woman, you have an amplified sexual experience.

Now think about being at a sports event, convention or a dance. Remember the energy in the air, the shared excitement? That is the collective consciousness. You may have been swept up in the "crowd vitality." You may become addicted to these group energies. Then you want to go these events to feel the thrill, the group consciousness again.

Another case is the stimulation and sexual arousal you can feel within a group or with a certain person even if you do not care for them. Now compare this feeling with the time you felt unconditional love or you were falling in love or during a sexual event. You may have felt totally open hearted, open to all sensations, to all thoughts, to all possibilities of the infinite Higher Power. You can learn to feel a merging, perhaps a sense of the infinite. You may desire the feeling of collective consciousness of your best woman and you alone.

You may be able to learn a new way of being a part of a group

The notion of separateness from other people and from everything else is an illusion. Granted, it is an illusion shared by everyone. You may be able to feel like you are a part of everything around you and simultaneously feel you are separate.

Most people feel loneliness or a yearning for connection with others because of this shared illusion of separateness. But we are all part of a larger organism called mankind, or GAIA, the whole living Earth.

Now is the time to change this illusion into the reality where you are connected to your woman.

This one change in thinking will solve many of your social problems. You must learn to let people, not just your lover, into your immediate territory. The skill of letting people into your personal space allows you to be closer to your lover. But the skill of keeping everyone out raises a wall between you and your lover. So you will soften up your rugged individual in the course of studying and applying this book. You will gain the skill of letting people into your personal space. Then you will be capable of a higher level of love with your best woman as a Tantric partner.

To prove your interdependence on other people, try this mind experiment

Could you build a house by yourself? Maybe not.

How small an object could you build by yourself?

How many skills do you have that are needed to build a house? Probably a few but not enough.

If you were in a group of a hundred people, all of whom have different skills, could you build a house? Probably not. Because you would need lumber and nails which require factories full of people.

Whatever you do requires other people.

Are you getting the idea of depending on other people?

If you were alone on an island, you would die soon because you do not have the skills to survive.

We depend on each other for everything.

We depend on each other for love and sex.

What if you had all the materials to build a house and people with the skills?

But, what would happen if no one wanted to help you? You could not build the house without the group energy. This is the same requirement for making love. You need a profound collective consciousness to have a satisfying copulation. You need other people in a harmonious group.

Is a goal you want to achieve?

What do you want from a sexual adventure?

This question came up before. What you sincerely and forcefully want usually comes into your life. The dominating thoughts of you mind have a tendency to change into physical reality. You experience more sexual contact by thinking about it. Experience is a conscious process in the brain. Without the brain, there is no pleasure, no movement, and there are no exquisite memories. Your sexual experience will become memorable after you have thought about it for days beforehand. Planning it out in detail and pondering your hours of sustained orgasm puts you in a state of anticipation. Then you are sexually excited before you see your lover. Explore it. You'll feel the buildup. When you meet your lover you will send electric sparks to her.

To get the best results, think how to improve your sexual experience. Then experience the sexual game again with the improvements. One way to immediately intensify your sexual play is to get your body in tip-top healthy form. Read on to learn how and why.

For now, look up these books at the end of this book. They'll help you to raise your mental picture of your sexual life.

Great Sex after 40: Strategies For Lifelong Fulfillment

Toxic Relationships and How to Change Them: Health and Holiness in Everyday Life

The Anger Trap: Free Yourself from The Frustrations that Sabotage Your Life

The Power of Commitment: A Guide to Active, Lifelong Love

Making Contact

Love Is Letting Go Of Fear

Aesthetic Vedanta: The Sacred Path of Passionate Love

Chapter 15
Physical Preparation for Extreme Connection with Your Most Appropriate Woman

Prepare for success the same way you'd prepare for any major life adventure. If sexual contact were your career, would you jump right in without reading, studying, practicing? Never! Would you jump off a cliff without looking ahead? Never! How would you prepare to safely survive the jump? You eat right, plan the details of the jump, practice various ways, wait for the right weather, strap on a parachute, then go.

To gain the full potential of your sexual life, look at it as a major life adventure. Construct your ideas about sex so it's part of a larger life pattern of achievement. In the last chapter, you experimented with conditioning your mental state to achieve better sexual goals. This chapter will give you ideas about developing your body so it can sustain the vigorous efforts required by a sexual event. In another chapter below, you will make sex part of your spiritual life.

Sexual combination with the woman you have chosen to be your wife and the mother of your children requires preparation of your emotional maturity, preparation of your physical body, and other preparations noted in the following chapters.

Thinking is the basis of sexual bliss. How you use your mind to prepare your body is crucial to achieving sexual bliss. Make the following lessons part of your physical preparation.

Physical approach one: Your body needs the basic preparations

Your body needs the right food, the right sleep, and the right training. Make your body alive enough to sustain vigorous aerobic exercise for many hours. Get fit by using the equipment at a gym or in vigorous sports. The study of nutrition is a whole profession. It cannot be addressed in this short book. There are 1000 books published on this. The shortest clue it that you need protein. fat, carbohydrates, water, vitamins and minerals to continue to live. You need eight hours of sleep every night. Your body is more efficient if it sleeps the same hours each night.

Physical approach two: Sexual experience is so demanding that you must provide all your physical body and other basics if it is to rise to its possible payoff

Your potential for loving is enormous; maybe close to infinite. The word "potential" means all that is possible for you to release when you create the right conditions for sexual expression. You will release mental, emotional, physical, and spiritual energies. This is the opposite of animal breeding, the quick lay, or "wham, bam, thank you, ma'am." This method is taught in Tantric books. It is difficult to find a teacher of the Tantric Way.

Physical approach three: Your body must be built so it can withstand 1 to 5 hours of aerobic exertion.

Full sexual expression is aerobic in addition to demanding other resources from you. If you have a fit body, you can enjoy the whole dynamic, the movement of most of your body. I am guessing that the longest you have made love is 15 minutes to an hour. As you become a master of love on all possible levels, you'll be in a passionate embrace for 3 hours, even 15 hours. Is that worth making an effort for?

Making physical love is more than pumping, grinding, kissing, and changing positions. As you train for the Tantric Way, you'll gain control of the small muscles in you abdomen, legs, and genitals. You will feel the expansion of muscles you don't even realize you have.

How do you gain control of all your muscles? You practice movements while you consciously control certain parts of your body just like lifting weights. The more you practice, the better you get. Start with a course in hatha yoga. Search for a teacher. As you get better, get a better teacher. Yoga will improve your flexibility and sensitivity to moving each muscle when you want to move. You need to practice sensing each part of your body. When you experience an orgasm, your experience is only as excellent as your ability to sense all parts of your body. This means that you focus on consciously flexing a muscle or moving a body part.

Many muscles and internal organs respond during orgasm. You can use books and videos to learn the hundreds of muscles. Search for them. Some are listed at the end of this book.

During sexual intercourse, you are energizing many muscles for hours. Have you ever felt the frustration of running out of steam in the midst of passion? Perhaps, you felt cheated or embarrassed or some other emotion. You never want to have that happen again. The antidote is to be in top aerobic condition. Then you can actually do what you imagine. All those imaginative moves and experiments are possible if you can last long enough at the energy level you desire.

Aerobic exercise means you're consuming more oxygen than usual. Walking up stairs could be aerobic. The more vigorous exercises require rapid breathing. Perform several types of aerobic exercise so that all your muscles are prepared to last for hours of effort. You must flex and them stretch each muscle. The minimum suggested amount of aerobic activity is 30 minutes of walking each day. You need aerobic exercise, which is similar to the movements of love-making.

The Tantric Way does not require heroic physical action. It requires more subtle action over many hours. For example, the man may sit up while the woman is perched on his lap during copulation. Many positions demand flexibility, strength, and vigorous movement. This could go on for several hours. During those hours, your passion and your emotional excitement will be rising. Just the strain of sitting with small movements will cause fast breathing. The excitement and mental energy will also cause aerobic breathing. You cannot reach the greatest heights of pleasure unless you are in shape.

You need to exert muscular effort. You need strength training such as weight lifting or using the exercise machines like the Nautilus. These are common training methods. You can do much of this at home or at a gym. Increase the strength especially in your, arms, legs, and abdomen. You'll need them all to get into the positions and to hold your sexual partner.

You will get in shape over a duration of time. You can be completely overweight and lack muscle tone right now but you will improve after a while. Start hatha yoga, aerobic exercise, and muscle strength training right away. You will continue to improve your physical shape. As you improve, your sexual experience rises beyond your present concept of what is possible.

Your mental training energizes your physical performance. Your physical training enhances you feelings. There are physical sensations that you can-not begin to experience today if your body is not prepared. When you properly strengthen your body and begin to luxuriate in these new sensations, your feelings of pleasure and thrills will take on a new dimension.

Physical approach four: Plan how to express your love through massage or other physical touching

Your physical reflexes toward your best woman and the range of positive feelings you express during lovemaking increase your satisfaction and your woman's satisfaction. When you are making love, you will use your feelings, your mental abilities, your physical training, and your spiritual aptitude.

This is possible if you make the effort. You can succeed at it if you want. You have the time, the energy, the ambition, and it's the worthiest of goals. Just make the choice to succeed.

In the next chapter, you will learn where to get all this sexual energy. Love can be expressed in a surprising number of ways. You will study the seven levels of love.

Chapter 16
Emotional Preparation Is the Source of Vitality for Sexual Games and for a Long Term Marriage

Prepare your feelings for the full connection
with your best possible woman

You will build up your connection in stages: like flirting, dating, sexual behavior and marriage. These stages are driven by instinctual feelings to make babies. You may be convinced that these stages, and especially sexual enjoyment, are to enjoy pleasure and feel good. But sexual action is attractive for many reasons that you may not have considered. You desire sexual contact for your own reasons. You've gotten yourself a copy of this book to learn about how to have a deep and meaningful relation with your best possible woman. A total relation with your woman can consist of many parts. These parts correspond to the level of love. When you are cultivating your total relationship, sexual yearning becomes interconnected with love.

The seven levels of love

This information was in Chapter 9. Next is a little more information. If you love your sexual partner, you'll connect emotionally as well as mentally and physically. Prepare yourself to rise in love consciously. This is in contrast to "falling in love" by accident. There are at least seven levels of love, but there may be even more. You may ponder how you can experience love.

First level of love: Attraction

The power of love attracts women toward you. Women find you charming, fascinating, captivating, and enchanting. The positive attracts the negative. The yin (female) has allure for the yang (male). The man who feels authentic is attractive. The natural man is charming. Opposites attract. The profane is fascinated by the sacred. The forbidden man draws the pure woman. Learn to be attractive. It's an art.

Second level of love: Infatuation

When attraction is intense, the door of perception opens to the magical vision of life. The object of infatuation, your woman, becomes saintly; appears to have no imperfections. You, the infatuated subject, worship the saint. Through the magic of infatuation, the whole world becomes new and extraordinary. Limitation is erased by a timeless kiss. A thousand kilometers distance to the beloved woman does not seem far in the unbounded connection of infatuation. You can only perceive that everything about her is right; nothing is wrong. Everything is connected to everything. A new spiritual awareness is born in you.

Third level of love: Communion

Communion is the sharing of spirit, a spiritual connection of souls. A rapport and communion are the end of loneliness. You are the lover who becomes the beloved. To experience communion, the lovers must drop their defenses. They must abandon their illusion of separateness. The boundaries between one person and other living beings must dissolve.

Are you convinced that you are an individual? Probably If you have an investment in the notion of individuality then communion can be threatening.

Many different barriers deny communion depending on a lover's attachment to being different. To pass the barriers, communion is assisted through ceremonies such as Christian communion or Buddhist tea ceremony or marriage. After the ceremony, lovers express deeper communication.

Fourth level of love: Intimacy

Intimacy is a close association, familiarity, or contact of a private nature. Intimacy merges body with body and spirit with spirit. Sexual energies are connected. Sexual orgasm becomes a communal act. The human energy fields blend together. The psychic part of the spirit comes alive with sensations. Awareness of each other's vitality is awakened. Intuitive understanding is manifested.

Yes, you realize suddenly that you have intuition. The realization that sexual energy is the creator of all living things comes over the lovers. The lovers perceive that sexual energy is inherent in passion, inspiration, mental alertness, excitement, and long life. Intimacy is the gate to interconnection with all living things. Intimate lovers are on the way to freedom from insecurity, from loneliness, from need, and from conflict.

In the state of intimacy, lovers can clearly know that sexual play is sacred and divine.

Fifth level of love: Surrender and non-attachment

The act of giving yourself up to another person is also the act of releasing obstructions created in your mind.

Before the profound experience of surrender changing into non-attachment, the lovers have thoughts of I, me and mine, called the root of suffering. The lovers realize that their essence is the source of reality, the spirit at their core of mind. The essence is recognized as a witness of the thought processes. By dissociating the essence from the root, from the thoughts of I, me, and mine, the lovers rise to a higher plane of existence. Lovers usually feel that they have attained a higher heaven in the first four levels too.

The dissociation of the essence is the entry into the non-attached existence, where love has no bounds. Then the lovers can love all living things. All fears are diminished. Fear of loss is diminished. There is less fear of abandonment. The fear of poverty is dissolved. There is no fear of rejection. Fear of breaking the rules is gone, and so on.

This is the opposite of attachment. Attachment is sometimes mistaken for love. Attachment is based on fear of loss or abandonment. It is based on insecurity, and the delusional belief an unchanging world. Attachment results in acts to control. Non-attachment is based on allowing changes to occur without fear.

Through non-attachment, sexual behavior and saintly intention are joined. They're joined because defenses are dropped and many delusions are removed.

Sixth level of love: Passion

A strong emotion, passion is a focused mental state. It occurs most often in the absence of a logical state of mind. The object of a strong affection or enthusiasm is also called a passion. In this book, the passion for the man is the woman and the passion for that woman is that man. Each lover senses a higher reality. The reality is the experience of the merging of yin (feminine energy) and yang (masculine energy). The reality is the merging life and love. In the higher reality, events unfold as passion creates them. This is different from events unfolding due to the control of the lovers. Passion seems to be the work of a divine higher power. Hindus consider it to be the energy of creation. The source of masculine creation interacting with the source of feminine creation. This is the merging of opposites. Merging of opposites is a central ideal in Tantric sexual union. Loss and gain are merged. Creation and destruction merge.

The play of the divine source of reality consists of creation, protection, destruction, concealment, and revelation. When you're awakened to the merging of your mind, your feelings, and the divine source of reality in the state of passion, you perceive these five facets of the play.

When you are awakened to this merging and you are also merging in these six levels of love in the physical and mental, and emotional and sexual Tantric union, you realize a kind of enlightenment.

Even though this state sounds beyond your reach, you can do it.

Seventh level of love: Ecstasy

Ecstasy is intoxication of extreme emotional excitement, the thrill of rapture, is a kind of spiritual enlightenment. The lovers are awakened to their true original nature. Christians call this Divine Grace. Buddhists call this Buddha Nature. Ecstasy is ineluctable: here are no words to describe this experience. You must live this for your self. This experience is ineffable. It cannot be transmitted from one person to another. Perhaps ecstasy is the merging of the lovers with the collective consciousness, the source of underlying reality. Hindus say, "Thou art that."

Maybe ecstasy is when there is a mixture of human experience of mind, emotion, physical copulation, and spiritual awakening, mixed with the unknown non-conscious. This paradise is then mixed again with the unknowable spirit often called Brahma, Buddha Nature, or GOD. It's not possible to describe. When you experience it, you'll recognize it.

How high do you want to rise in love?

What level of love can you achieve? Write down the levels of love you want with your woman. Once you've identified your desired levels of love, the next step is to find that perfect partner. This book is showing you how.

But first, look up these book descriptions at the end of this book. They'll help you to raise your spiritual dream of your love life.

Better than Chocolate: 50 Proven Ways to Feel Happier

Boundary Issues: Using Boundary Intelligence to Get the Intimacy You Want and the Independence You Need in Life, Love and Work

Chapter 17
Spiritual Preparation for Extreme Sexual Fulfillment and for Married Bliss

Read *The Marriage of Sex and Spirit.*

This chapter could be called Eleven Weeks to Sexual Thrills beyond the Earthly plane.

There is also a spiritual part of sexual congress. Part of your preparation for the ultimate union between yin and yang is spiritual development. You are capable of joining your lover in a state called collective consciousness. To raise your sexual experience to a higher plane, perform the following suggested course.

The main benefits you will gain are as follows. Correct preparation to meet your lover. Understanding the many concepts of love. Experiencing love. Removing the barriers to love. Learning to love another person.

Unskilled people make love for about 15 minutes. Some skilled people make love for 15 hours. Is that kind of pleasure worth the effort of learning?

Please consider what you can gain from this spiritual preparation. You have thought about the fundamental human need for love and connection. You are capable of feeling deep love for other people or for one other person. You can experience profound love and other feelings that you didn't know were possible. You can develop a deep connection with your best woman. You can develop a connection with your best woman that is satisfying and constantly improving. You can rise in love by learning the many faceted sexual, emotional, mental, and physical connections.

A diamond is a many faceted crystal where all the atoms are connected to all other atoms. Diamond is the hardest substance. It lasts forever. You and our lover can be that diamond. But as always, the decision is up to you.

Please try a mental experiment. Remember when you were at a group event like a football game, concert, or conference. Remember your increased wakefulness or perceptions or intensity at the event. Not everyone had this increased intensity. But if you did, then you experienced the vibrations of the group energy. Later you noticed less energy and mood. Consider that you can join with your best woman in this vibrant oneness.

To join your lover in this high state, it is your responsibility to throw yourself into the following course. You must release fixed thinking about the limits of love and sex.

Once you have opened up the possibility of harmony, you will feel an energetic presence. Even if you think you grasp the intellectual meaning of the concepts, you will sense an entirely new level of meaning during the course.

Caution: the high energy you may feel may be pleasure but it can also be pain

Buried memories of pleasant or painful past events may come to your mind. Forgotten and repressed feelings may come up from the subconscious. They may cause physical symptoms or disordered thinking. The opposite may happen. Symptoms and troubled thinking may disappear.

A group will often generate a mental field which may affect each person's emotions or may cause changes in perception of space and time. New ways to conceiving ordinary events may occur.

Try another mental experiment. Remember a time when you were extremely tired and worn out. Remember the poor attitude you had. Perhaps you spoke harshly to someone who you normally love. Perhaps you had an accident like walking into something because you did not see it. Now remember a time when you were well rested and under no stress. You know you would not speak harshly or drop something. You can conclude that your different levels of attitude or consciousness or energy lead you to different perceptions.

Try another mental experiment. First, think of yourself, your sad feelings, and your immediate craving for things. Second, convince yourself that you are 30 years older, your feelings are joyful, and that all your needs are met. Consider that everyone you meet loves and respects you. Do you grasp at the first thought of yourself? Are you able to shed your first thought and believe the second, 30 years later?

Try another mental experiment. Imagine a pool. Into the pool, unknown things are being thrown. The surface is wavy. You cannot see the bottom. This is like your mind when it is confused and stressed. Now imagine the pool after it calms down. You can see the bottom. The things being thrown into it were gold coins. This is like your mind when you have learned to meditate in the course below.

If you take the course with a group, one or more people in the group may be healed of mental or emotional discomfort.

Deep understanding or accelerated learning may take place. In this course, you may change your notions of what you are. If you can allow this, go ahead. If you are afraid of what you may find, go to the next chapter. If you know you have repressed memories that are painful and you are afraid of them, do not take the course.

If you take the course, you may quit at any time. If you take the course, you may find treasures beyond the earthly plane. Love for another person allows them to enter your feelings. You could imagine that your lover enters your heart. Your lover enters into your root.

This is the opposite of being a rugged individual, separate from your parents. Part of the American culture is to separate from your parents and be a rugged individual. This removes the support of your family. It often leads to loneliness and alienation. You want love but you do not allow yourself to receive love from your parents. You want another person to enter your heart and share your root. So, you may feel this internal conflict.

Suppose you are a rugged individual. You make an effort to keep people out of your root. You are proud of being independent. You may be egoistical. You may only have goals that serve you alone. Simultaneously, you want to let one person, your best possible woman, inside your defenses. And you want to screen almost everyone else out. It may be easier for you to let many people into your root. They you will have the comfort of the collection of people. This is a contradiction. You must let many people into your root, your ego. You cannot let just one person in.

You will decide how to cope with this need to be separate and also to have one woman as a part of your sense of self. Or you will decide to let many people into your sense of self. No one else can decide this for you.

Do you have the aptitude to allow yourself to be a part of a large group or even a part of all human kind?

The notion of separateness from other people is an illusion. Granted, it is an illusion shared by everyone. And most people feel loneliness or a yearning for connection with others because of this illusion. Maybe a person feels lonely for a different reason. In any case, each person decides how to perceive his world.

We are all part of a larger organism called mankind. We are all part of the organism called Gaia, the Earth and all living beings. Now is the time to change this illusion into the reality where you are connected to all people. This one change in thinking will solve many of your social problems.

You must learn to let people into your world, not just your lover. The skill of letting people in allows you to be closer to your lover. But the skill of keeping everyone out raises a wall between you and your lover. So you will soften up the rugged individual in the following course. You will gain the skill of letting people into your personal space. You will let people into your ego space, your root space. Then you will be capable of a higher level of love with your Tantric partner, your best possible woman.

This opportunity may not agree with you. This unique experience may frighten you due to your own past experiences. Your discomfort is normal. Discomfort, butterflies, or other negative feelings don't mean that you can't have the experience of falling in love or rising in love You may receive the treasure of love even if you're afraid today. You may panic when you get too close to someone. You may feel alienated from other people when you think of being rejected. You may prefer to be left alone.

You may learn to lead yourself out of panic or alienation. If you decide that this is not for you, you may quit. You're in control of this process and of your whole life. If you decide to continue, you'll give yourself a course on rising in love with your spiritual nature.

Requirements of the environment of this as a group course

The objective of this course is to guide each person into communion with a Higher Power. The next objective is that each person can bring this communion into Tantric love with his best possible woman.

If you want to find a guide for a group in the following course, there are requirements.

1. A multi-dimensionally awakened individual who can initially provide the presence, wisdom, an experience to move the interaction safely into new dimensions.
2. The individual is able to set his or her intention for the process. Activities that do not add to the intention must be removed.
3. The setting or environment must be appropriate: a special inspiring location, secure and harmonious.
4. Deep and mature commitment on the part of each participant to enter an open-ended exploration of Beingness. Each must be willing to release some old patterns and transform into new thinking and feeling.
5. The intention is an infusion of a basic sense of well-being and a new sense of love. Painful aspects of reality must be eventually embraced by love.
6. Each person must receive some direct experience of a Higher Power, an expanded consciousness.
7. Grace and luck.

Although the course is long and difficult, it's less painful than what you were doing. It is easier than all the relationship problems, loneliness and emptiness.

There are 3 types of people practicing this spiritual exercise:

1. People who want to stop now. Those will leave this course.
2. People who are skeptical and want to ask lots of questions before making up their minds to invest the time and effort in this course. Those people should read this entire book and some of

the other recommended books. Convince yourselves that you are ready to rise to a higher level of love and sexual expression.

3. People who are eager to rise in love and rise in spirit right away.

Which kind of person are you?

The following is a guide to a course in love leading to a higher state of Being leading. This is the ultimate connection with your best possible woman

A committed couple or a group of couples may study and apply themselves to this course.

Week one: Preparing to rise in love

Before meeting your lover in a private space, purify yourself. Remove stress. Feel love. Relax your mental defenses so you are open minded to learn. Increase your vitality level. Do not eat heavy food like meat or fatty foods for at least 3 hours before study. Eat vegetable snacks. These will calm down your food preoccupations. Do not eat to stuff yourself.

Remove mental habits that prevent your connecting to people. Remove habits that result in isolating you, in your feeling lonely, in your feeling separated from other people. Remove habitual of feelings of being the rugged individual. Open your mind to the Diamond Connection, the experience of opening up to all other people.

Do this for at least a week or until you think you have made these principles into permanent changes.

Week two: learning overall concepts of love

Think about the following questions. Write your answers in your journal.

What does connecting with another person or thing mean?

What is the feeling of love: what is it? Is it possible to put it in words?

What does thinking of love mean?

What are your actions that demonstrate love?

How do you speak of love?

What do you say to convince your woman that you love her? Discuss these questions with your woman.

Week three: experiencing the state of being in love

Focus on the feelings and reality of love. Can you describe it in words? Are you convinced you are in the same couple with your best possible woman? Do you want to improve your membership in the couple? You could call it a higher form of organism or a higher level of mind.

Week four: removing barriers that exist between you and your best possible woman

You will have a heavenly experience with this woman. There is a high probability that you'll feel harmony, respect, tranquility, and admiration, and other desirable qualities toward this woman. You have the exquisite privilege of being in an exclusive couple. Few are qualified to experience rising in love like you will.

Removing barriers between you and your best woman

More about the Root. The Root is similar to the invention of ego, or a component of ego. However, the psychiatric profession has defined ego as a part of your mind that does certain things and is in conflict with other parts of your mind. To avoid confusion with the psychiatric definition of ego, we will limit the concept to the following and add to the definition in Third week above.

The Root as used in this book means:

1.) The thought of Me, Myself, and I.
2.) The thought, "It belongs to me." Example, my arm belongs to me.
3.) "I belong to it." Example, I belong to my country.
4.) "I am real and important." Example, I am better than anyone.
5.) "It is part of me." Example, I am a person who is polite.

This book could guide you to a higher level of mind. If you study it and make the effort to learn, to modify your thoughts, your speech, and your actions of your body, the result will be a change of your view toward your woman. You will change your point of view toward most people you meet. This new point of view is called "Sukhavati." This is a Sanskrit word which describes a kind of paradise which is enjoyed by those who live in the highest level of mind. If you finish this course (or "graduate," if you prefer) you will be connected with your best possible woman like the atoms of a diamond.

You'll be able to rise in love. You'll be able to rise in love when you want to; perhaps all the time. You'll have a deeper understanding of what love is. You'll be capable of feeling love that you've not yet experienced. You'll have resources of love that you are not aware of today. You will become powerfully interconnected like the atoms of a diamond. The process is called Sukhavati Diamond.

Discuss this question with you lover. Do you feel insufficient love for yourself?

The quality of loving oneself is the limiting factor in loving another person. Feel the illusion of separateness as a limiting factor in loving another person.

Feel your life stress. Stress is many things. One stress is worrying about external factors over which you have no control, like the weather. Stress may be a limiting factor on loving another person

What are the most likely barriers to love that you've built? Think about barriers between you and strangers.

Exercise: Be still and quiet with your mate for 15 minutes. Then look within and feel the barriers between you and your mate.

You could feel love when you prepared to join with your woman. Now release the defensive parts of your personality. You can feel love when you prepare to join energies of feeling, thinking, spirit, and bodies.

You could rise to a higher level of mind when you mentally and emotionally

reduce the barriers to love,
reduce the barriers to joining with your woman,
then feeling connected (not feeling separately), and
thinking as a connected person (not thinking separately).

Therefore, when you're about to meet your lover, prepare yourself to be this rare loving person by forming the habits of the first five weeks.

Week five: allowing yourself to concentrate on your best possible woman

A definition of concentration: holding the mind on a center of spiritual vitality in the body or fixing it on some divine form within the body or outside it.

Your best possible woman is a kind of divine being. The fullness of your appreciation of her may be starting, or it may be blooming.

You can learn to concentrate on your feelings.

After you have learned about feelings, you can concentrate on your woman's feelings.

You can learn to concentrate on the many elements of your own spiritual foundation.

You two lovers concentrate on each other. Greet each other. Shake hands. Note your feelings toward each other. Is there a lack of connection? You'll observe changes in feeling and connecting.

Practice this exercise often. You and your woman sit facing each other.

Week six: learning to meditate in a specific way

A definition of meditation: an unbroken flow of thoughts toward the object of concentration.

Meditation allows you a different view of reality. It reduces the illusion of separateness. It allows feelings of connection with other people. When you feel intimately joined with a group, including your woman, this called the feeling of Sangha, congregation, fraternity, sorority, brotherhood, or sisterhood.

Meditation is a non-denominational practice, not dependent on a particular religion. You refine this process each week.

You can learn to meditate on your feelings.

You can learn to meditate on your woman's feelings.

You can learn to meditate on your spiritual foundation.

After you have learned about your spiritual foundation, you can better comprehend your woman's spiritual foundation.

After you have been able to apply concentration and meditation as stated, you will have questions such as:

How does concentration, meditation yield extreme sexual fulfillment?

Nothing happens during concentration and meditation except that you notice your troubled mind. What good is that?

You will discover the answers as you practice concentration and meditation.

You can begin to rise in love starting now

Whatever you think about all the time, will tend to become part of your physical world. Experiment with the following affirmations. Sit upright in a comfortable position. Let your body relax. As much as possible, let your mind relax. Stop pondering issues, plans and preoccupations.

You begin by learning to love yourself more. You can only love another person as much as you can love yourself. Repeat the following affirmations many times silently.

May I be filled with loving- kindness.

May I be well.

May I be peaceful and at ease.

May I be contented.

The first jhana

Experiment with this meditation every day for a week. You refine this process each week.

First level jhana is seclusion, in a quiet place, body erect (neither lazy nor lying down) and, free from temptation. Concentrate on your heart. Examine your thinking.

Possible results from the first jhana

You reduce the stress of the external world. You relax defenses. Meditation tends to reduce barriers between you and your woman. It reduces mental defenses, and external preoccupations.

Week seven: Learning to meditate the second way

Start with the first jhana from the previous week. It may take weeks or months to feel comfortable with the level two jhana.

Imagine that you are a lovable child. Imagine that you are feeling the effects of love by other people toward you.

If you are ready, expand your own feelings of loving-kindness to include your woman. Think about a love experience in the past and recall an experience that was satisfying. Feel rapture and pleasure borne of seclusion and non attachment.

Repeat these affirmations silently to yourself,

"May she be filled with loving-kindness.
May she be well.
May she be peaceful and at ease.
May she be happy."

You will be ready to extend your meditation to a higher level.

Relate to your best woman in several ways simultaneously

Practice eye contact: lovers, sit in a way that you can remain for 20 minutes at a time without discomfort. Sit facing each other and deeply look into each other's eyes. The left eye of one partner looks into right eye of the other, and the right eye peers into the left eye of the other. Focus far away and you'll perceive that your lover's eyes become one eye. Hold this gaze. While holding the gaze, examine your feelings. Name your feelings silently or aloud. Let yourself relax, or tense up, or whatever happens naturally. Examine your body. Name the sensations you receive silently or aloud: heat, cold, pressure, sound, smell, noise.

Prepare for second level jhana

Method of preparing to meditate. After you have done the first jhana, you and your woman sit facing each other. Greet your lover and shake hands. Note your feeling toward your lover. Note any lack of connection. After a few minutes, practice loving-kindness. This will reflect on the pleasures of lovemaking. When you cultivate loving-kindness, your life will seem easier.

Make the effort to do the first and second jhana every day upon awakening and before sleeping. Do this meditation 10 minutes each time. The following second jhana exercise is really difficult. Try it out. Do not feel bad if you cannot do it. Persist and you will be rewarded.

Exercise in consciousness

Think about your left foot. Your focus of attention goes there. This is the consciousness communicating the sensations of your heel to your brain and mind.

Move your focus slowly from the heel to your nose.

Move your focus of consciousness to your heart area.

Without thinking, feel openness between your heart and the heart of your lover.

Move your focus to your eyes. Move your focus behind you eyes.

Now you may feel your consciousness in the center of your skull behind your eyes.

You are thinking differently now. Maybe you are not thinking at all.

This is the opposite of mental defense.

Second level jhana

Remove from your thinking all thoughts of the past present, and future. Remove the memories of today, feelings of today, bodily sensing today, do not pay attention to your senses right now. You think, "With the falling away of all thinking and investigating thoughts from my mind, I enter and abide in the second jhana."

Think about the part of your head five centimeters behind your eyes. Your focus of attention will move there. You will notice that you do not think the same. You may think, "I feel pleasure and rapture borne of concentration on the "golden flower" behind my eyes.

Feel rapture and pleasure borne of concentration on the vitality behind your eyes. You will enter pure Being. This is the second jhana.

The intensity of this experience, Being with your spirit, may be difficult. However, this is the opportunity to find the benefits of the second jhana. After you do everything suggested in this course, you'll agree it's worth the effort. Please continue next week.

More affirmations using auto suggestion

The dominating thoughts of your mind have a tendency to change into physical reality. That is the reason for affirmations. In addition to thinking correctly, you can suggest your achievement or your future experience. The method is called, "auto-suggestion." You consciously put ideas into your mind. You mind uses these ideas as true information about the world today and about the future.

This means you affirm what is wonderful, or whatever you want, in your life. Then everything will have a tendency to be wonderful or whatever else you want. This is a tendency not an absolute cause and effect. Affirmations are used to suggest positive results to your own mind.

With your woman, discuss the level meditation results. It may have felt blissful. It may have raised irritation, anger or awkwardness.

Week eight: Adding the third jhana

Experiment with feeling gratitude, not thinking about gratitude.

This is very hard to do because you are always thinking about things. You may have a mental argument or conflict. Almost everyone has two or more streams of thought that do not agree with each other.

Method of preparing to meditate. After you have done the first jhana, you and your woman sit facing each other. Greet your lover and shake hands. Note your feeling toward your lover. Note any lack of connection. After a few minutes, practice loving-kindness. This will reflect on the pleasures of lovemaking. When you cultivate loving-kindness, your life will seem easier. Try to feel compassion. This is similar to sympathy.

After you have been in level one jhana for a few minutes, notice whatever your senses are sending you. Watch for the problems that you are having in your mind. Do not try to solve the problem. Just watch your mind going on. As you watch the struggle, remember to relax. Watch your breath.

Then do the second jhana. Remember, level two jhana is after the falling away of thinking and investigating. It is listening, not thinking.

The third jhana

After you have been in the second jhana, you come out of it. You think, "Rapture has fallen away. I enter and abide in the third jhana."

Establish the third jhana, thinking, "With the falling away of rapture, I enter and abide in the third jhana, a pleasant abiding with equanimity and mindfulness."

Think about the part of your head five centimeters behind your eyes. Your focus of attention will move there. You will notice that you do not think the same. You may think, "I feel pleasure and rapture borne of concentration on the "golden flower" behind my eyes.

After you have come out of the third jhana a while, expand your loving-kindness beyond yourself and your lover to include friends and neighbors.

Practice the three jhanas every day upon awakening and before sleep.

Other concepts of love

As you rise to higher levels of mind, you are capable of understanding higher levels of love. Consider loving non-human animals and beautiful objects. Besides loving people, you can love sounds, sights, smells, taste, touch, pets, magnificent art, music,. inanimate things, vacation places, sports, and so on.

Watch yourself to note when you feel loving-kindness. Watch to find times to feel compassion.

Another kind of love is sympathetic joy. When you observe someone feeling joy, raise joy I yourself also in sympathy to their joy. What ever they are joyful about; you also feel joyful about.

Remove barriers to love

You can reduce Root through meditation, through mindfulness of ego, or watching mental defenses. You cause increasing love for yourself. You remove the limiting factor on loving.

Think of how to open your heart and allow another person into your ego space; into your Root.

Making it easy to love more people. Experiment with feeling the presence of your woman, as well as her energy.

Exercise: Openly observe her look, her facial expression, and her body language.

Week nine: the fourth jhana

Begin with the first jhana. After you have done the first jhana, you and your woman sit facing each other. Greet your lover and feel her vitality without touching. Note your feeling toward your lover. After a few minutes, practice loving-kindness. When you cultivate loving-kindness, your life will seem easier.

Then do the second jhana. Remember, level two jhana is after the falling away of thinking and investigating. It is listening, not thinking.

You think, "The thinking and investigating are falling away. Excluding memories of today, feelings of today, bodily sensing today, I enter and abide in the second jhana. I feel pleasure and rapture borne of concentration on the "golden flower" behind my eyes.

Then come out of the second jhana into the thinking mind. Establish the third jhana, "With the falling away of rapture, I enter and abide in the third jhana, a pleasant abiding with equanimity and mindfulness."

The fourth jhana

After you have been in the third jhana for 10 minutes, come out to the thinking mind. You think, "With the falling away of pleasure and pain, sadness and gladness, I enter and abide in the fourth jhana."

When you come out of the fourth jhana, consider more concepts of love.

Is jealousy love? Is attachment love? Is sexual bliss love? Is possession of another person love? What about demanding respect? Is admiration love? Are taking advantage of my woman and cheating love? When you take another person for granted, is that love? Is contentment with your lover love? Or is it boredom? Is dominating your best possible woman love?

A benefit of the four jhanas

All people have tendencies to get caught up in events of the moment. Some people would just call these situations, "Life."

The process of the jhanas will train you in the art of examining yourself. The you will take a more discriminating examination of your own ignorance, craving, clinging, sloth, doubting your ability to love, jealousy, pride, worry, and the wasted busy-ness of hurry.

More Concepts of love

Loving God or Allah, what is it? The word describing this is, 'agape.'

What is loving one person as family or loving many people as family. The term describing this is 'philos.'

Loving sexual contact is a kind of love. This kind of love is called 'eros.'

Tenth week: absorption

After you have done the first jhana, you and your woman sit facing each other. Greet your lover and feel her vitality without touching. Note your feeling toward your lover. After a few minutes, practice loving-kindness. When you cultivate loving-kindness, your life will seem easier.

Demand yourself to feel compassion for our woman. You may not be able to demand this. Maybe you can allow yourself to feel compassion.

Then do the second jhana. Remember, level two jhana is after the falling away of thinking and pondering. It is listening, not thinking. You think, "The thinking and investigating are falling away. Excluding memories of today, feelings of today, bodily sensing today, I enter and abide in the second jhana. I feel pleasure and rapture borne of concentration on the "golden flower" behind my eyes.

Then come out of the second jhana into the thinking mind. Establish the third jhana, "With the falling away of rapture, I enter and abide in the third jhana, a pleasant abiding with equanimity and mindfulness."

After you have been in the third jhana for 10 minutes, come out to the thinking mind. Think, "With the falling away of pleasure and pain, sadness and gladness, I enter and abide in the fourth jhana."

When you come away from the jhanas, you are ready for absorption.

Absorption

You have been concentrating and meditating for weeks. Some of the time or maybe all the time you are in meditation, you are having an insight into the true nature of many things in your life. Meditation tends to lead to the power of absorption.

Other occupations that lead to absorption are mathematics or writing a novel or scientific observation. In science, the observation is first a concentration of the mind. Then it becomes a meditation without thinking or investigating. Finally, the scientist is absorbed in the observation and the immediate phenomenon. This process, concentration, meditation, absorption, is the common way to gain knowledge about the environment or even about what is happening inside one's own body. Mastery of these mental and spiritual abilities leads to knowledge.

It is the way to deeply understand your best possible woman.

Increasing the power of concentration, meditation, and absorption

The senses communicate with the brain and the mind with a process called, 'consciousness.'

Experiment more with consciousness as in the previous section.

1. Feel your largest toe on you right foot. Do this by thinking of the toe.
2. Then feel your left hand thumb by thinking of the thumb. Then pay total attention to your thumb. Your eye consciousness sends a picture of your thumb to your brain and mind.
3. Focus on your left shoulder. Push you right hand against your left shoulder. Your consciousness intensifies the touching

sensation at your left shoulder. The skin on you left shoulder and your right hand communicates about the touch to your brain and mind. When you focus on a part of your body the sensations are amplified.

4. Then feel inside your skull behind your eyes by thinking of this location.

You've just proven that you can move your consciousness. You can choose what sense data to amplify in the focus of your brain and mind. When you move your consciousness, it forms a direct link between your sense organ, like your eye, and you perceptive brain and mind.

Constructive use of your emotions, your feelings

You can feel at least 100 different emotions. Some of the feelings are pleasant friends: joy, well-being, equanimity, love, kindness. Others are painful demons: jealousy, fear, anxiety, depression, on and on. Can you put a name on a few? Look in the Appendix C at the end of this book to see a list of feeling words.

Perhaps you are like most people; you do not notice your feelings. When you are mindful of your feelings, you can recognize them. Wouldn't you like to choose your feelings?

The demons tend to drain your life vitality and to tie up your mental time with useless thoughts. Often your feelings inform you of a danger or a reward.

In meditation, many demons and pleasures arise. They are mental creations. They do not weigh anything, nor can you touch them. When you can name your demons and your pleasures, you can discuss them with other people. You can ponder them. You can use them in your speech.

When you are meditating, you can name your states, "My mind is angry." or "This mind is filled with joy." Some states persist. They are called moods like anxiety. If you watch them, you will see that they do not last long. Most of your thoughts and feelings flit through your mind like butterflies. Then they are gone.

Some demons block your awakening to a higher state. Religions deal with difficulties, and demons more than pleasures. Buddhists call them Hindrances. Christians call them Sins. To achieve a higher level of love and sexual bliss, you must name your demons and your pleasures. You must observe them without the delusion that they are you.

This week, begin to rise in love by observing your demons and your pleasures.

Look around and relate everything you see. Note those that belong to you. Note which are a part of you. Which ones prove you are real. This is the focus on the ego.

Some feelings

Reduce aversion in combination with improving toleration. Watch your feelings as you meet or see other people. Ease yourself into acceptance of other people. Do this through mindfulness of other people all day. Forgive their faults and their insults. Tolerate their poor manners, their poor taste, or what-ever you find annoying. Instead, think of their joy. What gives them joy? Feel the same joy for the same things. This will erase ill will. The reason for this is that by becoming sensitive to other people, you'll become more sensitive to your woman. By being tolerant and accepting of other people, you'll be tolerant and accepting of your lover.

Autosuggestion for changing feelings

This exercise is extremely difficult. To counteract the difficulty, use affirmations. Suggest feelings to yourself. Suggest to yourself in a firm loud voice that it's easy. You'll soon believe it is. Yes, this really works. The key is to believe it is easy.

Experiment with changing feelings toward your lover. First think of something about your lover that annoys you. Then change your feelings. Try appreciation, acceptance, and other feelings. This will train you to watch your feelings and to change them into useful and positive emotions. This will train you to have romantic feelings, or joyful feelings or whatever you want to feel when you are with your lover.

Sometimes concentration and meditation improve the sensations from your senses

In the exercise above, you noticed that your focused consciousness amplifies a sensation of touch.

Skill in concentration, meditation and absorption also amplify sensations also. By now you may detect the improvement of your sensations. For example, your smell or your sense of touch may be better. If you keep up these meditation exercises, you will be able to focus on your body and senses much more than when you started practicing this book. If you can push yourself to do these exercises you will improve after while. Most people take several months to notice the benefits. And you can take these few weeks to feel the improved effects on love making.

Concentration, meditation, and absorption also improve your communication with your woman. You will begin communicating your relationship on several levels simultaneously. Lovers can be connected sexually. Their bodies can be connected physically. They can also be connected emotionally by opening their hearts to each other and reducing the Root defenses. They can be more mentally attuned because of learning the lessons in this course. And they can communicate on the psychic or spiritual channel.

Eleventh week: Loving on five channels

Put it all together. Like a diamond being created into a crystal. You could imagine you and your woman are connected by five channels of communication. Each carbon atom in a diamond is connected to other carbon atoms in several places: the diamond analogy.

Description of water crystallization

Imagine a liquid is homogeneously composed of one identical substance (water), except for a few dust seeds. As the temperature drops, the liquid collects at the seeds and solidifies. The solid is a regularly spaced crystal like ice. The crystals grow from each seed and connect to the crystals of the other seeds. Each atom is connected to all other atoms with a strong bond in all directions.

Imagine carbon, for example pencil lead or black ash. The atoms of black graphite are soft and formless. Under pressure, the graphite atoms fuse together and form a diamond that is strong due to each atom being interconnected to all other atoms. A diamond is hard to break because all the atoms are interconnected. This could happen to people. A fusing into a strong family like diamond.

You could adopt this as your goal. You and your best possible woman will fuse in all your parts into an unbreakable diamond. Read about love in Chapter 9. The Seven Heights of Love. It may help you to begin to understand how love is like a diamond.

In some ways, you two lovers are alike. For example, you are humans with the same spirit. During the past 11 weeks, some of your thinking has become similar. And some of your emotional responses have become similar. Some of your physical arousals have begun to resonate in similar responses. Your Root has been pressured to reduce defenses. Each of your Roots has extended your bonds toward each other. You've experienced many feelings toward each other as two people combined into a completed whole. You may have had a sense of merging with each other. You are ready to connect into an extremely strong diamond. You've experienced the various kinds of energy, feelings, and touching communications, that emanate from each other. This emanation reinforces the connections between the two of you.

You've opened your hearts and accept the unity of your lover with yourself. You may even realize the unity of all people. You have a feeling reaction, maybe a thinking reaction, and maybe your body responds to all people. When you look around, you may see, hear, or perceive love coming toward you. You may feel love in your heart going out toward others. You may be the seed that this diamond crystallizes around.

Because you are crystallized, you can bring sexual experience into your lives on four levels.

Other concepts of love

There is an old saying, "All the world loves a lover."

You've reacted to the many kinds of signals coming from your lover. When you rise in love, some other people may sense your open heart or the emanations of love coming from you. Have you noticed this?

There may be an energy field around the lover that transmits energy or positive feelings to some other people. You may have opened their hearts and they tend to feel love. Other people sense the energy of love. You may even feel loving when away from your lover. When you leave the presence of your lover, you may notice a drop in your personal energy. You may notice it's harder to love other people than to love your lover. A possible goal is to love people who are not your lover.

Take note of your changing concepts of love since you started this course.

The objective of this course is that you lovers create more ways to express love based on what you've learned. Make a sacred ceremony of extreme sensitivity. Then you make love on all levels; emotional, physical, mental, emotional, and spiritual. This ceremony is just for the two of you.

Continuous, never-ending improvement

You may realize that you could sense even more of these emanations than you do now. Keep following these procedures. However, in the last few weeks, it is likely that you've noticed that you have a higher level of feelings, a more positive mental attitude, and a higher ability to love.

Continue the four jhanas. Send out your energy to be mindful of all people wherever you are. This may be too much energy for you, so watch out. Stop if this is confusing.

If you're courageous, identify yourself to be exactly the same as all other people at a deep level. Sense their energy. You'll get better at each of these disciplines. Each progress you make is one step toward being crystallized in the perfect relationship.

Everything starts with the first step. In the next chapter, you will learn more. You know you are at a new beginning. You have entered a world of love on all levels. You can connect physically, mentally, emotionally, and spiritually all at the same time.

For now, look up these books. They will help you to raise your mental picture of your sexual life. They are described at the end of this book.

Loving Relationships II

When the Earth Moves: Women and Orgasm

Sex For Dummies, 2ⁿᵈ Edition

Older Couples: New Romances: Finding and Keeping Love in Later Life

Chapter 18
Finding Your Total Tantric Partner

The previous 17 chapters introduced you to a new way to perceive a woman, methods to find her, check her out, and preparation for totally involved sexual experience. This chapter ties it together. There are so many factors in this process that you must have realized by now that you are limited in how much of these methods you are able to achieve. The following points out where the limitations may lie.

Limitation one: Your pursuit of women and your enjoyment of sexual thrills cannot be the focus of your whole life. You must take action to be healthy, to earn income, to build up your network of people, and a connection with a Higher Power.

You can only achieve the ultimate sexual connection if your life is ready. Don't expect too much if you don't have the drive for the higher levels of desire.

In Chapter 4. How to pursue her, we considered the levels of desire. Ponder their relevance to your relationship with your woman.

Consider the levels of desire:

1. Air, food, water
2. Rest, making babies, and sexual relief
3. Shelter
4. Safety
5. The acceptance and approval of your family, work group and friends
6. Giving and receiving love
7. Independence

8. Status and function in a group
9. Understanding and controlling your perception of reality
10. Achieving your highest dreams
11. Spiritual enlightenment

You and your best possible woman must be somewhat close in your levels of desire. Consider that you are at level 2, so you want babies and experience sexual relief. You're also seeing the importance of levels 3, 4, and 5. Then you'll have difficulty learning to give and receive love.

The most attractive woman may be at levels 6, 7, 8, and 9. However, you may have a problem becoming independent and gaining status and function, levels 7 and 8. Levels 9 and 10 may be out of your reach until you make an effort which will take years. These stages take time and focused effort to develop, so be patient and take each one as it comes. You may never rise to her levels of desire. You must recognize you cannot be compatible with her.

Tantric connection is part of levels 9, 10, and 11. You could begin practicing Tantric sexual contact at level 2. This book is leading you to inspiring goals on levels 9, 10, and 11.

Now consider your sexual partner. Think about what would result if you are at level 10, achieving your highest dreams while your partner is at level 2, resting, making babies, and enjoying sexual relief. This will not work for long. You could relate on the physical level and have great orgasms. You could even relate on a high emotional level. But your partner could not learn the mental perceptions nor the spiritual sensibility necessary for a higher connection with you. This may not matter to you if you're satisfied with physical and emotional gratification. These are much better than anything you're likely to be experiencing now. But you may want more after you master the physical and emotional methods.

You may want to find a more evolved partner. This may not ever happen. You have to decide to be happy with what you have.

The opposite case may also cause friction. You are level 2 and your partner is at levels 6, 7, 8, and 9. You'll be satisfied by physical and emotional gratification, but your partner may want to relate to her employer's group, where you do not fit in. There will be conflict about how to make the effort: do you focus on rising to her level? Or do you focus on Tantric play.

So think about the consequences and the payoffs. You may have more than enough achievement using the improvements taught in this book. The search for the perfect match may be exhausting, and it may not pay off. You have to decide how much effort you're willing to put in. No one else can do this for you.

You do not live in a perfect world. You cannot have everything you want, all the time, as much as you want it.

Now write a list of characteristics you want in your woman. Find out her level of desire. Include ideas from the Introduction that explains how everyone is different.

Limitation two: Attract and pursue a woman who is a possible wife, not a woman who will be forever impossible to relate to.

Give thought to what women you have met and decide who is appropriate for you. You realize not all women will want to marry you. Many women will not like you or want to associate with you. Do not break your back trying for the impossible.

Even if you are only looking for love and sexual enjoyment, the process of reaching the highest level of love and sexual connection is long and sometimes tedious. It requires work and commitment. You must make yourself attractive so that when you meet the appropriate love, you'll connect. How do you know if a woman could ever be your best lover? Write down everything you want in a lover. As you search for this woman, rewrite your description to suit your developing understanding. When you find your lover, you must know how to pursue her. Then you must invest your time and energy in playing together until you attain the highest love you're capable of. You must have the correct lover, a woman at your level who is appropriate for you to be able to do this.

Limitation three: Your sexual life is best if it is a part of balanced life that you and your best possible woman are building together

A balanced life is not a one night stand. Nor is it a basic animal satisfaction as in levels 1 and 2 like eating or sleeping. It's part of a major creation that will return value to you for many years or even for your whole life. You and your lover must have the balance of all the desires listed above.

Limitation four: This book is most useful and efficient for a man who will invest the effort, who will focus on long term possible outcomes, and who will continue making the effort until he achieves the entire process being taught.

If you live in a big city, you have noticed the huge number available women but you may have difficulty establishing relationships. If you live in a small village you have noticed that there are only a few women who you can find and interview, most of whom do not attract yhou. Therefore you must realize this process is not quick and easy. However, it is thrilling to achieve your goal if you have a positive attitude.

The methods in this book have a massive payoff if you can follow directions. But you must be practical in the face of current American social life. Things can go wrong. You're not in control of everything. That is why one of the traits you must have is persistence. Do not give up. Go for the possible women not the perfect women.

What if your desired partner can't keep up with your rapid growth? No two people learn at the same rate. So tolerate her shortcomings and keep at it. Keep following the advice in this book and the other books listed at the end. You are the powerful support: How to make yourself a major attraction. Refer to Chapter 2. Directions for you to get the next book are given there. There are detailed instructions for your woman to get the companion book to this one:

The Art and Science of Dating: Use These Suggestions, Methods, and Tools to Get the Relationship with the Man You Want

After she starts to study this book, many of your troubles will disappear.

If your partner is growing in sexual intelligence much faster than you are, ask for patience. The wisdom in this book took hundreds of years to discover, not just my lifetime. I took over 30 years for me to master this vital part of life. Have faith in the proven process.

On the other hand, if your sex partner doesn't want to read this book and if she doesn't want to continually improve, get a new partner. Your sexual life is a mirror of your whole relationship with this partner. If she can't grow with you, your relationship will go stale and self-destruct. Move on!

In the last four chapters, we have considered aspects of the sexual life: mental, physical, emotional and spiritual. Since you want the most memorable sexual times, weave these four aspects into your sexual adventures.

Read and study about sex.

Discuss your sex life in detail with your partner.

See movies, videos, and plays about love and sex.

Plan a buildup to each sexual encounter that takes days or weeks. This will heighten the sensations when you touch.

Create habitual feelings of love and expectation.

Make a special place, a love nest, that reinforces sexual meaning. Make love in that place.

Can imagine the difference between falling into bed with a stranger and building up a competent sexuality with your lover over weeks, months, and years, with mental, physical emotional and spiritual layers?

How could you make the love nest, bedroom, the woods or the hot tub more sensual?

How many different ways could you make love if you researched it in books, movies, and videos? Perhaps 1000 ways. Trying out new loving ways will keep you interested for many years.

After you ponder these answers, look up these book descriptions at the end of this book. They will help you to find your Tantric partner for your sexual life.

Loving Relationships II

Older Couples, New Romances: Finding and Keeping Love In Late Life

The Authentic Heart: An Eightfold Path to Midlife Love

Betrayal, Trust, and Forgiveness: A Guide to Emotional Healing and Self Renewal

Addiction to Love

Heart Over Heels: 50 Ways Not to Leave Your Lover

Chapter 19
Mastery of Communication on All Levels Adds Depth to the Marriage

Marriage is an investment. You give a great amount and you receive an enormous amount in return for many years. Continue reading with the intent to invest what is necessary.

As you have noticed in the last chapters, steaming hot sex requires mastery of several skills, not just sexual skills on a higher level. As you gain the skills, your enjoyment and your connection with your woman will increase beyond what you can imagine now. For example, you will be able to concentrate on sexual pass-times for 10 to 20 hours at a time. You will never have another disappointing intimate contact.

Keep in mind that men and women are opposites who attract; this is the basic source of sexual energy.

You are becoming closer to realizing sexual ecstasy. You are getting close because you have trained yourself in the 11 week course to awaken to signals and sensations from your lover and from your own senses and your own mind.

If you have not experimented with all the ways to speak, think and behave in the first 18 chapters then you are not being honest. You re trying to deceive yourself. You cannot expect to have any quality success if you are not honest.

If you finished the 11 week course, and you have begun the never ending improvement in the first 18 chapters, then you are ready. You have proved yourself worthy of persisting. Assume you want the perfection of sexual life and the valuable investment of marriage. You will achieve this heaven.

If your mate is willing to actually begin the never ending improvement, to study sexual involvement on several levels, and to practice daily to experience paradise, then she is ready to join you in this magnificent adventure.

An example of the Tantric Way to Paradise

The couple practices the methods in the last five chapters. Therefore they are connected physically, mentally, emotionally, and spiritually.

The Sanskrit word for the male sexual organ is, 'Lingam' translated as 'Wand of Light.' In Tantra, the practice of sacred sexuality, the Lingam is respectfully viewed and honored. It is a Wand of Light that channels creative energy and pleasure.

The purpose of the Lingam Massage is to create an environment for the man to relax, and receive expanded pleasure through the channel of his Lingam. His wife is the giver. She experiences the joy of causing and witnessing the man surrendering to his softer, gentler side.

The Lingam Massage can be used as a form of safer sex when latex gloves are used. It is an excellent process to build trust and intimacy. It is often used to help men heal from negative sexual conditioning and damaged mental conceptions of sexual experience. Orgasm is not the only goal of the Lingam massage although it's often a pleasant and welcome side effect.

The goal is to give pleasure thru the Lingam, also including testicles, perineum, and Sacred Spot (the equivalent to the female G-spot)all which allow the man to surrender to a form of pleasure he may not be used to, or perhaps has never even imagined. From this perspective, both receiver and giver relax into the massage. Men need to learn to relax and receive.

Ordinary sexual conditioning has the man in a doing and goal-oriented mode. The Lingam Massage allows the man to experience his softer, more receptive side and experience pleasure from a non-traditional perspective.

Before the massage, the giver and receiver take a relaxing bath or shower. Both relax their bellies. They let go of the tension that they hold there. They go to the bathroom and eject waste before beginning the massage. The best results occur when the bowels and bladder are empty.

They let go of their thoughts of the past and the future. They connect with their partner: They listen to each other, feel each other's heart-beat, look into each other's eyes, smell the aromas of one another, taste the different body parts and creams. They concentrate all thinking on the experience. They allow total relaxation and trust. This is a full sensual moment.

The man lies on his back with pillows under his head so he can look up at his woman, the giver. He focuses on receiving. He has a pillow, covered with a towel, under his hips. His legs are to be spread apart with the knees slightly bent (pillows or cushions under the knees will also help) and his genitals and crotch area clearly exposed for the massage. The giver sits cross-legged between the receiver's legs. Before their bodies touch, they begin with deep, relaxed breathing.

The woman gently massages the legs, abdomen, thighs, chest, nipples, and so on. This helps the man to relax. The woman reminds the receiver, with a loving and low voice, to breathe deeply and to sink deeper into relaxation. She pours a small quantity of a high-quality oil (or water-based lubricant when using latex gloves) on the shaft of the Lingam and the whole area.

She begins gently massaging the testicles, taking care to not cause pain in this sensitive area. She massages the scrotum gently, causing it to relax. She massages the area above the Lingam, on the pubic bone.

She massages the Perineum, the area between the testicles and anus. She moves slowly, knowing she is giving a massage to an often-neglected area of the body. She massages the shaft of the Lingam. She varies the speed and pressure. She gently squeezes the Lingam at the base with her right hand, pulls up and slides off and then alternates with her left hand.

Then, she changes the direction by starting the squeeze at the head of the penis, sliding down and off. She alternates right and left hands. She imagines that she is using an orange juicer. She massages all around the head and shaft. She grabs his Lingam with both hands in tight fists. She moves her fists opposite each other like she is wringing out a washcloth.

She holds his shaft in one fist and, with lots of oil, rubs the other palm quickly back and forth across the tip of the head of his Lingam with firm pressure. She takes his Lingam in both hands with her fingers on its topside and thumbs its underside. She looks for the very sensitive spot on its underside, right at the very top of its shaft in the little triangle where the edges of the bottom of the head of his Lingam converge below the tip. She massages this area with the pads of her thumb tips, one following the other, with lots of oil, varying speed and pressure.

If he has an uncircumcised foreskin, she occasionally pulls it all the way down with one hand, and, with lots of oil, runs her other fist up and down its full length, "polishing" the head of his Lingam.

She holds his testicles gently but firmly in one hand, pulls them down as far as his ball sack will stretch, and grasping his shaft in her other fist, strokes its full length, occasionally polishing the head. With all these moves, which make a fist around his shaft, she alternately squeezes him hard.

In contrast, she makes her strokes without squeezing at all. She continues making it interesting and changing. Alternating among all these different moves, she remembers that the motion that most advances his orgasm is a long stroke surrounding his shaft and going all the way along its full length in each stroke.

A skilled Tantric lover knows that any given man's sexual responses are changing. So at times, his sexual energy is best advanced by a number of short strokes, perhaps only a couple inches, alternating with the full strokes.

The Lingam may or may not go soft as she performs various techniques. She soothingly relieves the man so he does not worry that it will not get hard again. She will show him that it will get hard, then go soft, then get hard again. She convinces him this is a highly desirable Tantric experience, like riding a wave, bobbing up and down. Hardness and softness are two ends of the pleasure spectrum. One is just as equally desirable as the other.

You may decide to release, to take the temporary pleasure at any time. Or you may retain the sexual vitality. Let it build up for hours into an ultimate peak of emotion, physical, mental, spirit, and vitality breakthrough. You can just experience the extreme of liveliness and energetic expression.

If it appears that you are going to ejaculate, she backs off, allowing the cock to soften a little before resuming the massage. She does this several times, bringing him close to ejaculation, then backing off. They remember that the goal is to raise the man to a high state of total pleasure including body and spirit, not orgasm in and of itself.

In this type of experience, you reach a high plane of existence. You and your best woman have merged. The masculine and feminine life forms merge. This is an analogy to birth; the birth of a total marriage. This is a new experience. The experience will depend on your and your woman's capacity to think, to feel, and to sense.

When you and your woman realize that you cannot rise higher in sexual pitch and that you are ready to return to the ordinary plane of reality, you decide that orgasm is the goal.

This is a brief example of what you can do based on the training in never ending improvement. With enough time and effort, you can join with your woman into the diamond Sukhavati state of mind.

This example is only one of hundreds of moves, places on the body to touch, words to whisper, sounds to create, and aromas to release. All of them raise the sexual tension of your and your best possible woman. You transmute into a different plane of reality.

By learning the methods in Tantric books listed at the end of this chapter, you and your best possible woman can increase their life vitality, Chi, by raising the pitch of sexual excitement and holding it without releasing it through orgasm.

On the other hand, if you choose to let go and ejaculate, your woman encourages you to breathe deeply during the orgasm and to enter the states of jhana one through four that you learned in Chapter 18. If you can enter the jhanas, and especially if you have almost ejaculated and then held back at least six times before ejaculating, you will enter a sublime mental state associated with a transcendent physical and emotional state. Holding back six times charges up the sexual battery with tremendous energy.

Remember, if you can maintain control, which most men cannot, you have the choice as to where you want to send this powerful energy. You can release the enormous energy outward with the sperm. You can choose to contain the potential energy inward for other uses. A man who masters the moment of ejaculation is able to channel this energy into other areas of his being.

One phenomenon that you will notice, if you withhold ejaculation of sperm, is that in the following days, many women are magnetically attracted to you.

Or you may wait until another Tantric lovemaking session to compound the power of the release.

When you feel complete with the Tantric session, your woman gently remove her hands and allows you to lie there quietly. She may want to snuggle up together. Or she can leave the room and let you drift off into a meditative state. She allows him to fully experience his childlike innocence and magnificent male beauty.

After receiving from your woman, give an equal or better experience back to her

As soon as it is possible, reverse the positions and you give back as much or more to your woman.

This is the description of one possible experience of you and your best possible woman merging into one another on several levels simultaneously.

You could approach the Tantric experience as a ceremony. After merging several times in such a ceremony, you will have a true marriage of thought, feeling, physical contact, and spiritual experience.

In this process, you learn the art of ejaculatory mastery and control by coming close to ejaculation and then backing off on the stimulation. You learn that deep breathing is a key that will soften the urge to ejaculate. Eventually, you gain mastery over ejaculation that allows you to make love as long as you and your woman want. You learn the ability to enjoy the pleasure of the higher planes of being. You become adept at the adventure of many climaxes in one sexual experience without losing a drop of semen. You confirm that orgasm and ejaculation are two different responses that you can learn to enjoy separately. You realize you have an expanded sex life.

Your woman will have similar experiences. She can retain the sexual energy instead of releasing into orgasm. When she does this, her mental and sensual abilities increase. Many men are strangely attracted to her, partly due to her radiance. But also due to unknown factors.

The Tantric ceremony can be a healing experience through release of blocked chi, vitality, thoughts, or feelings

You may have strong emotions come up during access to sexual experience. You may cry and remember a traumatic event from your past. Your woman, the giver is in a place of trust and intimacy. She approves of your feeling. She is loving you. She does not try to console or fix you. She just accepts your feeling whatever you need to feel. She encourages you to laugh, scream, cry, or moan. She is the best friend and healer you could have in that moment.

Tantric methods increase vitality and health

This is a delightful side effect. In Tantra, many nerve endings on the Lingam that correspond to other parts here are of the body are excited. It is possible that many ailments can be cured by receiving a good Lingam Massage.

Try out the Tantric methods. Read the books and experiment with the hundred ways described in the books for rising in love in the Tantric way. You may find liberation from stress, from loneliness, from memories that hinder you, and from bad habits. This is the bliss of the Tantric way.

Look up these book descriptions at the end of this book. You can achieve total sexual, physical, emotional, mental, and spiritual connection. Studying the books will help you to raise your mental picture of your sexual life. They explicitly state the positions, the moves and the imagery for the vast and unending enjoyment of total union.

There are many books about Tantric practice and Kama Sutra:

Chopra, Deepak (2006). The *Kama Sutra including the Seven Spiritual Laws of Love*, London: Virgin Books.

Mallanaga Vatsyayana (2003). *Kama Sutra of Vatsyayana*, Wendy Doniger, Sudhir Kakar, trans., New York: Oxford University Press

Swami B. V. Tripurari, *Aesthetic Vedanta: The Sacred Path of Passionate Love*

Amodeo, John (2001). *The Authentic Heart: An Eightfold Path to Midlife Love*

Sonntag, L. *Bedside Kama Sutra*

Hooper, A. *Anne Hooper's Kama Sutra*

Hooper, A. *K.I.S.S. Guide to the Kama Sutra*

Heumann, S. *Everything Kama Sutra*

Lecroix, N. *The Art of Tantric Sex*

Sarita, M. *Tantric Love*

Kuriansky, J. *Complete Idiot's Guide to Tantric Sex*

Heart, M. *When the Earth Moves: Women and Orgasm,*

Chapter 20
All this Knowledge and Wisdom about Dating and Sex Play Sets You Up to Be the Perfect Husband

You are evolving into the perfect husband

Remember all the effort and time you expended to get through high school and maybe college? What you learned there is a small fraction of what you need to know for a good marriage.

The education you obtain from reading this book will help your marriage. Using the knowledge from this book and other recommended books will push you toward your success. You can succeed in satisfying your need to be with people and to have close friends. You can succeed in relating to your best possible woman and other people while you make an adequate marriage.

Read *In the Spirit of Marriage: Creating and Sustaining Loving Relationships*

What is a happy marriage?

How is satisfactory marriage defined? Each individual person wants a different set of satisfactions in marriage. Each person conceives of marriage as a different institution. The reason for courtship is to screen out the unsatisfactory mates.

Maybe you are like many of the generation born after 1970 who have never heard the term, "courtship?" It means to date a woman and interview her for the position of wife. It is work disguised as play. Before about 1970, courtship was what men did. They looked for a wife. I suspect that contemporary women court men; reversing the old ways.

Most of this book is about courtship.

An ancient discovery about marriage

Try to guess when the following discovered and the country where it was discovered. "Women have no place where the curse of poverty is found. They belong with luxury. Just as bees in their hollow hives support mischievous drones, women were made mischievous in their ways and a curse for men. Just as the bees work busily all day till sunset making the white wax, while the drones sit at home in the shade of the hive and harvest into their bellies the fruits of another's labor, women were made to sit home and harvest the fruits of a man's labor.

Men must live with women. The home goes with the blessing of fire and other technologies discovered by men. Whoever seeks to avoid marriage, the troublesome ways of women, and refuses to marry, he finds old age a curse without anyone to tend his years. Though he does not lack livelihood while he lives, on his death his kinsmen divide up his estate. As for the men fated to marry, even if they get a good wife well suited to their tempers, evil is continually balanced with good in his life. If he should get sick or immoral children, the grief in his heart and soul is unremitting throughout life."

Of course you did not guess who wrote this. It was the Greek, Hesiod 800 years before Christ was born. The first woman was the goddess Athena. The titans and men were speechless when they saw how deadly and how irresistible was this woman with which the gods were going to catch men. Now you have some idea of the historic opinions men have of women and marriage. Be warned. Read *12 Hours to a Great Marriage: A Step-by-Step Guide for Making Love Last.*

That said, it is the fate of all men to be coupled or married with a woman. She is joined with a man to help him evolve. This evolution is similar to a hunk of iron being heated in the flame to be smashed into a plow. You have no choice but to accept this heating and smashing. The nearest thing to a cure for the curse of a woman is to gain wisdom and then carefully select a woman.

Eleven efforts you must make to create
a good marriage and family
First effort. Find a wife, the best possible wife.

Most of this book is about learning the skills necessary for finding, pursuing, and agreeing to marry the best possible woman for you, considering your valuable offerings but tempered by your limitations.

This is not easy to achieve. If you ask 1000 men how to find the best possible wife, you will get 2000 answers. Major parts of culture are built around courtship and marriage. In America, the term, "courtship" is not familiar to about half the population.

The main problem men face after marriage is that they did not have a methodical system to find a wife nor did they have a planned approach to interviewing her for the job.

To notice another complication, most women are convinced they will be the boss and the husband will work for them as an employee, maybe as a slave. Many men have grown up in with their mother as a boss and the father as the menial worker. In America the family tradition is different for all the different groups, classes, and for all the immigrant communities.

Another common mistake that almost all men and women make before marriage, is wearing a mask of deceit. The mask usually appears to match the expectations and traditions of the other prospective spouse. If the expectations and traditions are vastly different, the couple does not usually get married. However, they may get married anyway because there is no other person available or she is pregnant or the marriage is arranged by their families, or some other force that cannot be overcome.

In all cases, the couple did not frankly reveal themselves so their spouses could realize the seeds of destruction from another point of view. If the man and woman are not correct for each other, nothing will save the marriage.

Since you are reading this book, this will not be your problem. This book tells you how to pick the correct spouse. After you have read it and tried to conform to the wisdom then read it again.

Second Effort. Learn the skills necessary for getting along in a marriage condition.

If possible, continue improving forever. It is possible to have a satisfactory marriage. But about half of marriages end in divorce. Of the marriages that do not end in divorce, about half the spouses live separately perhaps in the same house. Of the one in four marriages who live together, the condition is discord and accommodation. If the couple learns the skills mentioned in this book, they can continue to improve until they have positive feelings. I have observed this type of marriage. In the few marriages that evolve into good feelings and prosperity, they all had horrible times that they had to learn to overcome.

Facing the truth, no one has a perfect marriage because humans have too many faults. The probability is tiny that a man can find a wife with the traits that will end in harmonious marriage. That is why I have employed the term, "best possible wife."

Consider the skills necessary for achieving the best possible marriage. There is no school where you can learn these skills. You have this book and the books recommended at the end. You have your efforts to experiment by meeting many women and trying out various approaches. There are a few classes you can take. Churches often give short classes on marriage to those who have requested to be married. Thus, the skills you gain are dependent on your ability to succeed. This is the same ability that you will use to succeed in a profession or in a major business. If you stop the effort, you will fail in any of these efforts.

Read *The Marriage of Spirit: Enlightened Living in Today's World,*

The world needs schools to teach how to get married and how stay married

You could found a school or college to teach how to be married. In my knowledge, this has never been done. It would be priceless to any nation that had such a school.

Marriage preservation is the major American problem of the twenty-first century. Most social problems are born in the destruction of the family system. This is just my opinion based on experience and education. My only answer to this major problem is to found a school.

Some of the skills necessary for a positive marriage

(A.) Negotiating.

(B.) Arguing with logic and debating

(C.) Persistence

(D.) Willingness to learn from books and from other people

(E.) Control of emotions

(F.) Etiquette

(G.) Loving kindness, compassion

(H.) Spiritual or religious foundation

(I.) Intention to improve continuously

(J.) Correct thinking, not disordered

(K.) Practice concentrating

(L.) Sympathetic joy in the accomplishment of your wife

(M.) Equanimity with your wife

(N.) Honesty and abiding by rules and laws

(O.) Sexual skills

Now that has been mentioned, if you have all these skills, then you can deal with the problem of selecting the correct woman. You can interview her and observe her to see if she has these traits. Notice that age, body, facial beauty, social class, and economic class are not mentioned. If you and your wife have most of these qualities, you will have an excellent marriage if you are lucky.

There can be no guarantee because there are too many probable influences.

Third Effort: General guidance. Create a basis of friendliness with your prospective wife.

Get to know her by interviewing her. Ask her about her thoughts and feelings. Do many different activities with her over 6 months to 6 years. Uncover her excellence, her faults, and her emotional troubles. Reveal your own excellence, faults, and troubles. Discover her emotional strength and mental superiority. Tout your own. Join her in various extremely demanding activities to establish long-term compatibility. Communicate on all levels about what marriage means.

You will need many extremely joyous, fulfilling experiences before you get married. These positive experiences are like a treasure you can call on after you are married when the outlook is dark. You need to be able to remember excellent times together to neutralize the coming troubles.

If neither you nor your woman are willing to learn and grow, to study and be flexible and the other qualities listed above, your marriage will have serious defects even if you stay together. Discuss this with her.

Fourth Effort: Learn skilled methods of relating.

Relating consists of communicating on all levels: thinking, speaking, feeling, relating sexually, actions of the body, listening, clothes, attitudes, helping one another, and so on. You need to learn to argue constructively, to persuade, and to negotiate with her to see how your relationship handles conflict. Arguing is an art. You will not discover it or the other arts listed. You will need books and mentors to teach you.

While you are doing this, agree on rules. The first rule is never, ever insult the other, never call evil names, never accuse without clear proof of the accusation. Never raise your voice and try to dominate or intimidate. It is better to forgive and not say anything if no solution is possible. Most things blow over if left alone.

Learn the skills necessary to get to know each other. This often takes years. Negotiate conflict, or argue, but do not physically fight. Persuade for an agreement but do not force it. If you ever feel rage, hate, or other extreme emotions, then leave the area where your woman is. Go away for a day or two if necessary until your emotions flatten out. Tell her you are not capable of discussing and you need to get way to think.

Discuss the topic that brought out the extreme emotion another day.

The healthy choice in a complicated interplay of two people who wish to smooth the rough edges of marriage is to keep communicating. Do not communicate when in a rage or other extreme emotion when reality can be distorted. There is insanity in extreme emotions. Attack will ruin any chance of solution. Pick your words carefully; harsh words and insults cannot be taken back ever.

Do not repress feelings such as hostility. State clearly what is offensive, disturbing or painful. This requires courage combined with gentleness, firmness and belief in the friendship. Emphasize your feelings and needs while considering your wife's feelings and needs.

Fifth Effort: The fourth effort is very difficult but if you can do it and she can do it, about half the major problems will not exist.

When basic etiquette is used, then all graceful and valuable relationships can take hold and grow. There are three rules that you must observe without regard for time, place, social rules, or traditions, or people of any class.

1. Be considerate. Consider the needs and feelings of other people especially your wife.
2. Be respectful. Learn how to show respect. This is different for different cultures. Learn the culture. Always show respect.
3. Be honest. Learn to tell the truth and to be honest. Soften a harsh truth. Learn to be tactful about harsh truth. Never, ever lie. It is harder than you think to persist in telling the truth. It is often easier to lie.

Lies will come back to bite you.

Sixth effort: The objective is to agree on a satisfying marriage relationship before the marriage is announced.

Put it in a legal prenuptial agreement. Write any other legal definitions you need. Dealing with the legal work beforehand does you two favors. First, you define your relationship and experience each other in serious and grounded terms. A prenuptial agreement brings up all the serious and unpleasant problems. Face them before you are married. If you have to fact them after the hardship, it may be too late. Second, you save a lot of legal fees and trouble in case of divorce. Face the legal issues.

In the USA, there is a substantial probability that you will divorce. To avoid divorce, make a tireless effort to succeed at everything in this book. You also can study other books listed at the end of this book to avoid divorce. Read *In the Spirit of Marriage: Creating and Sustaining Loving Relationships,*

When you announce your marriage, hidden troubles will surface. Convince all concerned people the marriage will work, even your lover's family.

Seventh effort: Plan the wedding in detail; way ahead of time.

Read the recommended books on planning weddings. The marriage ceremony and all the expected events will cause great stress which you cannot anticipate. It's really difficult, isn't it?

Read *Priceless Weddings for Under $5000*
Wedding Planning for Dummies
Dazzled, Frazzled & Back Again: The Bride's Survival Guide,
Emily Post's Etiquette, 18th edition
The Everything Groom Book: A Survival Guide for Men!

**Eighth effort: Lessons you must learn and use
every day with your intended wife.**

Go to the chapter on HOW TO PURSUE HER. Memorize the
two lessons about what women want and what men want. Together with
your intended wife, begin moving toward higher levels of desire listed
under the heading: SET YOUR STANDARDS FOR THE PERFECT
WOMAN.

Together, discuss

The basic needs of an ordinary person.

You and she must be convinced that neither of you has one of these
needs unsatisfied. If one of these needs is unsatisfied, there will be
substantial trouble.

Now that you are practicing the successful ways of relating, answer
this question. Why are so many couples getting divorced in America?
There are endless reasons. The main reason is that people have not
learned the lessons of this book and put them into practice. Another
reason is because most of us don't have extended families anymore. It
used to be that when a man and a woman got married, the bride got
a lot more people, especially women, to talk to about everything. The
husband got a lot more pals to tell dumb jokes to. His new pals did not
get mad at him.

Most of us have too few people to talk to when we get married. The
bride gets one more person to talk to about everything, but it's just one
more person and it's a man. The husband gets one more pal, but it's a
woman and she gets mad at him a lot.

When a married couple has an argument, they may think it's about
money, sex, power, housekeeping, or how to raise the children. But they

are really saying, "You are not enough people" or "I need more love and recognition and appreciation."

People are gregarious, a big word that means they were born to be around lots of people all the time. Sometimes when a couple fights, they are really saying "Love me more!" or "Give me more attention. Do not ignore me." or "Let's turn this argument into an exciting sexual game." Examine your disagreements, arguments, fights for underlying needs for love.

A married couple is not a survival group. The couple is not an extended family. They still feel lonely. They have a natural desire to belong to a group of people to call on for help.

A small number of people do not like to be in a group very much. They want to be alone most of the time. If you are one of these people, do not get married. Get a group of pals or a crowd of girlfriends you can talk to all night.

Ninth effort: Consider an extended family as part of your marriage plan.

The overwhelming majority of people on Earth belong to an extended family. Extended families have a very low percentage of depressed people. An extended family with three generations has low percentages of people with personality disorders (which you call crazies). However, sometimes the extended family makes things worse.

In the USA, there are a small number of extended families that actually communicate regularly. This is a factor contributing to why so many Americans get divorced.

Tenth effort: Understand male impotence and female loss of interest in sexual action.

Another factor involves the way men are raised. The last 100 years of education has been a disaster for men. The result is that many men have negative feelings about women. Another result is that more young men are impotent. Many men have difficulty with sexual activity because the changing role of women, liberation, aggressiveness, etc. And the changing role of men also brings stress on the couple. This was discussed above in

Chapter 18. Finding Your Total Tantric Partner and

Chapter 19. Mastery of Communication on All Levels Adds to the Marriage

Watch for these changes in the role of men which you are not prepared for.

Eleventh Way: Assess both of your levels of desire

Discuss these levels of desire. If you are too far apart, it is impossible to connect for long. Do you both pursue the same **levels of desire** in the chapter How to Pursue Her?

How do you find out if your intended wife has the character and values to make a partnership that lasts?

What level of desire are you, and what level do you aspire to?

What level of love are you enjoying and what level do you want to evolve into?

How can you learn skillful speaking, acting, and thinking for a happy marriage?

Since you will meet conflict, can you negotiate a fair agreement?

What must you avoid doing or speaking to remain married?

What can you improve in the relationship?

What can you not improve?

Who in the families, workplace, organizations, and friends want to stop this marriage?

When can the laws and the justice system cause you pain?

Now think of your own questions and answer them, too.

Your levels of desire will change. They may not change to be the same for both of you.

Answering these questions together is necessary for a lasting marriage. So discuss these topics as long as necessary to clear up problems. If you think you can do this after you are married, then do not get married. It is easy to talk about these things before marriage.

If you find out the differences after marriage, you will never solve your problems. Then you will have to answer about 100 questions for the lawyer and another 100 questions for the judge. Imagine answering 100 questions to a lawyer while you know you are going to lose everything, and you are anxious, afraid, furious, and crying.

Today you have a choice. You are not being dragged around the divorce court by your wife and her family who hate you.

Today you are lucky. You have this book and you have the time to get ready for a satisfying marriage.

Here you are, answering questions, discussing problems, planning your married life. These are quick, simple and easy compared to marriage. These are nothing compared to divorce and single fatherhood when you see your child four afternoons each month.

If you have arrived at this place in the book, you have a good chance at a good marriage. You are willing to work toward happiness and contentment. Have the courage to face the truth: Marriage is hard and endless work.

You deserve rewards in your life. A reward is the fame of being one of the few happily married couples.

Chapter 21
How to Make Your Marriage the One that Is Happy Ever After

You have gone through the studies, the experiments, never ending and continuous growth explained in this book. You have found your best possible woman. You have checked her out and found her to be the best possible. You have married her. You would think that, after all that, you should have an adequate and lasting marriage. However, there is more for you to develop. If the marriage does not grow into maturity, it dies.

Some questions you will face in this chapter: How do you grow the marriage so it does not become boring and hopeless? What skills do you need for family preservation?

Have the courage to face the truth. Surely you have heard about the troubles people have in marriage. The truth is that America has evolved a culture that destroys marriage. To avoid the extreme pain of divorce, or the worse pain and suffering of being stuck in a horrible marriage, you must work at preserving your investment in marriage. If you give up on your marriage, as about four of five people do, you will have pain and suffering. You cannot imagine the pain even though you have heard people complain about their marriages and you have seen television shows and read books about unbelievably rotten marriages. Yet, the emotional pain of divorce is hell.

If you have children, you have compound hell. About half the children of divorce have serious life problems as result of the divorce. It takes a man and woman to have a baby. And it takes a man and women to raise it into a healthy adult. Divorce destroys this availability of this development. You will feel the holes in their souls, unless you repress the pain. Then the repressed pain will come out in unexpected ways.

Therefore, do the work now before the horror begins.

The first 20 chapters gave you the opportunity to avoid most of the problems of marriage by taking the time and effort to screen your best possible woman before you married her. However, people being the cunning and imperfect humans that they are, can fool you and you can deceive yourself about who you are marrying. Also women have been known to be "gold diggers" or other predatory creatures who intend to change their personalities the moment the marriage is official.

You must have a plan to win all the games and to succeed in all cases.

That is why you must always pursue and attract your spouse. Taking aggressive action toward the goal of a good marriage is more effective than feeble defense. You will perceive trouble during the marriage preparations, soon after the honeymoon is over, Trouble will intensify during pregnancy and amplify after childbirth. You will find out the true intentions of your wife by the time the first child is three years old.

Power Struggle in Marriage

There is a tendency in humans to strive for power. Power means different things for everyone. Many marriages are destroyed by the power struggle. For example, a dictatorial style of the wife or the husband may be destructive or a sadomasochistic relationship with violence or the person with superior educations and social skills may surrender to the other who is crude but efficient or any of 100 other distorted marriages.

When people depend on each other in marriage or business or the factory, there is an interplay of power and control against fear and submission. Many other opposite characteristics lead to power struggles. A man must be aware of the intrigue, power, plots, or other evidence of a drive for power in himself or his wife, just as he is aware in his field of work.

The struggle over power is one of the many serious on-going problems that often arise in marriage.

Poor judgment can arise causing unintended consequences

Poor judgment can mean a wide variety of speech or actions. Speaking without considering the needs and feelings of other people is poor judgment. Spending excessive money for minor pleasures is poor judgment. An extra martial sexual affair is poor judgment. It is the opposite of prudence.

Consider the results if you persist in showing poor judgment. What happens if you stop pursuing, stop showing interest, and stop grooming attractiveness into yourself? The marriage disappears. You may live together in secret disappointment. You may divorce. You and she may have affairs. Unknown events will occur. In any case, the marriage will not provide satisfaction for your needs. You will have feelings of jealousy, hate, anxiety, and so on.

What If your wife persists in showing poor judgment or begins showing criminal intent? The marriage disappears fast. If both of you show poor judgment, the marriage may last only a few days. And the pain will be unbearable for both of you. Death, not necessarily murder, is often the result.

What are some clues to guide you into being perpetual best friends and lovers?

Some clues to guide you into being perpetual best friends and lovers. Read parts of this book out loud with your wife once a year. Discuss problems, approvals and improvements to be made. In particular, read Chapter 20. How can you use all this knowledge and wisdom about dating and sex play?

In Chapter 20 is a list. 'Some of the skills necessary for a positive marriage.' By the time you have been married a year, this list will have emphatic meaning for you and your wife. You will wish you had begun improving the listed skills long ago.

Any skill improves with repetition

Love and sex improve with time. You will have a better chance of improving if you perceive yourself as a master craftsman. All master craftsmen take years to learn to make beautiful products or services. Love and sex can be beautiful services. Love and the dance of sexual dalliance are the most exquisite creations of all the arts. All champion sportsmen take years of training to win the trophy. Sex is a kind of sport that takes practice, skill, and endurance. Work at it until you can play well.

What is a satisfactory marriage?

Since everyone wants a different satisfaction in marriage, the definition of satisfactory is difficult.

You cannot go to school to learn marriage. It is bizarre that the most important part of your life has no school for preparation. You must be your own teacher. You pick the textbooks. Start with this book and the recommended books at the end. Then you write down what 'satisfactory marriage' means to you. You read, study, and test out your notions of satisfactory marriage. Your wife needs to do the same. It is better if you do this long before the marriage.

251

There are a number of theories of happy marriage. You could to pick one and try it out.

This approach to defining a marriage will only work if your wife is willing to experiment, to change her ideas, to be loyal to the marriage, to resolve conflict, and to persist. You also must be willing to do the same. Do your best.

Another way of defining a satisfactory marriage is to research and wrote a 'pre-nuptial' agreement. This is a legal document that defines all the features of a marriage based on what the couple has decided and agreed upon. The research turns up hidden ideas or unwelcome facts which may be difficult or even painful to discuss. It is better to face these difficult or negotiable ideas before marriage.

What is the probability of growing an excellent marriage? About half the marriages in America end in divorce. Some marriages appear excellent by your standards, but still end. Of the marriages that last, most are convenient ways of living, but unsatisfactory. Often a marriage looks perfect from the outside and ends in divorce. Very few marriages are happy in any sense. Marriage is a game to produce children and to delegate wealth.

It is a growing game where people live in the fire, the way a ceramic pot is baked, until they become mature works of art. When you meet older married couples who seem perfectly happy. They may tell you about the wars they fought with each other. This is the fire that taught them to be worthwhile people. In the war of marriage, many people find the meaning of life, even the worth of life. They find that marriage forced them to become the finest people possible.

The definition of excellent marriage is up to the married couple. So there is no answer to this important question. There is only the process by which the couple evolves a satisfactory marriage.

Continuous and never ending improvement is a process to forge a satisfactory marriage

In general, you need to continuously improve everything in your whole life. You need to learn skills to improve the rest of your life continually.

In marriage, you need to continuously improve everything. Decide what you can improve in your marriage. Honestly identify the things that you can improve easily and also others that will improve with difficulty, if at all. Some arguments go on for a long time, perhaps years.

Decide on a few things, not all things. This will make the process into an achievement of a goal rather than a fight to win the impossible. Set goals for the relationship between you and your wife. Do not adopt goals set by your parents or a TV story or other non-participants.

Use this process as a way to relate. Be friendly and polite about helping each other to proceed to the achievement of each thing you are improving at the time.

All married couples meet situations that appear terrible or impossible

Using the skills suggested in this book the situations will resolve into nothing.

To get through the impossible while holding the marriage together, you can stop everything and remember wonderful events when you were joyful and inseparable.

During courtship and early in marriage, create memorable occasions to refer to in order to preserve the marriage when the conflict is unbearable. If you can remember how harmonious you were at times, you will persist when the fire is burning you.

Have the courage to face the truth. There are problems that cannot be solved. Experiment by testing solutions to the impossible problems. Maybe you can fix them. Do not insist on fixing such problems right away. Tolerate them and probe during various negotiations.

More skilled methods and masterful means of relating to your wife

Develop the following skills:

1. Controlling the speaking voice. This is a valuable skill used by actors. Never scream, yell aggressively, or insult your wife. Never! Only speak to your wife when you are both in the same room. Speak clearly in an audible voice and pronounce your words carefully. This will avoid major problems. Read *How to Disagree Without Being Disagreeable: Getting Your Point Across with the Gentle Art of Verbal Self-Defense*

2. Listening actively. When your wife is speaking, even if it is endless, never interrupt. Look at her; look at her eyes. Ponder what she is saying. Prepare to reply. Repeat her main points so she knows you are listening. Then reply with logic and real solutions. Do not force her to agree. You can win later. Do not Use puffery or endless insulting talk. Never yell to drown her out. This will never be forgotten. Nor will it ever be forgiven. Listening is the best way to make a foundation of love.

3. Acting sexually. There are times when seduction is appropriate. For some women, who are slightly annoyed or even fiercely angry, it is often because they are asking for love. Some women may not want to ask for sexual satisfaction but that may be what they want badly. Seducing them may be correct.

A wife will often flirt with you. You must notice this and flirt back in a sexual way. Acting sexually often relieves sexual pressure and opens up a clear avenue for deep discussions.

4. Thinking respectfully. If you are not brought up to be respectful at all times, learn to do this. Show profound respect for your wife in all situations especially when other people are observing you as a married couple. Show respect even when you are enraged over something she or someone else did to set you off. She will remember when you were humiliating her or degrading her and she will never forget it nor will she ever forgive you.

5. Feeling love and admiration. Show that you admire her. Tell her that you love her and admire her. Do not assume she knows you love and admire her. Plan ahead of time to show love and admiration of her in the company of other people. This is extremely valuable to her; more valuable than jewels.

6. Show honesty and integrity. Examine yourself for unethical or criminal intent. If you are tempted to lie, cheat, steal and so on, notice that you are about to fall into these disasters. She only has to catch you once or even to suspect once that you lack honesty to always and forever suspect you. She may have intuition or other means to know you are acting against your principle of honesty. Years of careful honesty and building up a persona of integrity can be destroyed in her mind by one act of dishonesty. This is true for anyone you know who observes an act of dishonesty.

7. Consider your wife's feelings and needs. You have built up an inventory of knowledge of what your wife needs in any situation. Give it to her. Do not neglect her. You know from experience what your wife will feel in a given situation or when she hears insults or praise. Do not hurt

her feelings. If you know her feelings are hurt, console her. This consideration is a basic rule for dealing with all people.

8. Remember to feel love for your wife. You can make a habit of loving your wife. Then your first feeling when you are with her is love. This will solve many problems. Your response will be tempered by love. Then you will not violate some of the advice above. Also she will know you are always feeling love for her. It will give her confidence.

9. Give something in return when you take something. When your wife gives you anything, even if it is a trifle, give something in return. This is a basic rule of interacting with people

Unskilled thinking of ordinary people would degrade and hinder your married life were you to think and act ordinarily

1. Doubting the truth and believing lies.
2. Hate, anger, irritation and bitchiness.
3. Laziness, sloth and doing nothing.
4. Greed, jealousy and lust may feel good but ruin your relations with your wife.
5. Hurrying up, worrying, anxiety, rushing about in wasted busy-ness.

Examine your thinking and feelings. When you realize you are unskilled, change your thinking and feelings.

Legal problems and real problems of family formation

There is emphasis on the legal web of marriage in American culture. There is a separate specialty court in each state that deals with Family Relations. The number of relations and the complexity of settling them is a whole subset of the law profession. This should set off the alarms in your head.

It is appropriate to investigate some of the details of the procedure of becoming legally married. Hire a lawyer or read some law books on the legal responsibilities of marriage.

While you are researching, answer the questions:

Why does the government care if you get married or not?

What makes the marriage legal?

Why should you want a legal marriage?

How can a prenuptial agreement and other agreements benefit the married partners?

Why does the government interfere with your children?

What are the legal responsibilities of parents?

What are the normal operating methods of the courts and the lawyers?

After you answer these questions, you will be shocked at the heartless laws. The laws are written with an extreme bias to reward the wife.

Here are some symptoms of the sick family court system. No one smiles in a courthouse. Everyone complains and feels cheated, even the lawyers. The courts are full of uniformed people who are suspicious of you and watch your every move with malicious intent. No one agrees on anything, thus they argue endlessly. Unfair and illegal acts are routine among the lawyers, judges and court staff. Legal procedures are very expensive.

Other legal aspects of marriage are the tax laws. If you are so inflexible that you get a divorce, you have to pay your ex-wife. This could mean you have to give her half of everything you bought and also you have to pay for raising your children who you may rarely see.

You may even have to pay alimony. After she spends the child support money on a vacation for herself while the children are in childcare, she does not have to prove she spent the money on the children.

You have to pay the taxes due on all these payments. All this income for her is tax free. See the Tax Code of the IRS. The IRS is another institution where no one smiles.

If this chapter is successful, you are now thinking with our feet on the ground and you are protecting yourself. The way you protect yourself is to use the methods in this book to select the correct woman and to create the best possible relationship. Then pursue your wife and attract her to you.

Read some of the recommended books.

Appendix A:
References in the Text and
Recommended Books to Study

The books are listed in alphabetical order of author's last name. Many of the subjects are covered by several books. Read, study, and practice as many books as possible. You direct your own study. You decide how much mastery to gain over the vital activity of dating. You cannot learn this in college.

Shido of Sukhavati (2012). *The Art and Science of Dating: Use These Suggestions, Methods, and Tools to Get the Relationship with the Man You Want,* Bloomington, IN: iUniverse.

Ackerman, D. (1991). *A Natural History of the Senses,* New York: Random House.

Do you have doubts that all her senses are giving you attention?

Do you want to be able to consciously use all your attractions to seduce her?

This book goes into immense detail about the smell, touch, taste, hearing, vision and even the mental fantasies. The art of kissing will open your mouth to explore. The relationship of sex with food is clearly explained so you can use both sex and food to enjoy your date more. Experiments in touching are suggested. You will be eager to pursue a date so you can try out all the new ways to relish the difference between men and women.

Adams, J. (2005). *Boundary Issues: Using Boundary Intelligence to Get the Intimacy You Want and the Independence You Need in Life, Love, and Work,* Hoboken New Jersey: Wiley.

Does someone violate your space?

Do you know when your lover has gone too far?

How can you be married and still be an individual?

This book gives assistance and wise counsel about being separate and connected, intimate as well as autonomous. Understanding and respecting your own boundaries and is at the core of a happy life. This book is a terrific journey into your own psychological needs, strengths, and weaknesses.

Amodeo, John (2001). *The Authentic Heart: An Eightfold Path to Midlife Love,* Hoboken, New Jersey: Wiley.

Are you ready for deep lasting love? Do you want to learn to open your heart to another person? Are you afraid love has passed you by?

So you are ready to learn what you must? The richest, most fulfilling love of your life is yet to come!

This book is full of practical wisdom. Authentic love takes time and maturity. At midlife, you hold the extraordinary potential to become more fully awake and alive in your relationships than ever before.

Barill, M. (1996). *The Wedding Source Book,* Los Angeles: Lowell House.

A serious assortment of wedding concepts.

Bien, T. and Bien, B. (2003). *Finding the Center Within: The Healing Way of Mindfulness Meditation,* Hoboken, New Jersey: Wiley.

Are you too nervous to have a good relationship? Does your worrying interfere with having a relaxing time with friends? Does your friend meditate but you do not? Would you be a better lover is you could understand why meditation means so much to your friend? Do you need better control of your feelings like anger, lust, andjealousy?

This book is a practical manual on the practice of mindfulness, which can help many people to embody their Buddha nature and become radiant and peaceful beings. It provides easy steps for practicing mindfulness in day-to-day living.

You may want to live a calmer, more peaceful existence. This book teaches that if you find the quiet void within yourself, then through self examination, you will have the capacity to live deeply and fully. You will have the possibility of boundless peace and happiness in any circumstance.

This book exposes an eleven week program for overcoming the qualities of our personalities that prevent us from actualizing our wise inner self. The book combines Eastern spiritual wisdom with the pragmatic wisdom of Western psychology, teaching us how to remove the habitual thinking that conceals who and what we really are.

The book provides the tools needed to:

Find a path to the center through mindfulness.

Bring meditation into everyday life.

Work with and transform negative emotions.

Cultivate healthy, healing relationships.

Blum, M., Kaiser, L. F. (2004). *Wedding Planning for Dummies,* 2nd Ed., Hoboken, New Jersey: Wiley.

Do you want to learn about the details of weddings? Are you about to get married and need to know a lot? Do you want to reduce stress of wedding?

This book features helpful planning forms and checklists Plan your dream wedding on a budget. This friendly guide gives you all the help you need to plan and enjoy a memorable, hassle-free ceremony and reception. You get tips on everything from setting the date and selecting the invitations to keeping track of gifts, guests, and thank you notes.

Discover how to: Get the most for your money Personalize your celebration. Handle tricky family dynamics. Hire caterers, florists, and photographers. Plan the perfect honeymoon.

Bodian, S. (2006). *Meditation for Dummies,* 2nd Ed., Hoboken, New Jersey: Wiley.

Does your friend practice mediation? Would you feel closer to your lover if you could meditate together?

Millions of Americans now practice meditation regularly. It's a great way to reduce stress, increase energy, and enjoy better health. This fun and easy guide is particularly good for meditation newcomers.

Guided meditations are keyed to topics in the book:

tuning in to one's body,

transforming suffering, and replacing negative patterns,

examining you thoughts,

finding a peaceful place.

Boothman, N. (2008). *How to make people like you in 90 seconds or less,* New York: Workman Press.

This is a short book that you can fit in your pocket. Then you can pull it out and try out the movements and phrases that open people up right way to be friendly. When you read the book, you know immediately that the suggestions will work.

Would you like a new group of friends?

Have you logically thought of the benefits of connecting with other people?

Do you know how to make a good first impression?

Why does likability work? What is rapport?

What is a really useful attitude? A useless attitude?

Do actions speak louder than words? Why is listening so important? Does listening speak louder than words? Where would you like to have fun?

Branden, N. (2008). *The Psychology of Romantic Love: Romantic Love in an Anti-Romantic Age,* New York: Jeremy P. Tarcher/Penguin.

What is love? Why is love born? Why does love grow? Why does love die?

How much do you know about love?

There are a lot of untrue beliefs about love. How many of them do you hold? It is vitally important to have a deep understanding of love. Then you can be loved and give love.

This book reveals insights into love and the cultural effects of love. The explanations are unique; not found elsewhere.

The evolution of romantic love.

The roots of romantic love.

Choice in Romantic love.

The Challenges of Romantic love.

Browne, J. (2013). *Dating For Dummies over 50,* Hoboken, New Jersey: Wiley.

Have you forgotten what do you say on a date? How do you talk to a stranger? What questions would you ask on a first date?

There millions of adult singles in the USA. Many are divorced or older than 50 years. This book informs about internet dating services, and singles nights at grocery stores and other unexpected places. It gives advice on dating someone who has been married, someone with kids, or someone who is significantly older or younger.

Carnegie, Dale (1998). *How to Win Friends and Influence People,* New York: Pocket Books imprint of Simon & Schuster.

First published in 1936, this book initiated the self-help industry. Hundreds of millions of people have learned the methods to win friends and influence people. A few of the many major lessons you can learn:
* Three fundamental techniques in handling people
* The six ways to make people like you
* The twelve ways to win people to you way of thinking
* The nine ways to change people without arousing resentment

Carter, L. (2004). *The Anger Trap: Free Yourself from the Frustrations that Sabotage Your Life,* Hoboken New Jersey: Jossey-Bass imprint of Wiley.

Are you tired of anger, rage, irritation, destroying your friendships? Do you want the tranquility of choosing to remain calm when events are stirring you up? Can you control your anger? Have you lost friends because your rage? Are you tired of your anger controlling your life?

Chopra, Deekpak (1994). *The Seven Spiritual Laws of Success: A Practical Guide to the Fulfillment of Your Dreams,* San Rafael, CA: Amber-Allen.

What are the laws of success that you invented?
What is the law of pure potentiality?
Can you receive if you do not give?
What is the Law of Giving?
Have you suspected that are results from your actions?
What is the law of Karma or Cause and Effect?
Where is there a fair chance? Why do you suffer?
What is the Law of Least Effort?
What are the Laws of Intention and Desire?
What is the Law of Detachment?
What is the Law of Dharma or Purpose in Life?

There are natural laws that cannot be violated. Man made laws can be broken. You can learn the unbreakable laws that will help you.

Chopra, Deepak (2006). The *Kama Sutra including the Seven Spiritual Laws of Love*, London: Virgin Books.

Covey, S. R. (2013). *The Seven Habits of Highly Effective People: Powerful Lessons in Personal Change,* New York: Simon & Schuster.

If you realize that true success encompasses a balance of personal and professional effectiveness, then this book is a manual for performing better in both arenas.

Before you can adopt the seven habits, you'll need to accomplish a change in perception and interpretation of how the world works. This book leads you to improve the way you perceive and act regarding productivity, time management, positive thinking. As you can imagine, the lessons are difficult because you are changing your basic views.

Demasio, A. (2005). *Descartes' Error:' Emotion, Reason, and the Human Brain*, New York: Avon imprint of HarperCollins.

Since Descartes famously proclaimed, "I think, therefore I am," science has often overlooked emotions as the source of a person's true being. Even modern neuroscience has tended, until recently, to concentrate on the cognitive aspects of brain function, disregarding emotions. Demasio takes the reader on a journey of scientific discovery through a series of case studies, demonstrating what many of us have long suspected: emotions are not a luxury, they are essential to rational thinking and to normal social behavior.

Downing, George (1998). *The Massage Book: 25th Anniversary Edition*, New York: Random House.

Elgin, S. H. (1997). *How to Disagree Without Being Disagreeable: Getting Your Point Across with the Gentle Art of Verbal Self-Defense*, Hoboken, New Jersey: Wiley.

Do you know how to negotiate? Can you convince someone to agree with you?

This book gives you the opportunity to learn how to respond clearly to hostile comments from others. You can learn how to deliver necessary negative messages of your own. You could learn how to keep your dignity and principles. You could learn to keep domestic disagreements from escalating. You could handle aggressive, negative comments. If you make the effort, you can learn these valuable skills and many more.

Engel, B. (2001). *The Power of Apology: Healing Steps to Transform All Your Relationships*, Hoboken, New Jersey: Wiley.

Are you ready to stop arguing? Do you want to know how to cure a disagreement? Did you make a mistake? Are you covering up a screw up?

Learning these skills is difficult. Can you learn something that is really hard?

Are you ready to discover the healing power of apology and put its magic to work in your life? This book could teach you why some people have difficulty apologizing while others tend to over-apologize, how to ask for an apology, and how to receive one. You could learn how to make amends with those you have hurt. You could begin to deal with someone who refuses to apologize.

This book shows you how to bring a healing new element of renewal into every relationship in your life. You can renew relationships if you make the effort.

Fromm, E. (1956). *The Art of Loving, New York:* Harper & Row.

This is the authority on all types of love. If you want to have a chance at love, read this and make it a part of your way of thinking. You will probably not have a good loving experience until you understand the basics of love. You must know all types of love. It is not likely that you have learned much about love because our society has built up a lot of delusions and lies about love. Get to the root of love. Many people believe that love is the basic reason for living.

Fromm, E. (1990). *The Sane Society,* New York: Owl.

Are America and Europe generating a sick and massive mental health disorder? What are the symptoms of a sick country? War, alcoholism, drug addiction, suicide, and family destruction are symptoms of massive insanity.

Gaylin, W. (1979). *Feelings: Our Vital Signs,* New York: Ballantine imprint of Random House.

You live in a sea of feelings: your own and the feelings of others. The fuel for life and emotion is Chi, psychic energy. You know you are alive because your feelings drive you. You want to avoid pain and to enjoy pleasure. You are seeking experiences to give you different feelings. This book explains how to use your feelings.

Gendreau, G., Peyser, R., Gentille, F., Arnold, C. (2010). *The Marriage of Sex and Spirit,* Santa Rosa, CA: Elite.

Human love relationships are one of the most fertile grounds for growth and transformation. They are also filled with difficulty, frustration and pain. The combination of sex and spiritual needs is like a theater for us to examine our addictions and wounds. This is the underlying value of relationships. If you use marriage to transform yourself, it can be a fast track to spiritual and sexual transformation.

Gilbert, R. M. (1998). *Extraordinary Relationships: A New Way of Thinking About Human Interactions*, Hoboken, New Jersey: Wiley.

Are you ready for a really excellent relationship? Can you focus on changing yourself and your friendships? Do you want an extraordinary relationship?

This book explains a new way of thinking about human interactions. It proposes a method to turn any relationship into and extraordinary relationship.

You may agree that, after food, water, and shelter, relationships are the most important factors in determining your quality of life. At work, productivity and efficiency depend on relationships. At home, relationships with your spouse, children, and friends are keys to success and happiness. And among nations, relationships start and stop wars.

This guide shows that only by further developing yourself can you further develop your relationships. It is a guide to better relationships that include intimate relationships, friendships, family relationships, single life, workplace relationships, international relationships, and your relationship with yourself.

Glass, L. (2003). *I Know What You're Thinking: Using the Four Codes of Reading People to Improve Your Life*, Hoboken, New Jersey: Wiley.

Have you ever noticed that her words did not seem to say what her posture was expressing? Like talking cheerfully and looking depressed.

The body, hands, posture, and head movement are usually more sincere and truthful than the words. So you have to observe her body, facial expression, and words to get the whole message.

Do you think she is lying because she will not look you in the eyes? How will you know if you understand her feelings? Would you like to know the whole story your lover is telling? Then you could ask sympathetic questions. You would be in close rapport with her feelings.

Consider this condition, she is laughing and sitting rigidly upright but she is telling you that her mother just died. You feel edgy. Something is confusing you. To be sure, you need to learn how to read her body in addition to her words.

How does the judge know when a witness is lying? Have you ever been court and asked yourself this question?

When you watch a movie, do the actors say the words that communicate what their bodies project?

Here are some skills you may learn from this book. You could know how to read people based on their words and their bodily actions. You could interpret their hidden cues. You could be more perceptive. When your words, your face and your body all show the same meaning, you could be more successful at dating.

Glocheux, D. (2004). *La Vie en Rose: The Little Book of Joy,* Berkeley, CA: Ten-speed-Press imprint of Crown.

Read this just before you go into a group or a serious affair. You will be in a tolerant mood. Paris in Spring time is unique. April in Paris, is miraculous. Learn to be joyful through this book.

Do you think you have a problem making friends? Then change the way you think about it.

If you perceived everything as though it were a rose, your point of view would change your relationship with your spouse.

Dominique Glocheux's life as a powerful Parisian businessman changed dramatically when he was struck by a taxi while walking along the Champs-Elysées in 1987. After spending four months in a coma, the author awoke to see the world in a new and inspiring light. Glocheux shares his powerful message of personal fulfillment and happiness in *La Vie en Rose*, an invigorating perspective on the challenges and rewards of everyday life; from believing in the magic of love at first sight to stargazing on a gorgeous night to letting go of trying to change the unchangeable.

Grandin, T. and Johnson, C. (2005). *Animals in Translation,* New York: Scribner.

If you want to understand body language and the subtleties of communication, read this book about understanding how animals talk.

Venture, J., Reed, M. (2005). *Divorce for Dummies,* 2nd Ed., Hoboken, New Jersey: Wiley.

What if you cannot stay married? Do you want a nice divorce or an expensive disaster that wears you down and ruins your life?

This book tells you how to cut legal costs and even how to cope emotionally. You can get through divorce proceedings and all the legal, financial, and personal stress. Divorce doesn't have to be about winners, losers, and huge legal bills. This book is filled with practical advice. This friendly guide demystifies the process. It explains family, divorce, and bankruptcy laws and current child support trends in plain English.

You could learn how to negotiate terms, avoid costly mistakes, cope with your emotions, find support and move on with your life. Discover how to assess whether you're ready for divorce. Understand your legal rights. Cut costs by negotiating terms yourself. Find and work with an attorney. Avoid going to trial. Help your kids get through it.

Gray, J. (1992). *Men are from Mars, Women are from Venus: A Practical Guide for Improving Communication and Getting What You Want in Your Relationships,* New York: HarperCollins.

Do some women seem to be on another planet?

Do you wonder if both of you are speaking the same language?

This book explains all the differences between men and women. There are several books by Gray dealing with several issues that commonly come up between even the best of lovers. Look for them.

Guilmartin, N., (2010). *Healing Conversations: What to Say When You Don't Know What to Say,* Hoboken, New Jersey: Wiley.

Do you want to know how to speak about difficult topics? Would you like to help your lover by talking thru difficult moments?

This book could help your intimate relationships.

Painful moments require accurate speech. You may face uncomfortable situations where you are at a loss for words. Can you learn to cope? What would be useful? What kinds of boundaries do you respect? How could you pause to listen to comfort someone who is afraid or in pain? Can we ask for what would comfort us when we are the one having a rough time? And are we able to receive it with grace?

This book addresses these tough situations

Hagen, S. (2010). *The Everything Groom Book: A Survival Guide for Men!,* Avon, MA: Adams Media.

Hall, K. (2004). *Reclaiming Your Sexual Self: How You Can Bring Desire Back Into Your Life,* Hoboken, New Jersey: Wiley.

Are you jaded by too much sexual exposure? Do you feel your sex life is dead? Are you ready to learn to raise your sexual pleasure?

At last, a drug-free, holistic program to restore sexual passion and desire. Lack of sexual desire does not necessarily indicate a hormonal problem. It may mean that something is out of balance in your live. This book explores ways to improve communication with your partner. The right conditions and circumstances to spark your sexual interest. How to maintain a vital sexual connection for the long term.

Heart, M. (1998). *When the Earth Moves: Women and Orgasm, Berkeley, CA:* Tenspeed Press Celestial Arts imprint.

If you cultivate your sexual relationship with your woman, she could have 6 or 12 orgasms while you have one. Does that seem like a thrilling sexual partner?

It is alright for your woman to admit her desire for lusty satisfaction. Men should realize that some women often feel embarrassed or uncomfortable when enjoying their body's possibilities. It is not right or wrong, good or bad, normal or abnormal. It is her blooming into full womanhood.

Study this book with her. Then get the other books relating to sex, like Kama Sutra, in this recommended list. You can communicate what you learn when you seduce your lover with the combined information.

Help her to experience being the extraordinary sexual vixen who has been hiding within her. Take the first and most important steps toward ensuring her sensual fulfillment by using this book. Your lover will be delighted to be a part of the thrills you bring to her. And she will love you all the more. She will seduce you again as soon as he can. Because she will think she has become the most skilled lover in the world. It is worth the time to memorize the many lessons in this book.

Your woman can learn to have deep orgasms that are electrical, coming in waves and ending in fulfillment.

Find out why some women have difficulty having one. When might she fake them and why? Redefine the word, 'erotic'. Experience the thrill of her multiple orgasms.

Hedva, B., *Betrayal, Trust, and Forgiveness: A Guide to Emotional Healing and Self-Renewal,* Berkeley, CA: Tenspeed Press.
This book reveals positive methods for healing emotional suffering.
The infidelities of a romantic partner.
Harsh words of a parent.
The failings of an aging body.
The devastation of a lost job.
The bigotry and prejudices of society.
All of these experiences are betrayals that encourage negative feelings of separation, alienation, and emotional distance. *Betrayal, Trust, and Forgiveness* is a thoughtful guide to resolving these conflicts and overcoming feelings of disappointment and injury.

Heumann, S., *Everything Kama Sutra.*

Hill, N. (1960). *Think and Grow Rich,* New York: Fawcett Crest imprint of Ballantine Books.
This is book that launched millions of people into wealthy lives. You can also grow wise or grow enlightened using the clearly stated 13 steps.

Hill, N. and Stone, W. C. (1977). *Success through a Positive Mental Attitude,* New York: Pocket Books imprint of Simon & Schuster.
This self improvement book has been a best seller since 1960. If you want to raise enthusiasm, ask someone to read this book.

Hemmings, J. (2005). *Be Your Own Dating Coach: Treat yourself to the ultimate relationship makeover,* Hoboken, New Jersey: Wiley.

Are you ready to stop making mistakes on dates? Are you ready to take the time to learn how to relate on a date? Do you want to have satisfying dates, not trouble and shame? Ever wondered why you make the same dating mistakes time after time? Do you rarely get beyond the first or second date? Do you yearn for a long-term relationship but find yourself drifting from relationship to relationship? Or do you feel trapped when you really just want to have fun?

Hooper, A., *Anne Hooper's Kama Sutra.*

Hooper, A., *K.I.S.S. Guide to the Kama Sutra.*

Jampolsky, G. (2004). *Love Is Letting Go of Fear,* Berkeley, CA: Ten-speed-Press imprint Crown

LOVE IS DEFINED IN THIS BOOK.

If you need it, you can learn to be loving while you study this book. Based on material from *A COURSE IN MIRACLES,* this book teaches how to let go of fear and how to remember that our very essence is love. Included are daily exercises that give a direct and effective method to bring about individual transformation. This simple life-affirming book will provide you with a lot of comfort.

Jampolsky, G. G. and Cirincione, D. V. (2004). *Simple Thoughts That Can Change Your Life,* Berkeley, CA: Ten-speed-Press imprint of Crown.

In the book, *Think and Grow Rich* is the following basic truth. If you can think it, and you can believe it, you can achieve it. The dominating thoughts of your mind have a tendency to change into physical reality.

We are what we think. Our thoughts determine what we see and what we experience. Perhaps the biggest gift that we have been given by God is the power to determine what thoughts we put into our minds. One simple thought can change how we look at the world, ourselves, and each other. One simple thought can totally change our lives.

Kaplan, B. (1996). *Winning People Over: 14 Days to Power and Confidence,* Englewood Cliffs, New Jersey, Prentice Hall.

This book gives you a hundred lessons that you will want to learn if you do not know them already. Now you can become the master of any situation: get people to enthusiastically follow you and control events to come out the way you want.

This book is a valuable treasury of workable tools and practical, step-by-step techniques for Winning People Over. This motivating 14-day program shows you how to take complete command of the people, events, and circumstances that shape your life and career. Day by day, this exciting guide provides revealing self-tests, easy-to-do exercises, and step-by-step plans you can implement right now to help you with the following:

overcome the fear of failure,

neutralize difficult people,

clarify your goals,

rebuild damaged relationships,

and win instant acceptance for your ideas,

recognize and overcome your worst enemy,

use office politics to get ahead,

eliminate the bad habits that silently rob you of success.

take control of your business and personal relationships,

generate the energy you need to make your dreams come true,

win instant acceptance for your ideas,

prevent job stress from draining your power,

get the dream promotion you've wanted,

persuade your boss to help manage bad situations to come out a winner,

get ahead without getting stabbed in the back.

Kemp, E. A. and Kemp, J. E., *Older Couples: New Romances: Finding and Keeping Love in Later Life,* Berkeley, CA: Tenspeed Press Celestial Arts imprint.

You're only old once; make the most of it.

You have knowledge based on long experience. You are better at love now. You could live to be ninety years old. Continue to improve.

Edith and Jerrold Kemp started dating when she was 66 and he was 75. They courted, they married, and now they've collaborated on a new book that challenges stereotypes about aging and intimacy.

This book discusses on the sexual, financial, legal, and religious issues faced by single, divorced, or widowed seniors.

Kennedy, K. (2000). *Priceless Weddings for Under $5000,* New York: Three Rivers Press.

Weddings are expected to be expensive, way too expensive, expensive enough to cause major conflicts between families and between those getting married. This book can help you to solve these problems.

King, L. (1994). *How to Talk to Anyone, Anytime, Anywhere: The Secrets of Good Communication,* New York: Crown.

Kolbaba, G. (2004). *Dazzled, Frazzled & Back Again: The Bride's Survival Guide,*
Grand Rapids, MI: Fleming H Revell.

Kuriansky, J., *Complete Idiot's Guide to Tantric Sex*.

Lacroix, Nitya, *Kama Sutra*.

Larson, J. H. (2002). *The Great Marriage Tune-Up Book: A Proven Program for Evaluating and Renewing Your Relationship*, Hoboken, New Jersey: Wiley/Jossey-Bass.

Is your marriage mature enough to improve? Are you ready to learn how to work toward a richer marriage? Are both husband and wife ready to focus on the work of a mature and satisfying marriage?

All serious couples reach a point where they feel frustrated, stuck, bored, disillusioned, and misunderstood. This book gives you quizzes, self-tests, and personal assessments. You discover why you're feeling the need to improve. You explain the underlying issues. You find solutions to specific issues and problems.

Lavington, C. (1997). *You've Only Got Three Seconds; How to Make the Right Impression in Your Business and Social Life*, New York: Doubleday.

Lecroix, Nitya, *The Art of Tantric Sex*.

Lidell, L., Beresford-Cooke, C., Porter, A., Thomas, S. (2001). *The Book of Massage: The Complete Step-by-Step Guide to Eastern and Western Technique*, New York: Fireside.

Livers, E. (1999). *The Unofficial Guide to Planning Your Wedding*, Hoboken, New Jersey: Wiley.

Are you in the dark about weddings? Do you want to learn how to have a reasonably priced wedding? Do you want to learn how to remove stress from the wedding?

Readers want a unique wedding, but they can't afford to spend that kind of money. They want to please their families, but not at the expense of pleasing themselves. They have questions upon questions, but they don't want a rehash of the same old information. This book gives advice from brides who have been there.

Luciani, J. J. (2004). *The Power of Self-Coaching: The Five Essential Steps to Creating the Life You Want*, Hoboken, New Jersey: Wiley.

The way to learn enough to find your best woman and to find out if she is the best possible woman for you is continuous and never-ending improvement. This is self coaching.

Are you ready to grow into a greater life? Would you like to discover your limits and rise above them?

This book discloses a program for freeing yourself from your mental and emotional traps. Then you can lead the life you want and deserve.

There is nothing more empowering than accepting responsibility for our own future excellence. This book will help you navigate through the difficulties of personality and behavioral change to more emotional peace.

Mandell, T. (1996). *Power Schmoozing: The New Etiquette for Social and Business Success*, New York: McGraw-Hill.

Protecting and enhancing Your Love Life.

Markman, H. J., Stanley, S. M., Jenkins, N. H., Blumberg, S. L. (2003). *12 Hours to a Great Marriage: A Step-by-Step Guide for Making Love Last,* Hoboken, New Jersey, Wiley/Jossey-Bass.

Mallanaga Vatsyayana (2003). *Kama Sutra of Vatsyayana,* Wendy Doniger, Sudhir Kakar, trans., New York: Oxford University Press

There are dozens of versions of this book. The classic English version was edited by the British Army Officer Sir Richard Burton. The title translates as "lust lesson." This book was written hundreds of years ago. It remains the most authoritative book on the pleasures of sexual union.

Although sexual material is found everywhere in the American culture, it is primitive. When you read this book you will understand how limited the vast majority of Americans remain if measured by sexual technique. Americans also are limited in knowledge of the many levels of being involved in the sexual play. You can try out the many forms of love with your partner. As an introduction to mature and fulfilled alliance of lovers, this is the best.

The Kama Sutra is the oldest existing textbook of erotic love. But it is more than a book about sex. It is about the art of living--about finding a partner, maintaining power in a marriage, committing adultery, living as or with a courtesan, using drugs--and also, of course, about the many and varied positions available to lovers in sexual intercourse and the pleasures to be derived from each. The Kama Sutra was composed in Sanskrit, the literary language of ancient India, sometime in the third century, probably in North India. It combines an encyclopedic coverage of all imaginable aspects of sex with a closely observed sexual psychology and a dramatic, novelistic narrative of seduction, consummation, and disentanglement. Best known in English through the highly mannered, padded, and inaccurate nineteenth-century translation by Sir Richard Burton, the text is newly translated here into clear, vivid, sexually frank English. This edition also includes a section of vivid Indian color illustrations along with three uniquely important commentaries: translated excerpts from the earliest and most famous Sanskrit commentary (thirteenth century) and from a twentieth-century Hindi commentary, and explanatory notes by the two translators. Use it as a manual.

Mandel, B. (1989). *Heart over Heels: 50 Ways Not to Leave Your Lover,* Berkeley, CA: Tenspeed Press Celestial Arts.

When the honeymoon is over, the power struggle begins.

Many people fail at relationships simply because they do not have the habit of succeeding. Here are 50 ways to stay in a relationship and help it to grow and to flourish.

Martin, J. (1997). *Miss Manners' Basic Training on Communication,* New York: Crown.

This is another classic manual on how to do things and say things so you do not hurt someone's feelings. This reveals how to show the proper respect within your position in the hierarchy.

Martin, J. (1982). *Miss Manners' Guide to Excruciatingly Correct Behavior,* New York: Atheneum.

Martin, J. (1999). *Miss Manners' on Weddings,* New York: Crown.

The wedding itself is a few hours, but the preparation is a few months of trouble. Study this book to reduce the trouble.

Metrick, S. B. (2009). *I Do: A Guide to Creating Your Own Unique Wedding Ceremony,* Berkeley, CA: Tenspeed Press Celestial Arts imprint.

How many different wedding ceremonies can you invent? You can make the promises you want to make not those your mother wants. Planning a wedding can be an emotional and logistical nightmare, especially if you want your ceremony to be as unique as you are. Well, forget about the three-tiered cake and make your special day a walk down the aisle less traveled. Use this book, a creative, accessible guide to designing unique marriage ceremonies.

Beginning with an explanation of traditional wedding elements, the bridal veil, the exchange of rings, the cake, the vows, This book offers inspired wedding alternatives drawn from ancient Greece and Persia, pagan Europe, and Elizabethan England, among other traditions. Planning guides include sample ceremonies and instructions for personalizing them. Not your typical bridal bliss guide, this wedding primer seriously considers the symbolic as well as the practical.

O'Connor, B. (2001). *Living Happily Ever After: Putting Reality into Your Romance (Family Matters)*, Hoboken, New Jersey: Wiley.

Do you know what long term love is? Has the thrill of first love or marriage worn off? Are you ready to learn how to make love last? Will you put in the work to have a fulfilling marriage?

Most people want to believe that being together and loving each other are all that's needed to live happily ever after. If you understand what really loving each other means, it can be all you need. But first you must understand what love is. Then make it happen.

This book shows how problems with sex, money, household chores and child raising are often caused by the need for power and control. This book incorporates a series of self-assessment and things to talk about such as:

Am I still in love with my partner?

Giving and getting Sexuality and sexual preferences

What do you want from the relationship?

Is there really a way to solve your problems?

By learning more about your own needs and desires and those of your partner, you will be able to help each other change and develop as your lives unfold.

Page, S. (2006). *Why Talking Is Not Enough: 8 Loving Actions That Will Transform Your Marriage,* Hoboken, New Jersey:Wiley/Jossey-Bass.

How would you act if you had the marriage you want? Are you ready to learn to improve your relationship? What are you willing to do to have a satisfying friendship with your wife? Could you preserve your family if you knew how to converse?

This book goes beyond the conventional programs that focus on communication, compromise, collaboration, working through exercises. It offers a simple approach to improving relationships in our marriage and with all whom we love and care about. It suggests eight steps that could help you learn to bring resolution to tensions.

Peabody, S., Allegra, S., Adler, K. (2005). *Addiction to Love: Overcoming Obsession and Dependency in Relationships,* Berkeley, CA: Ten-speed-Press imprint of Crown.

There are five million love and sex addicts in the USA alone! Have you heard of Alcoholics Anonymous? There is also a Love and Sex Addicts Anonymous.

Love and sex are more addictive than you would ever imagine. These cravings seem to be from heaven. And the American culture has a focus on love and sex. But chasing and clinging to love and sex can ruin your life, your career, and your health!

What kind of love is as destructive as this? If you think you know something about this craving, you may think it is an illness. Love addiction is the result of clinging to past feelings about love, sex and about the sensual experiences caused by sex. Love addiction can result from impossible expectations about what love can do for you. Have you been going from one love affair to another without satisfaction? Perhaps your addiction has resulted in disgust and aversion to sexual contact.

The greatest problem with sex addiction is that it is advertised as a good pursuit by the news, TV shows, movies, and novels. So it seems acceptable. But if it is ruining your life, sexual preoccupation does not seem acceptable.

If you think you already know everything about this disorder, you need to read this book. Right away! You can recover from sex and love addiction.

The book brings fresh insights. In everyday language, they explain the addiction to fatal-attraction. They explain the Casanova type. They describe the person who is trapped in an "I-hate-you-don't-leave-me" relationship. They reveal the love addict who breaks the law in the name of love--the kind of love addict you read about in the newspaper. What kind of symptoms do you have?

Did you know that even relationships with parents, children, siblings, or friends may be addictive? This kind of dependency is not always related to romantic love.

In this book, there is an in-depth and easy-to-follow recovery program for those suffering from this often dangerous addiction. There is even a 12 step program, Love and Sex Addicts Anonymous. Look in the phone book. But in any case, get this book and do what it says. You can create a loving and fulfilling relationship in place of an addictive one.

Love addiction manifests in many forms; obsessive lust to less extreme but nonetheless psychologically and emotionally harmful forms. The most common of these is staying in a bad relationship because of a fear of being alone. In this book, recovering love addict Susan Peabody explains the variety of ways this disorder plays out, from the obsessively doting love addict to the addict who can't disentangle from an unfulfilling, dead-end relationship. Peabody provides an in-depth and easy-to-follow recovery program for those suffering from this unhealthy and often dangerous addiction and explains how to create a loving, safe, and fulfilling relationship.

Peale, N. V. (1952). *The Power of Positive Thinking*, New York: Fawcett Books

It brought the concept of positive thinking into the American mainstream in 1952.

Post, P., Post, A., Post, L., Senning, D. P. (2011). *Emily Post's Etiquette*, 18th ed., New York: HarperCollins.

This is a classic manual on how to do things and say things so you do not hurt someone's feelings. This book reveals how to show the proper respect.

Potter-Efron, R. and Potter-Efron, P. (2006). *Reclaim Your Relationship: A Workbook of Exercises and Techniques to Help You Reconnect with Your Partner*, Hoboken, New Jersey: Wiley.

Is your marriage on the rocks? Have you had a big fight? And you need to make up?

Simple answer: show love in your words and actions. This book could teach you how to reclaim your relationships. The basic question is, "Are you and your friend willing to really work on making a wonderful relationship?"

Get this book and start the climb back.

You could also begin by saying, "I love you" several times each day.

Say, "I love you" when you hang up the phone. What do you say after "I love you"? Simple answer: Open yourself to receive love, accept love, and believe you are loved. This book has exercises to help you learn to feel your partner's love.

If you are having trouble squeezing out, "I love you," maybe that is part of your relationship trouble. You have a lot invested in this relationship. Put in more effort and get the payoff, long term love.

The simple phrase "I love you" is terribly important to people. This book may explain what keeps you or your mate from saying it?

Ray, Sondra, *Loving Relationships II*, Berkeley, CA: Tenspeed Press imprint Celestial Arts

A woman's story of creating a suitable relationship.

Reynolds, S. Kostecki, J. (2005). *Better Than Chocolate: 50 Proven Ways to Feel Happier*, Berkeley, CA: Tenspeed Press.

TESTS HAVE PROVEN THAT HAPPY PEOPLE LOOK MORE BEAUTIFUL AND HAVE MORE DATES

What could possibly be better than chocolate? How about good health, self-acceptance, loving relationships, freedom from fear and guilt, and a clear sense of purpose in life?

Understand Buddhist theory (fewer desires leads to less suffering). Kiss someone (kissing just feels great). Animated with cheery illustrations, this book is sweeter than a candy bar baked into a brownie and dipped in hot fudge.

RoAne, S. (1992). *How to Work a Room: A Guide to Successfully Managing the Mingling*, New York: Grand Central Publishing.

RoAne, S. (1999). *What Do I Say Next? Talking Your Way to Business and Social Success*, New York: Grand Central Publishing.

Roskind, R. (2004). *In the Spirit of Marriage: Creating and Sustaining Loving Relationships,* Berkeley, CA: Tenspeed Press.

Do you want to take your marriage to a higher level of commitment? This book explains how to overcome your fears, how to accept your partner's differences, how to forgive the hurts that creep into long-term relationships. This book intends to teach you how to avoid the emotional pitfalls that can stall, hang up, or destroy your relationship. Do you need to know how to get loving respect, maybe even everlasting joy? The book features practical guidance for old relationships and new ones.

Salmansohn, K. and Zinzell, D. (2001). *How to Be Happy, Dammit: A Cynic's Guide to Spiritual Happiness,* Berkeley, CA: Tenspeed Press.

Reading about happiness could enable you to feel better. It cannot guarantee to perk up even the most cynical spirit. This book the merges psychology, biology, eastern and western philosophies, and quantum physics. Peek within its colorful, uniquely designed pages, and you really will find pearls of wisdom to help you discover more satisfaction every day. And you'll find no saccharine sweetness here. This book tells it like it is, exploring the ups and downs of life in a straightforward, thought-provoking, and humorous way.

Sarita, Ma, *Tantric Love.*

Satir, V. (2011). *Making Contact,* Berkeley, CA: Tenspeed Press Celestial Arts imprint.

DO YOU WANT TO LEARN HOW TO CONNECT WITH OTHERS?

Satir draws on years of experience and observation—and a rich understanding of human potential and interaction—to show how to better understand and use the basic tools for making contact with others. She clearly describes reliable techniques that make it possible to work for change in one's perceptions, actions, and life.

Shido of Sukhavati (2012). *The Art and Science of Dating: Use These Suggestions, Methods, and Tools to Get the Relationship with the Man You Want,* Bloomington, IN: iUniverse.

Silverstein, J. and Lasky, M. (2003). *Online Dating For Dummies,* Hoboken, New Jersey: Wiley.

Do you want a blind date? Do you want to consider hundreds of possible dates? Are you ready to learn how to look for a partner? How do you start an email to an unknown person? Can you meet right away?

This book explains online dating. You may think that meeting people via the Internet is only for the disenfranchised or socially unskilled. This book has chapters on

Overcoming preconceived notions of who is online.

Talking the online lingo.

Enjoying conversation in chat rooms.

Considering date site options.

Establishing your screen identity.

Facing the consequences of not posting a photo.

Initiate your first e-mail contact.

Make your first in-person meeting memorable.

Identify frauds and players.

Simring, S., Simring, S. K., and Busnar, G. (1999). *Making Marriage Work for Dummies,* Hoboken, New Jersey: Wiley.

Do you have the communication tools for marriage? Do you admit that you are stumped by problems of a marriage? Will you work to learn about marriage so you reap the benefits?

Marriage is one of life's biggest adventures and a healthy marriage can be one of life's greatest gifts. But weathering the stresses and strains of married life and maintaining healthy marital bonds over a span of decades takes work. Sometimes you need help from a friendly expert: this book.

This book offers chapters on:

Make your relationship more romantic.

Work out big and small differences.

Argue in ways that strengthen you relationship.

Resolve disputes over money.

Cope with mid-life change.

Handle a spouse who cheats.

Deal with families and in-laws.

Reduce stress on your marriage.

Understand your partner's annoying habits and quirks.

Balance career and family goals.

Seek professional help when you need it.

This book explores such crucial topics as:

Deciding if marriage is right for you.

Six common marriage myths.

Understanding the roots of marital problems.

Communicating with your partner.

The do's and don'ts of fair marital fighting.

Making marriage sexy.

Examining the marriage life cycle.

Ideas for resolving money differences.

Succeeding with remarriage.

Smith, L. (2003). *Depression for Dummies,* Hoboken, New Jersey: Wiley.

Is your friend depressed? Does depression ruin your love life? Do you want to understand your lover's depression? Does depression block intimacy? What do you have to be depressed about?

These are painful questions for someone suffering from the very real plight of depression. Depression is a very real problem. The number of depressed people is increasing fast. It comes with all the gadgets, the hurrying, the busyness, and all the endless opportunity that is beyond your ability to achieve. It is part of city life and modern pace of living.

So why should you read *Depression For Dummies?* Because this book satisfies the need for a straight-talking, no-nonsense resource on depression.

Sonntag, S., *Bedside Kama Sutra.*

Stanley, S. M. (2005). *The Power of Commitment: A Guide to Active, Lifelong Love,*

Hoboken, NJ: Wiley/Jossey-Bass.

Are you tired of changing partners? Would you like to learn how to have one growing love in your life? Are you ready to learn how to have a mature relationship? The answer is the Power of Commitment

What is commitment and what's so negative about it? How can we better understand and appreciate the value of commitment and make it last for a lifetime? Too often, men and women find themselves in half committed relationships that lead to frustration, sadness, and, in many cases, divorce. But it doesn't have to be this way.

This book offers a five-step plan for understanding commitment. It includes learning to handle the pressures of everyday life, moving through the pain of unfulfilled dreams and hopes, overcoming attraction to others that might endanger a marriage, transforming your thinking from "me versus you" to "we" and "us," and capturing the beauty and mystery of lifelong devotion, loyalty, teamwork, and building a lasting vision for the future.

Amazing concepts!

Sternberg, R. J. (1996). *Successful Intelligence: How Practical and Creative Intelligence Determine Success in Life,* New York: Simon & Schuster.

This book gets past the dogma that schools and colleges hang onto. They define intelligence as grades on certain tests. But this is short sighted and mostly inaccurate. This book describes the qualities that you must have to be successful in achieving your goals. Achieving goals is a basic human trait. Having a fulfilling life means, in part, achieving goals. It does not mean getting good grades on a test in the sense of marking a paper that is graded. This type of testing virtually never happens outside school. The powerful tests in working life are performance in complex tasks over months or years. The valuable skills in the working life are complex emotional skills, taking responsibility and creative skills.

Summers, H. and Watson, A. (2006). *The Book of Happiness: Brilliant Ideas to Increase Your Happiness and Transform Your Life*, Hoboken, New Jersey: Wiley.

Do you think you are happy? What does it mean to be happy on your terms?

This book intends to be a happiness makeover to bring a smile to the world's face. Learn to develop the happiness habit. You can influence how happy you are in exactly the same way that you can change your luck.

You can think yourself into happiness. The reality is, you can create your own happiness by choosing what you do, what you say, where you go, what you remember, who and what your surround yourself with, what you think and what you listen to.

This book_explores the six levels of happiness based on extensive research and questionnaire gathering. It discusses Surroundings and Behavior, Skills and Capabilities, Values and Beliefs, and How to Identity Purpose.

Swami B. V. Tripurari, *Aesthetic Vedanta: The Sacred Path of Passionate Love*, Berkeley, CA: Ten Speed Press Mandala imprint.

This book brings you ways of lovemaking that you have never heard of. It provides you the science of love and the art of lovemaking.

Consider making love and meditating simultaneously.

Read how to get the best of two blissful experiences. You will find it in this book. Some Hindus believe that the Higher Power came to the earthly plane with the name of Krishna. The playful dance of Krishna with the goatherd girls is one of the most sublime love stories of India. Krishna was able to make love to many goatherd girls in a single day. Is that an interesting idea?

This book unveils this wisdom. It guides you to the power of transforming the energy of passion into divine higher states of consciousness.

Tracy, B. (2006). *The Psychology of Selling: Increase Your Sales Faster and Easier then You Ever Thought Possible*, Dallas, TX: Thomas Nelson.

What you want to know about convincing her to invest in you?

This book explains how to sell anything, even marriage. What if you could sell all the tea in China? How can you convince her to say yes? What if you could convince everyone to do things your way?

Tracy was one of the best salesmen in history. He was also one of the best salesmen trainers in history.

Tessina, T. (1999). *The Unofficial Guide to Dating Again,* Hoboken, New Jersey: Wiley.

How long as it been since you dated? Do you want to learn how to overcome fear or other feelings about dating?

A number of adults may find themselves single. Maybe they've postponed marriage to concentrate on a career. Perhaps they find themselves alone after divorce or the breakup of a long-term relationship.

This book explains the range of dating options available today and provides practical tools that will help readers assess their needs, research their options, and make decisions accordingly.

Thurston, T. and Laughlin, B. (2000). *The Marriage of Spirit: Enlightened Living in Today's World,* Santa Fe, NM: CoreLight.

Wachs, K. (2002). *Relationships For Dummies,* Hoboken, New Jersey: Wiley.

Romance; the specialist explains it. Her name is Kate. She can teach you a lot. She wrote the book. She can tell you everything. You need this book.

Do you want to learn how to have the relationships you want? Do you need the "tools" for building fulfilling friendships?

Does the "For Dummies" title insult you? Skim this book. It is still the best book to learn all the important habits for long term love. You are no Dummy. How do I know you are smart? Because you have read this far in this book. You are willing to learn, to study and to try out methods that win you the love you deserve. Let's face it, making a relationship work takes patience, perseverance, energy, and an unflagging commitment to maintain a happy healthy relationship.

I'm telling the truth.

The fourteen ways to get over the friction and reality of a permanent relationship are presented in this book. It is up to you to learn them.

Whether you've just started dating or have been together with that special someone for years, Kate can help you. You could learn how to tell the difference between a healthy and an unhealthy relationship. You could have a more loving, fun-filled relationship and enjoy a more vibrant and satisfying sex life.

If you try, you could be able to work through most relationship problems which were totally impossible before. You will find the positive and the fun in every relationship stage. After the novelty wears off, a new stage begins in your relationship.

There are new ideas in this book. They are clearly written. They are given to you in easy lessons. After all this effort, you will have the benefit of relating to that special someone.

Westheimer, R. K. (2000). *Sex for Dummies,* 2nd Ed., Hoboken, New Jersey: Wiley.

Do you need to learn more about fulfilling sexual contacts? Have you found yourself frustrated during and after sexual contact? Are you an accomplished lover but want to be better? Does Viagra work?

If you thought sex hasn't changed much over the years you have a lot to learn, and Dr. Ruth is the one to tell you all about it. Material includes expanded coverage of medical concerns, from prostate cancer and Viagra to birth control and sexually transmitted diseases.

Williamson, M. L. (2000). *Great Sex after 40: Strategies for Lifelong Fulfillment,* Hoboken, New Jersey: Wiley.

SEX IS A SKILL THAT IMPROVES AS YOU PRACTICE IT WITH THE SAME PARTNER. It takes effort, learning, and open minded search for ways to improve. Sexual fulfillment is the result of emotional compatibility, spiritual contact, and bodily fitness. That makes sense does it not? You change. Your partner changes. Part of you gets better and part of you degrades with age.

Is the sexual part of your marriage getting stale?

You can learn to have better sexual thrills as you age. You can keep emotionally mature. You can keep physically fit. Preserve your sexual function. You can adjust to disease, even prostrate trouble.

You can experiment with your partner to feel how close you can become. To have sexual function, you must be interested in your partner, even aroused. What if your wife is fat, ugly and not interested? You could still hug, kiss, caress your partner sexually, and have fun.

As our active years grow longer, what can we expect of our relationships? The truth may surprise you. Both sexes report a wonderful mutual discovery:

You'll find strategies you can implement yourself for lessening the impact on sexual function associated with diseases commonly encountered at middle age and beyond.

your relationship. Whether you're contemplating marriage, a newlywed, or well into your married life, this sensitive and realistic guide will show you the way to loving respect and everlasting joy. Features practical guidance for relationships both old and new. Features practical guidance for relationships both old and new.

Appendix B
Use the following learning system to master the wisdom in this book.

This is at the end because it is the hard part of identifying the best possible woman for you, dating her, interviewing her, checking out your cooperation, and persuading a woman to marry you. You have to change much of your thinking, your speaking, your actions, and your methods of relating to women. Since you are reading this, you have already realized you have a lot to learn. You are one of the best men in the world if you are reading this and you are practicing the lessons. You are best because you are willing to make the effort to have a better future life. You are going to have one of the best dates and the best marriages possible for you.

Because dating is the one of the most complex activities you will ever enjoy, you realize that you need to prepare yourself since there are no colleges teaching this. Marriage is an order of magnitude more complex than dating.

The more you learn, the better dates you will have. If you can get through these lessons, you will probably have an unusually wonderful marriage.

If you get some of the books recommended at the end of this book, and learn all the advice, and practice the advice until you get it right, you will be famous in your town, city, or country.

**The objective of this book is to guide you to a sacred
relationship —a connection that will enrich your life.
You can be so connected that you have a sense of completion
even if you are not physically near your lover or your wife.**

The end of loneliness and isolation is coming soon. This is the beginning of the art and science of dating for you.

Finding and relating to your best possible friends and lovers will take time; weeks and months, maybe even years.

**Use the following learning system to
master the wisdom in this book.**

Here is the 12 step system.

The first lesson is learn how to learn

1. Decide to use this book.

   Make up your mind to continue learning the lessons in this book until you finish. Decide you will open the book every day at least for five minutes. Or decide you will read a chapter each day. Or decide you will try out one suggestion each day. Browse this book until you find something you want to learn.

2. Read the book everyday to learn as fast as possible. Memorize a skill that you can use the day you are reading.

3. Immediately try out the new skill or knowledge on different people face-to-face. Try it on strangers.

4. If you do not get the result you want, change something and try it again. For example, you could change the person you are trying out the skill on.

5. Keep doing this until you get the right results.

6. Go back to step 2. And keep this up until you can successfully use all the methods suggested in a chapter or the whole book.

7. Turn to chapter 16, the list of books. Pick the one that will answer your questions about how to find your best friend or lover.

8. Invest in the book today.

9. Read the new book every day to learn as fast as possible. Memorize a skill that you can use the day you are reading.

10. Immediately try out the new skill or knowledge on different people face-to-face. Try it on strangers.

11. Go back to step 7. Read all the books that look interesting, that raise your curiosity. Use all the lessons on real people face-to-face.

Do you agree that, after you do steps 1 to 11, you will have better women friends and lovers?

Then step 12. Take courses or find experiences when you can learn what you do not know.

Decide what you want with a woman

What would you like in a relationship?

Would it be nice to have a lover with whom you feel completely whole and strong?

Would you like to feel like a valuable treasure—respected, admired, loved?

Perhaps feeling totally connected is what you need.

Feeling excited when you are together may seem like the clincher.

Would you like a woman who you could convince you are right?

Or perhaps a woman with whom you seem to agree on everything?

This is a learning process

Think about what you need to know and how you will learn it. Look for instruction given by people who know what they are talking about. Some classes allow you to try new behavior without embarrassment even if you fail. In a class, no one will either reject you or laugh at you.

Would that work for you?

It will be precious because it will improve your social life. It will open up opportunities for your happiness with other people.

Try experiments with various women. This is walking on thin ice through which you may fall because an experiment may fail. The best way to learn is to try out ways to thinking, ways of speaking, and ways of behaving. A man learns fastest when he tries so hard that he fails. You may lose out with one woman but you will be more confident with the next one.

Your change in thinking will show you the best possible woman

You do not have to get into a fight to learn.

You can learn about dating, connecting with people, deeply satisfying relationships.

You can learn about sexual events that last for an hour even 3 hours.

Perhaps learning never ends. Continuous improvement begins with learning the lessons in this book. By the time you finish reading this book, you will admit how little you knew before you started.

Your improvement takes time and practice

If you want to have a thrilling and sex filled date today or this week, then give this book away. There are no fast tips. You are not going to improve that much in one day. To master this art and science, you will need to persist and to be determined.

Your success with women depends on how you think. When you learn how to think, you will say the right things and you will do the right things.

Learning takes place one step at a time. You can give yourself a class directly from this book. This is where you will learn everything you will need to know about sex, relationships, meeting the best woman, convincing her to marry you, and marrying the best woman.

Yes this improvement is difficult but it will lead you to what you want

Are you able to admit that there are many thoughts, feelings, ways to express with words, and winning actions that you do not know? Things you never even guessed you need to know. You will learn all this in this book. If you do not see what you need to know in this chapter, go to the next.

Compare the small cost of this book with the cost of a single date which may be boring or may get you into trouble

New clothes $100 + 1 hour shopping

New shoes $100 + 1 hour shopping

Dinner $100 Liquor $30

Parking $10

Painful suffering date 7 hours

Recovery from disappointment and fright 48 hours (maybe psychiatrist)

Cost $340 and 12 hours of pain. I intend to help you to avoid this suffering.

Why I am giving you this information

I am giving this book to you because I have met hundreds of men like you. I know your emptiness, the vacuum of your loneliness. I know your jealousy of other men who have beautiful women who are loyal to them. I know your inner anger and frustration because you do not know what to do to have a devoted woman. I am doing all this for you because my heart hurts with compassion when I see and hear your suffering. I know how much you need to connect with another person. And I know you are not finding her.

This book is a safe place. This is your gift for being lonely. This is your gift for being honest enough to learn how to be a friend and a date and a spouse. Please pass on the title of this book to people you meet.

Please help to compensate me for making this book available.

I spent thousands of hours writing the lessons and researching the books for you to own. I have spent thousands of dollars getting this book available for you. This is the result of 40 years of dating and being married.

All I ask is that you tell your friends to buy the book to pay for my time, effort and expenses.

My intention is to guide you to the life you want with the woman you want. But I must pay for the time and expenses I have endured to being this to you. Enthusiastically tell your friends how much this book helped you. Recommend that they buy it.

You can believe this book is full of advice that will guide you to the best women and to the best possible marriage for you depending on your individual abilities and limitations

I have experimented with hundreds of women, taken classes, and studied women in a focused way in books. I am advising you based on a vast array of women I have known. I am also informing you of solutions to dating problems I have experienced with women. After pondering the troubles men have, I wrote about what men would like to experience with women.

What makes me think that I, an older man, can teach an accomplished person like you how to have the dates you have always wanted with women who are excellent enough for you?

Simple!

I know what women want. And I know how to succeed in finding good women who are worth dating. Do you think that all men know what women want?

No!

Men complain a lot about women but they do not understand women. Nor do men know what they themselves want (besides sex). So men cannot usually suggest improvements to their own dating habits.

Women have some of the same problems. They do not understand men. They have fanciful ideas about how men think. They do not know themselves well enough to decide whether a certain man will be an excellent husband.

Do you understand why it is do hard to find and marry the best possible woman?

However, I know what women want and I understand women. I provide you with this depth of information. Also, I am giving you methods I discovered in books written over the last hundreds of years. There are many books about these methods. I compiled a list of books for you at the end of this book. I took 40 years of trial and error, of study and practice, to learn what I am giving you.

I know you are lonely and need to talk, to tell your secrets, to confide your troubles. I know because I meet men (and women) almost every day who open up to me and pour out their hearts to me. It takes me about 10 minutes to create this trusting atmosphere for a man (Women take about 20 seconds to trust me. When you become an expert, they will take about 20 seconds to trust you too).

Knowing a woman has a beautiful body, youth and low body weight is not enough information to decide whether a woman is worth being friends with.

You would be more effective to notice confidence, open friendliness, intelligence and cheerfulness. When you appreciate these qualities of the inner woman, she will be on the perfect date. She will open her heart, and for a while she will feel relief. She will realize there is another dimension to relating to a man.

When you experience this instant openness, that is your beginning of the art and science of dating.

Focus on observing couples

You will observe couples who appear to be a single living being and others who are not at all together.

I see many couples who make it so obvious that they are not in harmony. I see so many couples that I suspect have grossly inadequate relationships. I am certain that most sexual encounters are poorly done. Most sex is inexcusable, little more than a bump in the night.

My intention is to save you time and unpleasant feelings or torment. This book will give you the opportunity to avoid the disappointment of losing a lover. This book will save you from the torture of discovering the information in this book by trial and error. I went through the trial and error so you do not have to do it.

It is clear that most of you are miserable when you try to think of a way to have your best woman. I listened to many a man trying too hard to pretend he liked some girl. A girl who knew very little about men and who was not having a good time. I suspected he thought she was inadequate for him. I observed men who were uninterested in their wives—even magnificently attractive and intelligent wives. Other people, not just I, could also read their forced smiles, their tortured body movements that betray their yearning for absorption in love making. That is why I want so badly to help you.

If you observe carefully, you can see the married partners completely ignoring each other. Look closely. You can notice these incompatible couples. You might be able to observe the unsatisfied couples from all the way across the street. You can read their desperation to feel love for each other. They have given up trying to get attention. They do not even know how to listen. You will feel sad, too.

I often see the young men and women who are obviously on the first date. The man is talking on the cell phone. The woman is tuned to her iPod. They do not know how to have a spirited conversation. They are disconnected. They feel the cold city. At the same time, they are lonely. They feel isolated and want to connect.

My heart is breaking as I observe the unmet needs of couples. I cannot stand it any more. I have to help you.

At last, in 11 lessons, how to get the best possible dates considering your excellent qualities and your limited abilities Lesson 1: If you continue to do what you have always done, you will get what you have always gotten.

Education and experimentation will teach you to get what you want, not what you got in the past. This educational opportunity will help you find friends, if you experiment, frequently read the recommended books, apply what you can learn, and make the effort. It will take effort, constant trial and error with real people, and real life experiences to learn how to find your best possible friends, lovers, and your wife.

If you are driven to have the dates that are even more fabulous that you can imagine today, use the guidance in the whole book. It will explain how to be on a date with the woman you want. It explains why you need to take the time and effort to learn the art of dating.

Change your way of thinking and doing

Memorize the main suggestions about thinking, feeling, acting, and speaking.

Try out new thoughts, feelings, acts, and speaking.

Try out the new ways with many people until you have mastered them.

Lesson 2: How to relate to a woman who does not understand men and who has inferior relationship skills.

There are lots of these women. You probably noticed. Is it ever possible for such women to relate to men like you?

Yes.

How are ordinary women going to learn how to treat you right?

Read this book and use the advice.

How a man can relate to women he does not know or understand.

Practice using the advice again and again until you can succeed.

Lesson 3: Persist.

Persist in reading and trying out the suggestions in this book. Read the whole book a little at a time and try out the methods. These methods work. I have spent a lifetime experimenting with people. It cost me a lot of heartbreak and suffering. And money. And I achieved excellent results. You do not have to experience heartbreak and suffering. You just have to follow the directions.

When you persist, this book guides you through the processes of education so you can connect with practically anyone. Some of the topics suggest that you invest in books that will help you immensely. Other pages explain some clues and ideas about specific problems without suggesting books. You can use these lessons to accelerate your finding friends and lovers.

If you do not learn to keep the interest of the startling women who will date you, keep trying. The reason you may not learn is because you do not try hard enough or long enough. Keep trying anyway. If 10 or 20 excellent women turn you down, learn from each one. Write in your journal what happened. Write what you can do better next time. Be honest with yourself and admit your mistakes.

Not all dates will be wonderful. If you have a date that is not turning out the way you want, ask her what happened. Ask what you could do better. Sound painful?

Which is more painful, another rotten date or hearing your true problems? Another painful but effective way to improve your dates and to pick better women is to ask your acquaintances or enemies why you messed up your date or why you pick inappropriate women.

Why ask enemies? They will not spare your feelings. They will tell you the truth or an exaggerated truth. It is less valuable to ask your close friends because they will spare your feelings.

Next time, think it through and plan your date in more detail. Then do what you have to do to get what you want.

PERSIST!

When you persist, this book guides you through the processes of education so you can connect with practically anyone.

Lesson 4: Improve the probability that a specific woman will have an outstanding relationship with you.

You may know a woman who seems right for you. She may appear to know little or nothing about how to relate to men. How do you feel; frustrated and angry? Do you feel, compassion, sadness, hopeless?

She may be arrogant thinking that she knows men. You may have to save her from her own ignorance.

How will she know how to be as perfect a spouse, lover, sexual partner as you can desire? She will learn to act, think, speak, and go out for a fulfilling date. She will do these things within her own personality. Then you will know a woman who will be skilled enough for you to love.

You may open up to her so you both study having better dates. She can learn along with you. This will bring you closer together.

Keep reading. You can learn how to make yourself available, to attract like a magnet, to select the best women. You can learn how to plan out a date that is everything you deserve. You can learn how to communicate completely in speech, body, and actions. You need to learn more about communication. If you passionately persist with the lessons, and follow the advice, one or more women will love you.

Lesson 5: Nothing is free; pay for what you get. Pay with time, effort, and money.

You will never figure out how to find friends, lovers, or a wife without effort.

Look for new safe experiences to try out what you have learned—safe courses where no one will laugh at you or reject you. Dances are good practice events. You will hear approval and acceptance at dances. You can experiment as many times as you need. When you achieve your desired results, you will hear appreciation and encouragement.

Or you could be lazy and do nothing.

Lesson 6: Communicate effectively

Do things, say things, and think things that work in real life. Do not live in a virtual (internet, smart-phone, and television) world of make-believe. Do not insist that the world obey your rigid rules. No one else is going to live according to your rules. If you are inflexible, you will find discord, disappointment, and fights. Do not cause friction with your friends by setting down standards. A matrix of details smothers a friendship. On the other hand, basic morality is useful.

However, if you have rules and morals that are inflexible, tell her about them. Do not make her guess your code of honor. Ask her to adjust to your code. Note her reaction. If you will win persist. This will be a decision point for her. Her reaction will throw a shadow on your future together. Be easy to get along with if you know you will lose the fight. If you will lose, run away and try again later. Do not fight losing battles.

Since conflict is inevitable, make the effort to learn how to argue, to debate, to fight, and to negotiate. I did not suggest learning how to win. You can win an argument and lose your best friend. Pick your fights. Pick arguments when you know they will end the way you want. Debate your need for morality and respect. Be positive but firm. Never, ever, insult people or show disrespect. There is no forgiveness for this. Negotiate your desired outcomes without losing your lover, or your wife.

Get a book on negotiating. There are hundreds of them at several levels of ability and experience. However, I read 19 books on negotiating. I have negotiated practically everything. I know that studying this topic yields valuable results.

Lesson 7: An unanswered question can help you to learn

This book has many unanswered questions to help you learn. You will learn more if you have to work to answer some questions. You will learn by searching and feeling frustrated. Then when you find the answers, you will believe in them. The questions are here to stimulate you to think of the answers that fit you. Answer the questions! Write them down and keep them. Read them in a month or a year. Then you will see how much of an expert you have become.

Try out your imagination on these questions.

What is love?

What is our treasure that other people want from hyou?

What are your most attractive features?

How could you improve your attraction?

How do you pursue a particularly desirable woman?

How do you plan a date to get what you want?

Where do you find women who are looking for you?

When you find them, how do you meet them?

What women are eager to date you?

What skills do you need to keep their interest?

How can you endear yourself to a special woman even if you have average appearance?

How do you motivate women to respond to you?

Lesson 8: Men do not communicate the same way as women

Don't insist that women speak like men. Do not expect your woman to use words the same as you do. Keep reading and you will find out why.

Lesson 9: Women change their minds

You may not find the exact woman you want. Because you may never become skilled enough. Because you may have unreasonable specifications for the perfect friend, lover or wife. Because you want a famous or impossible person. And after you meet what seemed to be the perfect person, you may find she is not at all what you expected. Or after a few dates, she may be bored with you. Or you could be the one who changes your mind.

For your own peace of mind, accept that women change their minds. One day she shows no interest. The next she shows focused attention. She changes her mind.

You may accept this easier if you realize that you are changeable, too. In spite of women's changing their minds, continue taking action toward your goal.

Lesson 10: Give and take

Please notice that connecting begins with give and take. You must have something to give before you can take. And before other people will give you something, you have to give something. You can give a wonderful personality, money, power, a rugged powerful appearance, stimulating conversation, fun parties, and many other things. Make yourself into an attractive treasure, a powerful support that women will pursue.

If a woman does not give in return for what she takes, get another woman.

Lesson 11: Words women use

Women use words with different meanings than men use them.
<u>FINE</u>

This is the word women use to end an argument when they are right and you need to shut up.

<u>FIVE MINUTES</u>

If she is getting dressed, this is half an hour. Five minutes is only five minutes if you have just been given 5 more minutes to watch the game before helping around the house.

NOTHING

This is the calm before the storm. This means "something," and you should be on your toes. Arguments that begin with 'Nothing' usually end in "Fine"

GO AHEAD

This is a dare, not permission. Don't do it.

LOUD SIGH

This is not actually a word, but is a non-verbal statement often misunderstood by men. A "Loud Sigh" means she thinks you are an idiot and wonders why she is wasting her time standing here and arguing with you over "Nothing"

THAT'S OKAY

This is one of the most dangerous statements that a woman can make to a man. "That's Okay" means that she wants to think long and hard before deciding how and when you will pay for your mistake.

THANKS

A woman is thanking you. Do not question it or faint. Just say you're welcome.

WHATEVER

It's a woman's way of saying *!#@ YOU!

Send this to the men you know to warn them about future arguments they can avoid if they remember the terminology

The guidance in this book will work for you if you make an effort and take action. Read a page of advice every day. Use the advice the day you read it. If you do not get the results you want, change something (for example, try it on a different person)

Try again.

There are over 100 suggestions and guidance in this book. If you use one suggestion each day, you will have better meetings with women every day for over 100 days. And you will soon have the dates you want (not dates that are boring or horrible). After while, you will have fun and excitement if you want them. After an extended effort and learning, you will have the attention and seduction of women if you want them. More valuable than these, you will have the women friends that you have always needed.

Main lessons of the book

Go through the chapters in this book and find out how to open up women's hearts to you. Learn how to find women friends, actively find them in the chapter How to Pursue Her.

You can learn how to have sexual thrills. You think you know a lot about sex. But you are probably a gross beginner. There is a chapter about excellence in sexual events; sexual thrills that you have never allowed yourself to imagine. If you are married, you can make a deeper connection. Or you can get married and continually improve your marriage. Sexual communication in marriage can heal many mistakes.

Your first goal is to become a treasure, a powerful support, a person whom your woman values above all others. You offer your treasure to attract the friends you want. Other people need to know your treasure.

It does not matter how old you are, or that you are overweight, or what you look like. This book does not discuss body fitness or looks or age. These aspects are superficial and only mean a lot when you first meet. True, the first meeting can make or break the connection.

However, some women care too much about these superficial aspects of a first meeting. When you first meet a woman, she is interested in your face, build, age, and the feelings you project. She is at least vaguely aware of how she feels around you. As you know, these appearances do not support a long-term fulfilling relationship. But you have to jump the hurdle of appearance. Luckily for you, this is a hurdle you will learn to get over in the chapter You Are the Powerful Support.

When you are the powerful support, appearance has little importance.

You will have to learn a lot to keep women interested. Most likely, you can learn enough from this book to keep your lover devoted to you.

If you are not confident that you can rise to heights of love, go to Chapter 16: Emotional preparation is the source of vitality for sexual games and for a long term marriage. In the chapter are The 7 Levels of Love. Do this now. When you realize what towering possibilities exist, you will go for it passionately. Enjoy the seven levels of love. Understand where you are going. Then read this whole book.

Three concepts you must know to use this book effectively

1. All women (and other people) are different from one another.

Consider why women are different. To start, women communicate differently from men. Some communicate mostly by speech and hearing. They like to listen to music a lot. Their ears collect data on the world.

Some women collect information about their world with their eyes. They think a lot. The look of food or a lover has a relatively high meaning to them compared to how a lover smells or how his voice sounds. You can spot these people because they tend to talk fast.

Some women relate to their world mostly through their bodies. They communicate through sports, or touching you. They tend to talk slower. They may like the feel of luxurious fabrics or your tender skin.

Other women have their own unique mixture of communication.

Some women are non-sexual and do not like to touch. Yes, there really are women like this. "Technical" women, for example, or nerds are more interested in ideas and computers.

Some women are functioning alright and make a lot of money and have great power. But they are "disordered." What do I mean by disordered? They are difficult and a little crazy. Extreme ambition or the lust for power is a kind of mania.

Another example is the narcissist. She is mainly interested in herself. Such a woman is not interested in you unless you are primarily interested in the details of her life.

Some women, maybe one in a hundred, are homosexual. They only like sexual contact with women.

There are "directors" who want to control everything.

There are "socializers" who lead a group by attracting obligations through friendship.

There are "relators," people who just want make friends with lots of people. There are endless types of women.

Do not expect any woman to behave the way you want. This will lead to disappointment. Ask questions. Discover who each woman is. Appreciate her for who she is. Do not expect her to change.

Don't expect. Just adjust.

That said, if you ever find a woman who molds herself to your desires, you have a rare treasure. Accept this woman and give her what she wants. You could flow into her mold. On the other hand, a woman who flows into the mold you set for her may be faking it. She may cast off this attractive trait later. If you want this flexibility, find a woman who wants it, too. Or who will change herself into what you specify. These women are rare.

If you find a woman who is everything you want, later she may not be what you want. You may become bored with her sooner that you could imagine. Boredom may result because she is not a challenge. She is too easy. Maybe she is too much like you. Boredom usually ruins a relationship. The challenge in most relationships is to keep them interesting. Keep reading to find out how to keep things hopping.

You change your mind. She changes her mind. Keep up with the changes. Or you can purposefully make the changes in your affair. For example, some women want a relationship that is predictable and stable. You might like this too. Neither of you want big changes or surprises. In any case, most people want changes to keep their interest. Make small changes to keep her interest. If you want this steadiness, find a woman who wants it too. Or who will change herself into what you specify. Such women are hard to find.

2. The advice given in this book does not fit all women (or people).

It is impossible to give advice on each type of woman. This book is written about the tendencies of women. Not about all types of women.

The advice given does not fit all women. Some women behave in ways you cannot imagine. You have to find out the difference between the advice given here and the individual woman you are relating to. Start out by following the advice given in this book. Then test your new friend to see how she is different. Adjust to the changes.

3. Women are different from men in almost everything.

They think differently. They use words differently. Many want specific things and detailed requirements, unusual pleasures, odd surroundings, and so on. They respond to events with unexpected emotions. This will not change. There will be surprises. Enjoy the difference.

Wake up men! Think, about this. Remember how you think women are peculiar because they do not understand your feelings? Or because they do not automatically know what to do with you? Please take note. Women think the same thing about men. Do not bother trying to change this. You will just cause trouble. You will not succeed.

Get the book *Men Are From Mars, Women Are From Venus* by John Gray. Study it.

Read a chapter a day and let it sink in. It explains the details of the differences between men and women. After you finish reading it, wait six months and read it again. If you have been trying out new dating methods, it will seem like a new book.

Appendix C
Feelings and Feeling Words

After you learn the language of feelings, you will notice that your communications are more accurate. Experiment with these words. You will find they improve most communications. This is a list of words that describe feelings.

You use these words in the following formulation.

"I feel (feeling word)"

OR "I feel (feeling word) when you (other person's word or action)"

OR "I feel (feeling word) when you (other person's word or action) because (what you are thinking or what you remember)"

BELOW IS A LIST OF NEUTRAL FEELINGS OR LACK OF FEELINGS	BELOW IS A LIST OF LOVING FEELINGS OR COMING CLOSER
Equanimity	Loving
Calm	Romantic
Tranquil	Sexy
Flat	flirtatious
Blasé	Accepting
Satisfied	Loving kindness
Fulfillment	Compassion
Indifferent	Sympathy
Lackadaisical	Sympathetic joy
Empathy	Rapture
Contented	Friendly

Infatuated

Amorous

Openhearted

Embracing

Respect

Harmony

DEPRESSED, LOW CHI, SAD,
FEELINGS IN THIS LIST

Lazy

Hopeless

Sloth

Torpor

Listless

Heartbroken

Flat

Deflated Self-conscious

Crushed Scared

Enervated Jaded

Defeated Distrustful

Failed Distressed

Lowdown Concerned

Gloomy Disquieted

MORE DEPRESSED, LOW CHI, SAD, FEELINGS IN THE LIST BELOW	ANXIETY, FEARFUL TYPE FEELINGS IN THE LIST BELOW
Dejected	Uneasy
Dispirited	Troubled
Oppressed	Hounded
Dull	Unsettled
Heavyhearted	Afraid
Melancholic	Alarmed
Exhausted	Consternation
Blue	Dread
Idle	Horror
Indolent	Panic
Sluggish	Terrified
Tearful	Apprehensive
	Appalled

ANGER, ILL WILL, HATE TYPE OF FEELINGS IN THE LIST BELOW	JOY, HIGH CHI, HAPPY, POSITIVE TYPE OF FEELINGS IN THE LIST BELOW
Frustration	Effervescent
Irritation or irritable	Exhilarated
Vexed	Thrilled
Impatient	Rapture
Short tempered	Excited
Grumpy	Delighted

Cranky	Enchanted
Snappy or snappish	Content
Bitchy	Motivated
Rage or enraged	Energetic
Outrage or outraged	Pleasure
Pique	Jovial
Vengeful	Glad

ANXIETY, FEARFUL, NEGATIVE FEELINGS IN THIS LIST	JOYFUL, HIGH SPIRITED POSITIVE FEELINGS BELOW
Worried	
Flurry	Intoxicated
Jealous	Vivacious
Inflamed	Vigorous
Envy	Vital
Restless	Jubilant
Edgy	Euphoric
Overwhelmed	Ecstatic
Nervous	Overjoyed
Displeasure	Merry
Hostility	Spirited
Indignation	Cheerful
Ire	Fortunate
Infuriated	Lucky
Maddened	Benevolent
Fuming	Inspired
Boiling mad	Elevated

Seething

Blocked

Annoyed

Fretful

Peevish

Petulant

Sore

Elated

Animated

Exalted

Uplifted